# A PACIFIST'S WAR

Frances Partridge was born in London and was educated at Bedales and Cambridge, where she read English and Moral Sciences at Newnham. She worked for some years in David Garnett's and Francis Birrell's bookshop in Taviton Street, then Gerrard Street, in London; it was a centre for the Bloomsbury circle, and she became a member of their Memoir club. She married Ralph Partridge in 1933. She has translated many books from French and Spanish and helped her husband edit the Greville Memoirs.

By the same author

*Memories*

# A PACIFIST'S WAR

Frances Partridge

ROBIN CLARK
LONDON MELBOURNE NEW YORK

Published by Robin Clark Limited 1983
A member of the Namara Group
27 Goodge Street, London W1P 1FD

First published in Great Britain by the Hogarth Press,
London 1978

Copyright © Frances Partridge

Printed in Great Britain by
Nene Litho and bound by Woolnough Bookbinding,
both of Wellingborough, Northants

**British Library Cataloguing in Publication Data**

Partridge, Frances
    A pacifist's war.
    1. Partridge, Frances    2. Pacifists—Great
    Britain—Biography
    I. Title
    940.53'162'0924    JX1962.P29

    ISBN 0-86072-063-2

# CONTENTS

# Preface

It is hardly necessary to say that the following extracts from my diary of 1940-5 were not written with any idea of publication, but as a means of relieving the various emotions aroused by the Second World War, ranging from boredom to horror, fear and disgust. Why publish them? The suggestion that I should do so has come from two directions – firstly from some who want to be reminded of it, even down to the details of our adjustment to the daily grind, secondly from others who want to know (and do not because they are too young) what living through those years was like. As will be seen, few people passed a more sheltered war than we did at Ham Spray, and this may be considered a disqualification, though we were not ostriches: we thought, felt and talked about it endlessly. And I have also been concerned to give some picture of the life we led there, conversations, thoughts and activities, our values, and the people we saw. Any of our friends' remarks here quoted – and some may possibly find them hard to believe now – were, of course, written down at the time and I can vouch for their accuracy. I have also included various different reactions: those of a young woman whose husband was fighting at Alamein, the relations of an airman killed on his first flight, the baker, the daily help, my old mother and five-year-old son.

But perhaps my chief purpose is to testify to the pacifist beliefs I developed in my teens during the First War, and which I shared with my husband, Ralph Partridge, whose statement before the Tribunal for Conscientious Objectors is printed below. He is, of course, the central figure in the years covered by the diary, and for that very reason may well remain rather shadowy. We were always together, communicated all our thoughts; he was the focus of my life and I had no need to describe what he was like *to myself*. I will therefore try to fill in the outline a little.

He has, I think, been "hard done by" in many books on Bloomsbury; the first source of his portrait was his very old friend and rival, Gerald Brenan, whose assessment (inaccurate in my view) was accepted in all innocence by Michael Holroyd in his life of Lytton Strachey, and has "type-cast" him, as it were, in other subsequent accounts. I am anxious to remove these distortions and substitute as detached a picture as I can.

A brief summary of his record is relevant: having won a Classical scholarship to Oxford from Westminster, where he was head boy, he went up to Christ Church in 1913. Two fellow-undergraduates describe him as "one of the best brains of his year", "a man of wide reading who was expected to go far in law or politics", "noticeably more intelligent, quick-witted and forceful than most of his contemporaries". He joined up in 1914, when he was nineteen, and served all through the First War as an infantry officer with considerable distinction, gaining the Military Cross and Bar and the Croce de Guerra. By the age of twenty-three he was a Major commanding a brigade, and by the end of the war he had been twice wounded, and buried alive (narrowly escaping death); moreover he had become completely disillusioned with war itself, considered both ethically and practically, and decided that all he could usefully try to do was save the lives of as many of the men under his command as possible. In 1918 he resigned his commission and returned to Oxford, where he was academically idle (though he passed his finals with distinction), and devoted much of his time to rowing with outstanding success. His friend Noel Carrington took him over to Tidmarsh Mill House, where he fell in love with his first wife Carrington and got to know and made a lifelong friend of Lytton Strachey.

As with others of his generation, those ghastly years of trench warfare had knocked nearly all the ambition out of him. His war experiences had moved him deeply; his memory of them was extremely vivid and he often described them to me in detail. When the Second War began he knew what was at issue; what I knew was second-hand, but unforgettable.

To quote others, he was "a good-looking man of powerful build with the brightest blue eyes I have ever seen and marvellous Rabelaisian high spirits", "always immensely alive". He was physically active in fields he enjoyed, such as swimming, walking and tennis; but he certainly made an impression of indolence at times – perhaps because he could happily sit reading a book the livelong day, for he was a passionate reader with a remarkable gift for remembering and synthesizing facts. And he was never bored; thinking, talking and arguing were the breath of life to him. In terms of work his achievement was not very great: after a spell at the Hogarth Press with Leonard and Virginia Woolf he trained and practised as a book-binder, helped Lytton Strachey edit the *Greville Diaries* in eight volumes (acting also as his business secretary and literary agent), spent a number of years reviewing books on history and crime for the *New Statesman*, and published a book on Broadmoor which is still in print. He died in November, 1960.

To sum up his character: he was a man of deep and strong emotions; his chief relationships were life-lasting and provided an incalculable

10

sense of support to those at the other end of them. To some he could be formidable. High-spirited and excitable, his eyes would flash and his voice rise in an argument so that the uninitiated thought him angry though he was in fact having the time of his life; laughter-loving and -producing; a great enjoyer and immense fun to be with, having a rogue-elephant streak which could be irresistibly comic. But some people undoubtedly found him aggressive and he was quite aware himself of a tendency to "lose his wool" or "blow up" as he described it. To his excellent brain and memory must be added realism with a strong vein of scepticism. He was a dedicated rationalist and almost shockingly truthful. His strong interest in other people was the only feminine thing about him and he was much in demand as a confidant and adviser. Many of the friends who visited us during our thirty years at Ham Spray have told me what a strong influence he had on them.

# Ralph Partridge's Statement to the Appeal Tribunal for Conscientious Objectors in 1943

I joined the Army in 1914 because I was persuaded that I should be fighting for civilisation in a war to end war. During the course of that war I had plenty of time to reflect on why I was trying so hard to kill my fellow men. All civilised values had disappeared, my country was dominated by fear, hatred, anger and revenge, and the object of the war was reduced to punishing the Germans. The 'war to end war' had degenerated into a war to stave off the next war by punitive peace terms. I resigned my commission in the Army as soon as the war ended and became a pacifist, not out of a revulsion from fighting but from a conviction that wars never lead to peace but only to the next war. I met pacifists, argued with them on moral grounds, and found the pacifist argument overwhelming. I had already found from experience that war defeats its own end. When I considered the matter more deeply I became convinced that war is wicked as well as irrational.

The ethical basis for my profound conviction that war is wrong in itself and all its consequences, is that I believe human behaviour should be governed by reason which is all that distinguishes us from brutes, that men can only be reconciled and united by reason; that in disputes between human beings a resort to violence, being irrational, is recognised as wrong both by the laws and conscience of mankind; and that the organised violence of war is infinitely worse than individual acts of violence because for political reasons it is exonerated by the State and even glorified. It is the doctrine by which the Inquisition was justified. The outcome of a war can never prove that one side is right and the other wrong; it only proves which side has superior force. The only lesson nations learn from war is the need for superior force to obtain victory. That is the lesson Germany learned from the war of 1914-18. It is the only lesson that will be learnt from this war.

I have the firmest belief in the sanctity of human life and the brotherhood of man, and I am convinced that no civilised life can endure in this world until these universal conceptions override national jealousies and mistrust, and are accepted by the governments of states as well as private individuals. I respect the authority of the state wherever my conscience is not at stake, but I claim the right to refuse

13

to take lessons in murder, which is what military service would be for me.

I do not object at all to civil defence, as I regard my neighbours and fellow-countrymen as companions in a common misfortune, but I consider that at present I am of far more real use to the community producing and distributing food than waiting about for emergencies that have so far not arisen in the remote part of Wiltshire where I live.

1939

During the first months of the War — the phony War as it was after-wards called — Ham Spray House, Wiltshire, was crowded to overflowing with 'refugees' from London, where air-raids were daily expected. These were mostly the young families of friends. At the worst we had six children, three nannies, parents at weekends, and two adults. When week after week passed uneventfully here in England, they gradually took wing. By the start of 1940 our only permanent winter residents were a friend with two children; and of course we had "visitors" — quite a different thing.

1940

As midnight struck, Ralph and I went out into the garden to see if we could hear the bells from the village church. But only total silence met our ears, and 1940 crept its way in, in a dense cold mist. We gathered up the prophecies for the New Year, made that afternoon with Faith and Nicko Henderson, and R. sealed them and put them away in an envelope. How wrong will they be? Then he brought us tiny glasses of neat whiskey to drink to the future.

*January 3rd*

Cold, cold, cold. An east wind blowing and a hard frost on top of the scattered snow. Across this bleak landscape a horse and cart trundled to and fro all the morning carting manure with a hollow rumbling sound, like a tumbril carrying bodies dead of the Plague. This perishing vision, and also the frightful accounts in the papers of arctic warfare in Finland and of the Turkish earthquake — war, cold, fire and blood — all combine to turn one in upon one's nipped and frozen self, and fasten powers of satisfaction on to small sensual things, pots of cyclamen, the shine on holly berries and cats' fur, the texture of materials. The foreground has in fact become all-important, leaving the vast grim background to fade into chaos.

Rachel and David [Cecil] arrived to spend the night with us. Unceasing talk till bed-time. David is unconscious of his body as he talks but is never still, sometimes flopping on his knees on the carpet to emphasize a point, or with his feet hopping and dancing like two live rabbits in his bedroom slippers. But no-one is better company. Talk almost entirely about the war.

*January 4th*

A letter saying that the Nichols[1] family are not coming back. So here we shall be, after those first congested and gruelling few months, alone and rattling in our delightful humdrummery. If only the war wasn't grumbling in the background. The sight of a letter from Joan[2] to her "soldier" on the hall table, waiting for the postman, filled me with despair; their happiness seems to hang by a thread.

Thawing. With Burgo[3] in the garden, carving the remains of old snowmen on the lawn. After his lessons with me he ran up to the nursery shouting: "Nannie! King Alfred's dead, did you know?"

[1] Phil (Foreign Office), Phyllis and their three children.
[2] Maid.
[3] Age 4½

Tea nowadays is an extremely snug meal, with hot buttered toast and the shutters drawn, and my beautiful jardinière (which I have painted white and filled with cacti, cyclamen and hyacinths) adding to the greenhouse effect. Three huge pots of arum lilies stand in the corner on a tin tray. After tea today I set to work to wash their leaves, which looked dusty, with an old sock and water in a child's pail. I felt like a zoo keeper washing his elephant's ears. I get intense pleasure from the richness and intensity of my awareness of our circumscribed private world, contrasted with the bleakness and horror of the public one.

War rumours brought us by Paul Cross, who came to lunch: how the Germans have a new kind of bomb no bigger than an orange, which can be  stowed in millions in their bombing planes. How the A.R.P. authorities were expecting 70,000 deaths in the first raid on London, and had enough papier mâché coffins ready.

*January 7th*

Mist. Cows meandering in the park like lost souls, while on the lawn a moorhen paced up and down with a donnish gait, slowly lifting its large feet and peering about. Soon after lunch (made cheerful by the remains of yesterday's rosé wine) we drove to visit Gamel and Gerald [Brenan] at Aldbourne. Road crowded with soldiers, lorries and guns. Aldbourne itself looked rather French. A girl pulled an unwilling-looking soldier along by the arm. Girls, girls everywhere, older women and children leaning out of windows. We hear that these troops are leaving for France tomorrow. A young worried-looking officer in high boots directed the manoeuvres of a lorry. We all went for a walk, R. and Gerald shooting ahead, the rest of us slowly climbing a grassy slope towards Upper Upham. Gamel, stooping as she walked, carried her face like the figurehead of a ship. Remarks of Gerald's to R.: "Gamel is like an iceberg, only one sixth of her shows above water — the rest is submerged and it is best left alone." "The truth is, no-one in the world could put up with me but Gamel, and  no-one could put up with Gamel but me." At the moment Gamel is grieving for Llewelyn Powys, who has just died. Gerald "can't bear Gamel's Powys mood".

For some days a kind of philosophical attitude to the War has been taking shape in my head, in which optimism and pessimism are combined. Something like this: though there is no intellectual reason to believe that the Universe is mainly good — rather the reverse — I feel that all experience, whether painful or pleasant, can have an essence squeezed out of it which is the main source of happiness; that the process of tasting can be good and valuable even when what is tasted is not.

To London by the early train. The Great Western Hotel embraced us, warm and womblike. Left the hairdressers in full blackout lit with minute crosses and balls of light, like a dance in May Week, festive. Avenues of huge trees appeared to loom up and sweep past — a very queer blackout illusion: they are really houses. Then there is the feeling, which one likes to exaggerate, of possible danger — a distinct sharp thrill. I thought, "Supposing there was a sudden crash and I was smashed-up and dead, how foolish to have spent the last hour of my life having my hair washed and curled." R. and I had a night out, dancing at the London Casino and watching performances by naked girls who stood about in senseless attitudes but were often young and lovely. Human dramas were evolving around us, among officers on leave with their wives or tarts, débutantes and relentless bony youths.

The glass dome of Paddington Station looked beautiful out of our hotel bedroom in the transparent morning light. Icy cold. London seemed full of pathetic couples having last flings together, their possibly dull and ill-assorted lives suddenly sharpened by a stab of acute anguish.

Dined with Clive, Raymond and Eddy[1] at the Ivy. Eddy spotty and tired. Raymond arrived saying, "I'm in a *frightful* temper, *madly* irritable", and was quite the reverse. We ate oysters and little bleeding plovers.

These nights we sleep the sleep of the dead — as if we never wanted to wake up again. Perhaps we don't. Facing the bitter cold last thing at night and first thing in the morning is an ordeal.

R. and I took Burgo for a walk to see the threshing-machine at work on the Inkpen road. It was a very vigorous scene — an academy picture of Energy. Some whacking great cart-horses stood rocking their carts to and fro, dead rats lay about, and all the time the machine was forcing its thick snake of straw relentlessly along; it was like a section of a vast and constipated digestive tract, and the brilliant air was full of whirling chaff. Burgo would have liked to stay for ever, but the freezing cold soon sent us home.

Michael MacCarthy turned up at tea-time with a chicken house. The chickens are coming next week, another step towards making ourselves

[1] Bell, Mortimer, Sackville-West.

23

self-supporting. Michael was on the whole uninterested in the war, but is doing well on it farming for Bryan [Guinness].

*January 13th*

R. had some interesting ideas about Anxiety during the night, and we lay in bed discussing them. He thinks that both he and I dread it obsessionally, and will go to all lengths to avoid situations which produce it. It seems to me realistic of us to dread Anxiety, because it is a great distorter of facts, and creates the paradoxical situation in which one suffers more pain from imagining a thing than from the thing itself. The only, or best, defence against it is knowledge.

Skated with Gamel, Kitty West and Noel and Catharine [Carrington] on the pond in the park, to a gramophone playing Viennese waltzes. On we went till the sun disappeared in a pink haze behind the Downs, and a crescent moon rose high above the black trees of the Russian Wood. Gamel crouched by the pondside in shawls and rugs, looking like an Irish samphire-gatherer. She seemed in very low spirits. I asked after Alyse [Powys] but we were soon uttering banalities about death and bereavement. I told her about Ray [Garnett][1] but there was no intimacy. The waves between us broke on our separate coasts.

Indoors we found Anthony [West] who had been writing a review.

A discussion at dinner as to whether girls look attractive from behind. Anthony twinkled ferociously and said, "We like to see the whites of their eyes when we shoot."

After they had all gone R. looked preoccupied. I asked him what he was thinking about. "Well, I was trying to compose a Latin hexameter for Anthony and Kitty, if you must know."

Anthony is a conscientious objector, or so he feels at present, but wants to prove he's no coward by enlisting on a mine-sweeper before he's called up.

*January 15th*

This extraordinary procession of perfect iced days is like something kept in a refrigerator — not quite real: sub- or superhuman. Before we started off to skate at the Wests' I saw the headline in *The Times:* All Leave Stopped for B.E.F., and as a result there was an under-current of emergency and alarm running beneath our fanatical ice-life. Skated on the moat, where the ice was quite black and not very thick, between high banks criss-crossed over with trees. It was wonderful racing over this sinister transparency, and trying to cut a few wobbly threes and

[1] My sister, very ill with cancer.

24

eights, but we were well aware of the water beneath, and the ice cracked with reports like pistol shots, so loud that Anthony came out to see who had fallen in.

After lunch we drove to the canal between Bedwyn and Pewsey. Some reaches of it were quite unfrozen – open rippling water, a shocking sight to our ice-mad eyes. But we soon found a long untouched stretch, and shot along it till we were tired, seeing quantities of fish scurrying up and down beneath the ice, terrified by the strange thunder over their heads. It was lovely to whizz along, looking down at them, and also at some pale rhubarb-like leaves imprisoned there as if in aspic. Three soldiers and two little boys ventured on and slid. One soldier fell whack on his back. Catcalls and hee-haws from the others.

This ice madness fills up the days, and in the evenings we succumb to ice-memories and ice-thoughts and great physical fatigue. Tried to listen to a Haydn symphony, interrupted by shrieks on the wireless.

*January 18th*

Michael MacCarthy came to lunch, bringing us our twelve Rhode Island Red hens. We are rather excited about our new protégées.

In writing a diary all the most important things get left out. Only the decorations get mentioned and the shape of the building is taken for granted. Far the greatest pleasure I have almost every day of my life is simply being with R., or, when I'm not with him, from remembering everything to tell him afterwards. In some ways the outer bleakness created by the war has intensified this very great happiness.

*January 21st*

*Bon mot* by R. in bed this morning: "Time and weather are the hoary old beaters who put up us pheasants" (or partridges?) "for the guns of God."

A conversation about logic in music. Music, R. said, was a cure for anxiety, because by its formal qualities it solved the problems it set itself, and this symbolized the solution of one's worries reassuringly. I find this logical component of music (propositions, and statements depending inevitably upon them) one of the things I most value in it. I see no counterpart to the marvellous sanity of Bach or Monteverdi in modern composers. Analogies between composers and painters: Haydn – Giorgione: Debussy's musical pointillism – Seurat; Piero della Francesca's great sanity and Handel's. Et cetera.

Spent most of the morning reading Vera Brittain on Winifred Holtby – frightfully bad, but it aroused various reflections. It is a glorification of the second-rate and sentimental and reeks of femininity. Why should woman on woman so painfully lack irony, humour or bite? And it's too winsome and noble, somehow. But much of that belongs to the First War, and not to women only. (There it is in Rupert Brooke.) A musty aroma of danger glamourized and not understood by girls at home floats out of this book. Vera Brittain writes of the number of women now happily married and with children who still hark back to a khaki ghost which stands for the most acute and upsetting feelings they have ever had in their lives. Which is true I think, and the worst of it is that the ghost is often almost entirely a creature of their imagination.

Drove into Hungerford. A horrid young sergeant was drilling a platoon of soldiers outside the fishmonger's, roaring at them with a scarlet face: "Look sharp! Stop that fiddling!" in such a very insolent way that I fumed inwardly at such indignity being inflicted on these nice harmless men. However, looking at their faces, I saw that they were slightly irritated but nothing more.

I tried to analyse why it pleases me to find time slipping by so fast and uneventfully. Is it because every day got through brings one nearer the end of this hateful old war? I deliberately set myself to cultivate tastes like reading and music, which seem – at present anyhow – inviolable. As far as the war is concerned, I have entered into a phase of shying away like a horse from the news in *The Times*, and trying just to get the gist of the headlines without reading it properly. So much of it rouses a reaction of impotent fury or despair. We have missed listening to the wireless news several evenings.

Today the long long freeze broke at last in rain, to a tremendous orchestral accompaniment of roaring, shrieking, hissing, rattling and pattering. The rain lies in lakes on the frozen ground. We shall soon be an island – water everywhere.

R. and I, both coughing, stay in the library with our log fire. I have begun to dust the books, climbing on the steps in a smock and Pobble-like pink cotton gloves.

"Is it raining?" we asked Edie[1] this morning, when she called us. "Why

[1] Maid.

no, I don't think so, but the trees are all covered with icicles." A sharp frost on top of the rain had encased every twig in ice as thick as a man's thumb — a fabulous sight. Each leaf and each blade of grass had its glass envelope and the plants in the rockery were solid coral. The sound of the ghostly glass trees swaying and clanking in the wind was enough to freeze the blood.

Towards evening boughs began to break from the laden trees and fall crashing to the ground. I felt I knew what it was like to be in an air-raid. Crrrash — Crrack — BUMP. And then a terrible sound like a giant's fart; and all the time the wind rose, and whirled those poor icy skeleton trees until they cracked again. It was awful to think of our poor old friends out there, the beech, the aspen, the ilex, and wonder which would be struck next. R. and I sat over the library fire, and while I tried to read he was finishing his review for the *New Statesman.* Then I got out my typewriter and typed what he had written. We were sitting thus, R. writing, I typing, at quarter to twelve when all the lights went out. We groped about in the kitchen, found some candles and took them to bed with us, where we lay for some time listening to that fearful, unceasing, shattering Crrrash, BOOMP, Crrack.

"I believe this is Hitler's secret weapon," said R. "If it is, I surrender at once. I can't stand it."

*January 29th*

Woke at six. The crashes were still resounding, and as soon as it was light we got up and looked at the damage. A huge piece off the beech, several from the ilex, all the elms along the wall decapitated and the big oak in the field reduced to a joke. It now began to snow. No postman; no newspaper. The scene in front of the house is one of savage desolation. It has a prehistoric look; one expects to see a Megatherium cross the park. During the morning the water gave out and there was no electricity to pump more. The avenue was like a story by Hans Andersen, with the wych elms dangling long fingers covered in glassy ice, and underneath them several little gnomes dressed in black, with faces red with cold, trying to remove fallen branches. In the lane the telephone wires lay tangled and looped in hopeless confusion like wool played with by a monstrous kitten.

*January 30th*

The last day of this extraordinary month. Very slowly, drip by drip, the thaw began. In the afternoon R. and I with a trowel and a rake hit the branches of some of the trees and shrubs — the cherry, the magnolia

— to free them from their ice. They drew themselves up, very slowly, like people stretching themselves. As for the European War, this local war against the elements has practically put it out of everyone's head.

Seven partridges, fluffed out as round as seven footballs, ventured on the lawn in search of food. A steady thaw goes on, but the electricity supply has become unhinged again, so we sat by candlelight. You would think to hear Nannie talk that she's the only person suffering from lack of hot water and light.

An evening of the utmost peace, however, writing letters and reading Madame du Deffand.

*February 2nd*

The sun did its best to come through, illuminating the glass trees with a pale waxy light. The shepherd drove his flock across the waste land of the park; they looked quite black against the snow. Poor things, they eagerly nibbled at the blades of grass in their glass cases.

Nannie has been insufferable all day, popping toads out of her mouth with every breath. I took her two books this evening, to mollify her. She replied instantly with two toads! I was so furious, I left the room instantly, banging the door quietly behind me. A few minutes later a tap on the library door. Would we like to borrow her wireless? NO NANNIE, WE WOULDN'T. It was delightful gazing owlishly at the red logs, with Tiger [our cat] warm and soft on my lap, and the smell of the candles reminding me of Christmas trees. Like the light of the candles, each of us has our own fitful flame.

*February 6th*

Joan Cochemé to stay. I have retired to bed with 'flu. R. and Joan spent yesterday evening, so he tells me, sitting in the library, talking about the last war until far into the night, with the tears running down both their cheeks. I wish that everyone could hear R.'s vivid and detailed description of his war experiences — they are infinitely moving, and pacifism seems the only conclusion to draw from them, as he found himself.

F.: "I wish Lytton was here to discuss Madame du Deffand with me."

R.: "I know. I often wish Lytton was here. Life would be very much improved."

*February 10th*

My first day up. When I got downstairs the sun was filling the sitting-room, whose familiar colours — blue, dull purple and honey — acted as

28

balm to my spirits. I looked at the glowing row of Spanish plates on top of the book-shelf and thought with pleasure and some pride how we had contrived to surround ourselves with a great deal of visual beauty. Clive arrived in time for lunch, staggering in with a huge bundle of washing, like a jovial Father Christmas. James [Strachey] had written to R. suggesting getting Lytton's letters typed with a view to publication. This led to a discussion, Clive throwing up his hands in horror. "Old Bloomsbury would be dead against it, and if they were published no-one would be on speaking terms with their oldest friends."

Surely it's very odd for the Apostles of Truth to be so queasy about facing it when it concerns themselves?

*February 16th*

Nicholses to stay. A discussion with Phyllis about martyrs. She said how important it was that there should be people prepared to suffer *anything* for their ideals. This somehow got my stuffy old rationalist goat, and I suggested that the only way to change people's opinions was by persuasion, that unless one changed their opinions one had done no good. It's possible to admire and pity a martyr while being left unconvinced of the truth of his belief. Martyrdom is in fact a form of force on the part of the martyr. All to no purpose, for the light of St. Sebastian was in Phyllis's eye. The two Phils embarked on their usual argument with each other about Winning the War: Phil's best remark was: "This is nothing but a confession of opinion wrung from an idealist who believes we are living in the Jungle."

This evening I finished reading Madame du Deffand. She must have remained mentally alert till the last week of her life. I feel exactly as if I had just lived through that last year in her house and her society. Mme du D. on war: *"L'horrible chose que la guerre! Quel bien peut-elle jamais produire? . . Je frémis en pensant que dans le moment où je suis dans mon tonneau à effiler mes chiffons, mille coups de canon partent, et emportent bras, jambes, têtes à d'honnêtes gens qui n'avaient rien à démêler avec ceux qui les assassinent; la guerre est de toutes les folies la plus atroce."*

*February 27th*

To Rockbourne to spend a night with Desmond and Molly [MacCarthy]. Desmond came in from having his portrait painted by Henry Lamb, who he said had made him look "a sly old Yid". He was dressed, like all Henry's sitters, in a great many waistcoats, one red. He said: "I must tell you I had a message from ON HIGH the other day. It said 'Armistice Day will be on August 16th.' " Later he spoke about some "very fine hogs" there were in the neighbourhood; he took us to see them and although actually sows, they were of enormous size and rootling about in the richest mud. Desmond delighted in scratching their backs with his walking-stick, making them squawk and grunt. Molly stood aloof, saying she didn't like pigs, she couldn't see any point in them whatever. At dinner she suddenly dropped a bottle of claret on the floor with a bang; it fell over but didn't break. It is, I suppose the sort of thing that happens daily and Desmond didn't turn a hair. Afterwards, Desmond and Molly sat one on each side of the fire and Desmond read aloud to us while Molly lay back and snored gently. Then she woke up and read us Joad's views on picnic food (which had somehow fascinated and re-pelled her) with great expression and explosions of laughter. Conversa-tions with these two masters of the art charmed us until bedtime. Stories of Desmond's: "I was sitting with Logan [Pearsall-Smith] in the garden, in front of a stone path with a bust at the end of it. I said, 'Logan, what would you feel if that bust came hoppity hop along the path towards you?' 'Disgust.' " And "Once when Molly and I were walking back from Ampthill in the dark, I suddenly said: 'Molly, are you sure it's *me*, Desmond, you're walking with and not a spirit from another world?' and Molly *screamed* and *boxed* my ears."

*February 28th*

Our morning at Rockbourne flew by in talk. If conversation were always so absorbing and effortless one would never want to do anything else.

Lunched with Pansy [Lamb] and her children — a thin, serene Madonna with her little boy Valentine in her arms. He has a wonderful head with a great forehead and speculative blue eyes. The Lambs' life is uncorrupted by respectability, which I find sympathetic. There were holes in the sofa cover, and books and mess everywhere.

Driving home through Salisbury, I noticed that whereas in 1938 the Green had been an untidy mess of trenches, rubble and earth, they are now neatly roofed over and beginning to cover with grass, and have entrances and steps like Public Lavatories. They look commonplace in fact, and I suppose in this lunatic world that is what they will be — in every town in England.

*March 2nd*

Raymond for a few days and much talk — war, books, people. We drove to a local tea-party reminiscent of the last war. There were two subal-terns, one shy, one talkative, a golfing lady, a learned elderly gent, dogs, excellent cakes and innocent jokes. "Do you read the *Bystander* much?"

one subaltern asked Raymond, who said he had "had a job not to giggle".

*March 10th*

The Wests to lunch. Anthony discussed his military service. He finds that CO's aren't allowed on minesweepers as they carry guns, but has more or less decided that a minesweeper shall be his fate none the less, and reached calm with the decision.

While Burgo and I were planting some primroses we had dug up from the woods, Edie appeared looking surprised and said, "There's a corporal to see you." In the darkness of the hall I saw some big tin-hatted shapes entering the front door. It could only mean billetting I thought. But one stepped into the light, and it was Justin Vulliamy and a friend, who had motor-biked from Newbury. Burgo couldn't under-stand that they were going to have tea with us. When I said they hadn't always been soldiers, but friends of ours, he said, "Are they really *men*?"

*March 13th*

To London to the dentist. In Oxford Street I was struck by the fierce animal faces of the passers-by, and felt like a tame rabbit away from its hutch, among so many dogs, birds, wolves and monkeys, ranging the streets and boarding buses. Every chance remark was concerned with food. "WON'T eat sausages, WON'T eat macaroni", I heard at the bus stop; and "Beef irritates me", inside John Lewis.

I visited Julia [Strachey]'s flat. Lawrence [Gowing] came in carry-ing a bag of eggs which he laid before her like a dog a bone. He's so amusing and so full of intelligent ideas that his stammer must be a great curse (for I don't believe Alix [Strachey]'s famous remark: "Never feel sorry for stammerers. They *enjoy* it.") Julia advised him to stammer as much as possible at his C.O. Tribunal: result, he made a long speech without faltering.

*March 18th*

At Rockbourne, talking to Rachel and David till past twelve. Only last thing did we talk of the war. Ralph, Rachel and David all in cheerful, hopeful vein; I had to testify to my gloom. For about the war I am utterly gloomy and hopeless. It amazes me to hear people talking of reconstruction, Federal union, reforms, as if we were now at this moment working for them, instead of being engaged in nothing but disintegration and destruction. If any reconstruction is to come it can only be in peacetime, and now that we are at war we are much farther from it than we were last summer. I think I must have wanted to make the others share my depression. David was cheerfully bellicose. In bed though very tired I couldn't sleep, and at last about four o'clock I got out Peter Lucas's diary of the September crisis and read it while the wind rattled the curtains.

*March 19th*

We talked of the varying intensities at which people required to live. I said, thinking it was axiomatic, that my great — almost my only — object in life was to be as intensely conscious as possible. To my surprise neither Ralph nor David agreed in the least. What I most dread is that life should slip by unnoticed, like a scene half glimpsed from a railway-carriage window. What I want most is to be always reacting to something in my surroundings, whether a complex of visual sensations, a physical activity like skating or making love, or a concentrated process of thought; but nothing must be passively accepted, everything modified by passing it through my consciousness as a worm does earth. Here too comes in my theory that pleasure can be extracted from experiences which are in themselves neutral or actually unpleasant, with the help of drama and curiosity, and by drama I mean the aesthetic aspect of the shape of events. The exceptions are physical pain and anxiety, the two most stultifying states; I can't hold intensity of experience to be desirable in them.

Back to Ham Spray, where we found the Wests. I had written to Kitty to suggest that she should come and live with us while Anthony was at sea on his minesweeper. Anthony came up to the library and said he thought she might like to come for the summer. I wish now I had asked him more about his own feelings about going to the war, and if I have another chance I will, but I feel that with this subject one broaches a source of misery.

*March 23rd*

Alix and James [Strachey] arrived before dinner in their little car, well muffled up against the dreaded cold, with their gas masks, wireless and a jigsaw puzzle. There was a conversation about psycho-analysis after dinner. They view Karen Horney's recent book with suspicion, as she is a Freudian who has deviated from the Scriptures, and won't accept the universality of the castration complex. James brought out the last number of the *Journal of Psychoanalysis* which he now edits. It had a large photo of Freud, and he and Alix discussed this in detail, much (I can't help thinking) as if he were Jesus Christ. They told us of the

32

schism in the psycho-analytical ranks among the followers of Anna Freud and Melanie Klein, describing it as "about the presence or absence of cunts". They laughed a lot over this. They say the Viennese refugee analysts now in London are "snapping up all the patients".

In the dining-room an argument about the war started, which took an old-fashioned Cambridge shape, mainly because of Alix saying, "Now — one moment — I must ask you to say *exactly* what is your reason for saying that." The Wests are much more emotionally affected by the war than the rest of us: they had to blame someone for their present misery and Mr. Chamberlain was the Aunt Sally. He must be wicked "because he represented big business". James, who said little and that explosively, declared that Chamberlain could *not* be wicked because he had a passion for Beethoven's last quartets. Kitty kept a wonderful control, even when her polite "Surely that's true isn't it?" was met again and again by Alix's firm *"No"*. Anthony mumbled that naturally he felt more strongly than the rest of us as he was of military age, and he was in a frightful muddle and hated talking about the war.

*March 25th*

R. and I were in the bathroom when we got a message that Mr. Garnett was on the telephone. R. went along to answer it, and it was to say that Ray died last night. R. said, "I'm afraid I sounded too brisk." F.: "What did you say?" R.: "I said, 'That's a very good thing.' " R.: "And then what?" R.: "Then Bunny said goodbye. He sounded in a terrible state." I could think of nothing but poor Bunny, faced with the horrible strangeness of death.

Alix hadn't even heard she was ill, though James had known all about it from Noel [Olivier] for two months, showing a remarkable lack of intercommunication. I had a craving to be alone and talk to R. about it, but he hung about with his hens and a bonfire and I felt hurt and abandoned. Later I relieved my feelings by telephoning Bunny and asking him here to meet Richard and William.[1]

*March 29th*

Bunny and both his boys are with us. Went to meet the boys' train, which was late, so I had time to watch everybody else on the platform. An officer was talking to a sergeant of about the same age, physique, intelligence and apparent value as a human being. This equality made the difference in their demeanour and movements ridiculous somehow — the drawling upper-class voice, casual gestures and slight stoop of one, and the braced attention and fixed eyes of the other. Trivial no

[1] His sons.

33

doubt, but I have always been fascinated by the language of voice and gesture.

Richard and William arrived at last, Richard self-possessed and talkative, William sunk and hunched in tangible gloom. Bunny and the boys each seemed to be dumbly saying, "You see we still have each other."

Bunny and I listened to Winston's broadcast, which he liked and I hated. He said with a distorted face that we ought to broadcast to the Germans that "we're going to bomb them to blazes". When the boys had gone to bed, Bunny, who looked quite exhausted, gave us a long account of Ray's death, talking till one, and leaving us flattened by the pathos.

After the Garnett family left R. and I talked it all over. I never stop thanking my stars for the way we completely understand each other's ideas, even when we don't share them.

*April 3rd*

Bunny writes that "it was a blessed weekend for me, and how good it was for the boys to feel the world was full of friendly faces. The piano and Burgo's kite ought perhaps to be thanked personally for their existence."

Spring is now making great strides, a forest of grape hyacinths in the rockery, daffodils in the grass, green on lilac and honeysuckle, hands of the chestnut tree spreading their fingers.

Gerald rang up to say he could not come over and see Helen [Anrep], as he and Gamel were off to Brighton. Would we apologize to her and ask her to come and visit them there? This gesture is purest Geraldine in style. The formula is that when one of your oldest friends visits your neighbourhood, although you have not seen her for a very long time, you leave for somewhere else *on the very day of her arrival*, and then beg her to follow you there.

Helen arrived this afternoon in an aura of flattery, amiability and vanity, wearing an eccentric hat with her pretty grey hair floating out in wisps from under it.

R. is reading Karen Horney, and identified Helen as the Super-ego type who cannot bear to be in the wrong. But she is not in the least neurotic. She merely has a blazing belief in her own knowledge how life should be lived, food cooked, children brought up and the "right" painters encouraged to paint. She hasn't a shadow of doubt that we would have had peace in Europe now, if she had been Prime Minister.

Shopping in Hungerford. Mr. Barnard, the greengrocer, was full of what sounded like wild rumours of Hitler having annexed Denmark and being now in Copenhagen. But it was quite true. We were jerked back into the war like fish that have forgotten for a bit that they are on the end of a hook. We drove home deeply disquieted, and for the rest of the day the wireless was dominant. For the second time the war is coming nearer, looming up large and threatening. Air-raids, invasion, refugees — one's whole body reacts with a taut restlessness, as though one had a lump of lead for a stomach and sensitive wires from it reaching to toes and fingers. The strangely casual voice of the announcer told us that at this very moment large-scale naval engagements were taking place, calling up visions of wallowing ships, shattering explosions, and soldiers sinking like stones because of the heavy equipment they carried. I put on records, Monteverdi and Haydn, hoping that music would have its usual magical effect in restoring belief in the existence of logic and sanity, but tonight it seemed impossible to correlate the two disparate worlds, the musical one of reason and the mad one of events.

*April 10th*

R. was stirring soon after seven, and at eight he went down to listen to the news. In a naval battle off Narvik, described as "wholly successful", we lost two destroyers and a third damaged. While these sensational events are happening all other interests are submerged in intense, painful excitement. Gaps between the news are intolerable; human feelings about drowning sailors and terrified civilians flash into my head and out again, leaving only a passionate absorption in the course of events. I can no longer relate them to my beliefs about peace and war — they are insulated. "Good", one says, hearing of an enemy troopship sunk and thousands of men drowned in the Skagerrak. The Downs tonight looked dry and colourless, with dusty rabbit-scars on their sides. Over them a heavy cloud the colour of a battleship and a crescent moon in a peacock-blue sky. Helen Anrep and I sat by the sitting-room fire talking about the future of Europe, and her belief in progress, which I do not share.

There seem to be two possibilities: an attack on the West through Belgium or Holland, and air-raids on London. Round and round goes my head.

*April 16th*

English troops have landed in Norway: this news makes most people more cheerful but no less anxious, and I see that even we pacifists may soon become like the Japanese schoolboys, whose photos I shall not forget in a hurry, egging on the perpetrators of an execution with male and bellicose "give-it-him" attitudes.

The campaign in Norway is our main interest and subject of conver-

35

sation. This evening I felt, not for the first time, what vast and horrid possibilities lie in the situation. Then, with a sudden click, we return to our quiet and beautiful Ham Spray and its garden. "I *like* my life", R. said this evening.

### April 20th

Yesterday's rain has produced miracles. I have to keep walking round the garden to see all the new arrivals — two red tulips in the rockery, and the blue anemones in the border. I feel about our garden and view as I do about the face of a crony: everything in it is familiar and charming, even the flaws in its perfection. The peculiar sound of the wind in the ironwork of the verandah is like a tone of voice. I'm worried by the changed silhouette of the hanger on the downs, made by the ice storm. The old friend has had an accident and got a scar which takes getting used to.

Gerald and Gamel came to lunch. Gerald has recovered from his trench mouth but can't get his false teeth in, and as he has exactly every other one missing he presents a peculiar machicolated appearance. About 10.30 at night, after they had gone, we went out into the sweet night air. There was a halo round the moon and a wind blowing the white flowers about in the rockery. The sky was partly covered with an eiderdown of small fleecy clouds. It was very like the sky of the first night of the war, I suddenly remembered, as I walked round the garden staring up and thinking of the contrast between the quiet eternity of the sky and the rumbustious frenzy of human existence.

### April 24th

R. said at breakfast: "I see some curious things dropping from the sky. What can they be? My God, they're wistaria buds!" He rushed out and found them being wantonly picked off and dropped on the ground by villainous sparrows who didn't even want to eat them.

Perhaps the badness of the Norwegian news was too much for us. R. was inclined to feel I was responsible for the nibbled wistaria, his lost knife, and a hen's having laid an egg in the shrubbery which couldn't be found.

I went off for a lonely walk across the plover field, due north from here. Two carthorses were harrowing the field and the plovers screamed over my head as I plodded up the long hill. I wasn't consciously thinking of the war, and only realized after some time that the plovers had been shrieking NAR-vik to my ears. Over the brow I got into that wonderfully strange region R. and I discovered last autumn, with short rabbity turf, deserted barns and groves of thorns growing in a bog.

There were masses of the biggest primroses I ever saw, violets, cowslips, celandine and blackthorn. I loved being in this sweet secret place, alone except for the scurrying rabbits and the birds singing in the trees.

Here I escaped from the war for a bit, which isn't so easy while the Germans continue to advance in Norway.

A conversation about the nature of our interest in the conduct of the war. A few weeks ago we thought very little about it, now we are absorbed in the strategic drama of the Norwegian campaign, and are of course delighted when our troops do well. "If we so much want the Allies to win, shouldn't it logically follow that we ought to help them to?" I asked. R. answered with an analogy: "It's as if all our money had against our wills been put on a certain horse running in the Derby. We may hate horse-racing, disapprove of it even — yet we still want that horse to win. If we are to remain sane we *must* follow the news with interest, and we *must* mind what we hear."

*April 28th*

Hester [Chapman] is staying here. A conversation between her and R. about what we are fighting for. "Because a Nazi regime, concentration camps, etc. are worse than death," says Hester. "Yes, but worse than whose death?" says R. "Your young men friends? If not, suicide is the correct answer."

*April 30th*

David and Rachel to a short quick lunch. It passed like a rattle of musketry. David maintained his optimism, but Rachel looked pale and ill. "You don't think it's *possible* we might lose the war?" she asked R. "Certainly it's possible." David managed to be cheerful even about that. "We could all emigrate to Canada together and lead a pleasant sort of Scotch life there." I'm sure he is concerned to shield Rachel from the despair that threatens to submerge her, and I felt afterwards we'd been unkind and had no business to threaten their defences.

*May 2nd*

After an access of hope yesterday, this evening's news told of our complete withdrawal from southern Norway. The announcer seemed to dislike his task and sighed deeply as he performed it. The effect on me was crushing and bewildering; I felt even physically sick. What has been painful about the Norwegian campaign has been the struggle to maintain hope, for which at last there seemed some basis. Now it's gone and here is another country to be "mopped up" by Germany. R. commented on my pinched serious expression. Why did I take it so heavily? There followed a conversation about what subjects one could joke about. I agreed that all subjects could be joked about, but thought not all emotions about those subjects were joke-producing. For instance, jokes arising from acute anxiety over illness would be hollow and false. R. said his ideal was to die joking like Mercutio, and he had seen many people do so. I defended seriousness. This I do with head as well as heart (which is indubitably in a serious mood). What I'm suffering from is the crushing of a hope, built on stronger foundations than I knew, of the war being ended quickly through the Norwegian campaign, and the realization again of the *immense* strength of Germany. Therefore two horrid and inescapable alternatives arise in all their grimness – either a German victory or a very long bitter struggle indeed.

In contrast to all this, it has been the most lovely May day, blue and green of the purest.

I sent Rachel a postcard of a battleship, saying I felt we had been depressing company the other day. David rang up to ask if they could lunch with us today, and I felt warmly to them both for taking it in such good part.

*May 8th*

Visit to London. So long since we'd been that it was quite like going abroad. Would the crossing be rough and where were our passports? Harrods' sandwich bar was full of spending, cormorant women who were avidly stuffing food into their mouths. To Raymond's flat, where we were joined by Clive and Dora Morris. "If only there wasn't a war on," said Clive at one moment.

"Do you still want the war to stop?" asked Raymond. "I'm not arguing about it. I just want to know." Clive and I both answered "Yes".

*May 10th*

Gerald rang up soon after breakfast. "I suppose you've heard this morning's news." "No – what?" G.: "They've invaded Holland and I believe Belgium too."

So the blitzkrieg has begun at last! I felt a grip of fear and excitement mixed, as if a giant's hand had seized me round the waist where I stood by the telephone, picked me up and dropped me again. I called out and told R. At one o'clock an incredible story of waves of bombers swooping over the flat land, and German parachutists dropping out of the sky just before dawn like flocks of starlings. I thought of the jackdaws dropping out of the hole in our great aspen. Then I felt calmer than for a long time. Now it's going to begin in real earnest – and it's almost a

38

relief, as if one had lain for ages on the operating table and at last the surgeon was going to begin.

Julia [Strachey] rang up to know if there were likely to be raids on London and if she might come down on Tuesday.

Gerald arrived unexpectedly for tea, in pensive mood, very charming. He talked all through dinner about the situation in Spain, but showed a touch of the old spirit when he said that Fascists and Pacifists should both be interned, since they were ranged on the same side. Saw him bicycle off into the sweet-smelling darkness.

Chamberlain has abdicated, handing over the premiership to Winston Churchill.

*May 13th*

Everyone makes jokes about the likelihood of German parachutists landing in our Wiltshire fields dressed as nuns or clergymen – a good farcical subject on which to let off steam. This afternoon I was alone in the kitchen when the doorbell rang, and there on the step stood three tall bearded men who addressed me in strong German accents, and wore something between clergyman's and military dress! Aha! I thought, the parachutists already. But when they asked for Mrs. Nichols I realised that it was some of the Brüderhof, a community of Christian Pacifists of all nations who live the simple life near Swindon. Curiosity was too much for me, so I asked them to have some tea. Two were very unattractive redheads with scarlet mouths above their beards. It was the maddest of mad hatter tea parties, consisting of me and these three Jesus Christs, all looking at me sweetly and speaking in gentle voices. I told them we were pacifists. "Are you persecuted much?" they asked, rather taking the wind out of my sails. I felt as if Jesus Christ had mistaken me for John the Baptist.

*May 14th*

Drove to the station to fetch Julia and M.A.M.[1] Julia and I walked along the grassy terrace under the Downs. I was almost brained by a wounded pheasant. "Perhaps it's a disguised parachutist," said Julia. On the wireless we hear ghastly stories of the German advance, calling up a picture of columns of giant machines, a sky black with aeroplanes, and the unceasing crash of bombs and explosives. "Well, it's fucking awful, that's all I can say," said Julia. Yet I think a strange calm possesses us all.

[1] My mother.

39

Returning to bed this morning R. said, "Well, that's what comes of listening to the early news. Holland has surrendered to Germany." It has now become a familiar feeling, this dropping of something inside one with a sick thud, an internal bucket into an invisible well of despair. So now the Germans, their armies and aeroplanes, face us across the Channel. In no time — days even — we may all be enduring the same horrors as Holland and Belgium. We talked about suicide. I thought with envy of Ray, and longed to have some safe way of dying within my power. R. said we could easily gas ourselves in the car, all three of us. We were still talking of this as we went along to the bath, and of how happy our lives have been, and so has Burgo's, though there has been so little of it.

We are told that parachute descents upon England "are now extremely likely". Everyone must shut up their cars every night or disconnect their engines. How MAD to be sitting listening to such things.

My greatest preoccupation is with the question of how to get a supply of lethal pills. I turn it over and over in my mind. I feel it would be the greatest possible help to know that we had death in our power. I look back at our state of a few weeks ago with envy, and hope for no positive happiness but merely for means to keep this acute misery at bay.

There were several calls on the telephone from Alec Penrose, who has bought a house at Eastbury. One made us laugh — it was to ask what he should do with his first and second Shakespeare folios. Should he bury them? Does he really want them to survive him?

Like the zooming that under war conditions affects the wireless, the war swings nearer and further, pendulum-wise. This morning it was booming right in our ears. "Hitler's weather" still blazes away uncomfortably; the world of the lawn is as hot as a furnace.

In the afternoon our attention switched to ordinary things nearer home, meeting Molly's train and shopping. When I got back the Wests had arrived for tea. Molly looked pale and tired, but was in wonderfully eccentric form, producing a characteristic stream of remarks and wild gestures. She kept looking out for Julia, having heard she was with us, and mistook Anthony, Kitty and M.A.M. for her in turn. Then when she did appear of course she failed to recognise her.

Everything — sitting on the lawn, Burgo's games of Snakes and Ladders — seemed so like the activity of a normal summer day as to blot out the war. But it was there, like some horrible virus working away under our skins, and in the evening it rose to the surface in the form of deadly fatigue and inertia. Talking to Molly was an effort, and we all yawned our heads off. M.A.M. and Julia went upstairs, but still Molly wouldn't go to bed, until we insisted.

*May 19th*

Very broken sleep all night. Soon after six I became aware that the rest of the bed was empty. Heard R.'s feet padding round the garden. It has become unnecessary to look out of the window, one knows there will be a cloudless blue sky and glorious sun. The perfection of the weather is getting on all our nerves. It is too phenomenal and everything super-normal is unnerving; also it's impossible not to remember that it is ideal weather for air-raids. The German advance into France goes on. I feel a strong desire to creep away, curl up and become unconscious.

The only happy people today were M.A.M. and Burgo, who spent the morning having a long, intensely dramatic conversation about fire-engines. As they moved from one place to another I heard Burgo say: "Come along Grannie, and we'll go on talking. I love talking, don't you, Grannie?" And then: "Oh my stars and stripes!"

I can't make up my mind whether it is better to force myself to realize the probable nearness of nightmare, or deliberately not think about it.

The Brenans arrived to tea on bicycles, Gamel wearing a divided skirt and with her arms scratched to pieces from having fallen off into a haw-thorn bush. Again the ordinary tenor of life was propped up during most of the day by invisible social supports, but as evening came it collapsed. The nine o'clock news brought no consolation, only a speech by Winston saying we must all prepare to suffer the war in our own country and be proud to share the experiences of our Brave Boys in France.

We all sank into our private worlds of despair. Julia sat with her head thrown back gazing at the ceiling. I stared woodenly in front of me. Molly buried her head in her hands. Only M.A.M. seemed stimulated and talkative.

*May 20th*

Molly and M.A.M. were taken to their trains. Before she left I sat for some time with M.A.M. on the verandah and tried to convince her we should like her to come back as soon as possible, which is not strictly true. I'm too anxious about the effect on her of R.'s occasional fierce-ness, though they are deeply attached to each other. Peace of a sort settles down again on house and garden. One is not fit to have visitors in this state we are all in; and to meet the extra strain a jerky marionette's response is developed, which relaxes with relief when they go.

The flawless weather and wholly bad news still goes on. Anxiety at full pitch. R. very jumpy all the morning.

*May 22nd*

Rain! Hitler's weather has at last broken. I woke feeling my brain had been cooled by sleep and rain, and began to wonder aloud what we should do if we heard the Germans had landed. I had a job to convince R. that I would trust entirely to his courage and masculine strategy in emergency.

"I don't know what'll happen when the fatal moment comes," said Julia at breakfast. "You have such totally different views on the subject, you'll never agree." (Julia doesn't like married couples to agree.)

But it became evident that we saw eye to eye.

R.: "Under the influence of fear one does one of two things. Either runs like a hare, or squats like a hare."

Julia: "Well what lesson can we draw from the hare?" She went on to say her plan was to make herself look very old and ugly so as not to be raped. R. laughed immoderately at this.

At six o'clock we heard the expected sinister news that there is fighting in and around Belgium. All our eyes meet and have the same expression in them. Went up to bath Burgo, feeling sick, but later unreasoning optimism came over me.

*May 24th*

My first thought on waking is – well, we have got through another night. And there is distinct surprise at hearing only the birds and farm noises instead of the expected explosions.

Went outside before breakfast to take a breath of the sweet air heavily scented with May. All the May trees have come out at once at the same time as the cow parsley, making a vision of powdered white on fields and trees together. We actually had a conversation about aesthetics at breakfast, quite like old times. The music of Mozart's clarinet quintet, which I played while writing, was like a voice coming from a very long way away indeed. Perhaps one should struggle more to keep in touch with such things, but there is no energy to spare for struggling. I wonder, supposing the war should get back to the eventless, dug-in stage of the old days, would the relief of it make one callous to the bloody horrors, now in progress and the agony of people with husbands, sons and lovers on the battlefield?

At lunch we heard news of the first bombs dropped on English soil, in Yorkshire, East Anglia and Essex. Not many people were hurt and none killed, and I almost felt relief – which I think is because I half expected the first raids to be on a colossal scale – shock tactics. Really dreadful depression settled on me after the news, and I wished I was dead in all earnest.

Audrey [Bonham-Carter] brought us our ducks this afternoon – two lots. Some very young ones, with a hen, were installed in a run on the badminton lawn. She told us that Victor has now received orders to "shoot all defeatists at sight". So one soon won't be able to speak one's mind to anyone. There's something deadly and cramping about these hedges of suspicion and misunderstanding rising up so rapidly.

"The situation is of increasing gravity hour by hour," said tonight's announcer. So it became one of those evenings when R. sighs, Julia and I yawn incessantly (a nervous symptom), and I end by falling asleep in my chair over my book.

*May 28th*

"They're evidently trying to prepare us for something awful," said R. I went down to hear a promised announcement by M. Reynaud from Paris. In the voice of a worn-out old Comédie Française actor he droned out: "*Je vais vous annoncer une nouvelle très gra-a-ave.*" It was that (on the order of King Leopold) the Belgian Army had capitulated without warning the French or English. What is to happen to the B.E.F., already in a terrible position, and now one must suppose cut off?

Nannie couldn't take it in when I told her. A *King* to behave so! Or was it really happening in Norway?

The implications are far from easy to grasp. That being so, I lapsed into a dim insensibility which rather shocked me. It almost worries me that I *can't* feel anxious. The ducklings flew about the lawn all day, followed by their worried clucking hen. Herded into their pen they nestled down, seeming to say, "We've had a *splendid* day." Lucky things.

*May 31st*

Julia and R. saw a lorry blazing through Hungerford, packed with uprooted signposts all pointing in different directions. We are told this is to confuse the invaders. Julia described it as "A blood-curdling sight".

We visited the Brenans at Aldbourne, finding them friendly, calm and sensible. Gerald thinks we have little to fear from bombs, that even if the French make peace we shall probably win the war in the end, and that even if we don't life won't be unendurable. (If so, why go through the horrors of a war *first*, I couldn't help reflecting.)

Anne and Heywood Hill to stay. Heywood expects to be called up before Christmas. He is taking a First Aid course, hoping perhaps to be able to join as a hospital orderly or stretcher bearer. All the morning, which was gloriously fine, they practised bandaging each other with a triangular handkerchief on which were printed parts of the body. So that one would see Anne with a small human bottom on her breast.

There has been intense anxiety over the fate of the B.E.F. in Flanders, so that stories of their arrival in England in great numbers are cheering to listen to, because they stand for hundreds of *individual* happy endings. Also the Germans believed they had our army encircled, and for once they were wrong.

Winston's speech in Parliament rounded up the Retreat from Flanders, which has now become almost a Victory. About 330,000 men have been brought safely back, thank God for that, but no retreat can ever have taken place with a greater blaring of trumpets and headlines.

The Wests came to tea; while waiting to be called up Anthony has bought a farm at Ecchinswell.

There have been air-raids on the East Coat of England the last two nights, doing little damage. To the Brenans and Bomfords. The Bomfords are giving shelter to a young German pianist; while he was playing Mozart and Schubert for us, two immense police sergeants arrived to see him and paraded past the window, inkpots in hands. Coming home we were stopped by two 'parachute' patrols, who asked to see our identity cards – vague young men, pointing guns at us, as if playing some stupid game.

Raymond arrived by train; we spent most of the day lying under the beech tree, taking refuge from the terrific heat, which goes on and on, parching the earth and withering the flowers and vegetables. Raymond said he felt there was bad news coming this weekend and that Ham Spray would be a good place to hear it. Apart from our Pacifism, he takes much the same view of the war as we do. Sitting in the cool of the evening among the exuberant pink roses and tall valerian on the verandah, we talked to Raymond about suicide. His French doctor friend has been asked by almost all his patients for a safe poison, generally by means of hints.

The wireless room has become a dentist's waiting room and I get at

44

times a superstitious feeling, "Switch it off quickly and it may never happen". Well, yes, it was bad news today and it was an effort to struggle back, as into one's saddle after being knocked off a horse by a branch.

*June 13th*

A black awakening. Germans are closing in on Paris. How *can* we win this war? Oh, if only we could then lose it quickly. I find my personal armour of fatalism getting more and more impregnable as disasters pile one on top of another, but only at the cost of blotting out a vast terrain accessible to thought and imagination, yet which for safety's sake must not be thought of or imagined. I can't help feeling this is a madman's escape, and it produces a very sub-human dead level of consciousness, without elasticity or scope for reflection. We are just pegging along a straight dusty road. Clive arrived to spend the night, very late, as more children are being evacuated from London and the trains are disorganised.

*June 14th*

Clive's philosophy is unshaken by the war. He has been admirable company. He is determined not to alter his way of life unless he has to, and to go on getting all the enjoyment out of it that he possibly can. And although I'm not sure what he thinks will be the final outcome, he manages to convey an impression of ultimate optimism going beyond the question of who wins. He was just the right person to be with when R., coming back from the one o'clock news, said: "You were right. Paris has fallen." Speaking for myself I felt absolutely nothing, almost indifferent. This war deals one so many blows on the head in such rapid succession that it's hardly odd that insensibility results.

Gerald came over on his bicycle, and the four of us sat discussing the news under the ilex tree. He has a horror of the idea of suicide; not so Gamel apparently. Everyone could easily be placed in one of these two compartments. In the first I can only include, with any strong probability R. and myself, Raymond, Gamel, Leo [Myers], Phyllis [Nichols]. The members of the other group (such as Gerald and Julia) are filled with righteous indignation against the idea. A few days ago a friend of the Brenans living near Swindon tried to get his wife to sign a suicide pact because of the war. She was very tenacious of life, and refused. So next morning he came in and shot her as she sat at her writing-table, and afterwards shot himself.

The Germans in Paris, in the cafés and everywhere! It's very difficult to imagine it. But it's a good deal less painful than to think of Paris and

Parisians being burnt and destroyed by bombs. I am certain the French will make peace in a few days. But will we?

*June 17th*

I got a reply this morning from Margaret Penrose[1] to a letter I wrote her exactly a month ago asking for her advice on suicide drugs. She writes, "I can't prescribe a poison, but I can produce a cure", and goes on to suggest our all packing up and going to start a new life in Canada. She also told us that Lionel was thinking of throwing up his career as a geneticist and starting a farm in British Columbia – which seems to me about as sensible as Casals throwing up playing the 'cello and starting to breed ducks. What would one feel like, I wonder, steaming across the Atlantic? That one was leaving a festering sore behind, very thankfully? R. says one thing and one only would occupy one's mind – was there a periscope anywhere about.

Well then, at lunchtime Marjorie Strachey rang up. She was hoping to take a party of children to America as soon as possible. Would we like to send Burgo? Mothers might get a passage but no fathers. I said I would think it over, though of course it's out of the question. How could one send poor little Burgo off, entirely away from everyone and everything he knows? And if the Germans beat us, as it looks as though they almost certainly will, we might never be able to join him again.

The French government has fallen and been succeeded by Pétain, Weygand and others. I told R. who was sitting reading by the weeping ash and he looked very shattered. He said he felt quite sick. I can't help thinking, "Thank goodness the French no longer have to fight."

*June 18th*

Julia writes, in a very good letter, that she means to stay with Lawrence in London for the present. "I don't feel anxiety any more personally – in any conscious form that is. I just feel that it is the end, and a stiffening up of one's motor resistances to greet the hail of destruction ahead. But there is a tell-tale nervous constriction all the while. Everyone here has bought themselves two-shilling boxes of ear-plugs to prevent concussion, and we all have corks on strings to wear round our necks and put into our mouths to prevent damage to the ear-drums! What a go!"

*June 19th*

R. and I to see the Brenans. Gerald, R. and I went for a walk, while Gamel had to attend a Red Cross meeting. Gerald and R. got into a

[1] A doctor, temporarily living in Canada.

political discussion that threatened to become heated, and I dropped behind and suddenly felt extraordinarily happy, tugging flowers and grasses out of the hedges. Gerald's new line about the war is that we are beaten now, and the thing is to make the best possible terms with Hitler. What a pity, he says, we can't raise a few better Fascists, Mosley is really rather too awful. If we could, he thinks we could get quite good terms – and what does the censorship of the Press matter? R. was fairly flummoxed by this *volte-face*, and tried in vain to drive it home to Gerald that it was one.

The last two nights there have been air-raids of over a hundred planes on various parts of England. Just before midnight I felt R. stiffen and hold his breath. The rumour is that some bombs fell near Swindon.

Phyllis rang up today kindly offering to take Burgo to America. She's going to try and take her children there and return herself, but Phil thinks it's already too late.

An Armistice has been signed between France and Germany.

A letter from M.A.M. today showing that she was quite shattered by the French collapse, because her unfailing optimism had left her quite unprepared. And now she will build up a new edifice of hope to be toppled over by the next blow that falls. Thank goodness that gloomy old crows like R. and me, who always expect the worst, don't have that special problem to deal with.

*June 23rd*

Jimmy Bomford was visited yesterday by a car containing eight policemen, one a Scotland Yard man. They thought it was about the German pianist, Peter Gellhorn, but "Oh no," they said, "we've come about *you*." They then went over the house from top to bottom, searched all the men bodily, and took away all Jimmy's papers and farm accounts. They would not say what were the grounds of suspicion, but they came to the conclusion it was village gossip, their having foreign friends, and Jimmy wearing a beard. When I tried to ring them up I was told the line was "out of service". I then tried to get onto the Wests and got the same answer. Surely *they* can't be searched too? But they had been, and came to tell us so. The police were there for about six hours and took away all their foreign books, maps and guides, and even some toy soldiers belonging to Anthony! They took him to Marlborough police station, where the Chief of Police was hectoring and disagreeable: "And by the way that's a pretty nasty shirt you're wearing." One of the things the police had against him was that he knew the Bomfords and Brenans! So I shan't be at all surprised if it's our turn to be searched next. I actually wandered round looking for things the police would be silly enough to carry off if they came here. Hugo's *German*, perhaps? Or

47

Clive's pacifist tract? Or this diary, I suppose.

There have been raids on England every night but one. Of course, even if they involve more than a hundred aeroplanes, as they generally do, they are nothing to what we must expect. At night when I hear aeroplane engines I feel differently about them, not that I assume they are German ones, but because I suppose they are up there because German planes are attacking somewhere.

*June 28th*

Mrs G., the Queen of Inkpen, met Audrey Bonham-Carter in Newbury and said, "Oh, Mrs. B-C, I don't know what you'll think of me for not having called on you before, but the fact is I was told your husband was a Conscientious Objector, so of course I thought it wasn't any use . . . " (He's not.) The general *dégringolade* of sense and wits into stupidity, crass suspicion and suggestibility, the lunatic sheepishness bred by this war are almost as bad as the brutality and destruction.

Brenans to lunch. I told Gerald (and it surprised him) that the police had mentioned him among the local suspects. "Oh, they have, have they? Well, they'd better not try anything on, that's all."

To meet Helen, who has come for three weeks' rest. We put her almost at once to bed, for she seems extremely tired, feeble and nervous. No-one could possibly have settled into bed in one's house more considerately and tactfully. She talked of the air-raid warnings in Suffolk and I felt her nerve was badly shaken. Talked too of suicide, but altruistically, not with reference to herself. If only she could drop her parade of living entirely for others, and of being an arbiter wearing Roger [Fry]'s mantle.

Meanwhile she lies in bed in the pink room as sweet and nice as can be, asking for nothing, apparently pleased with everything.

This evening she began to talk of her hopes for the future, the "new formula" that will be found, and progress — good God! I felt inwardly cynical, and indeed said I saw no spark of hope for the future. I find these conversations embarrassing.

*July 2nd*

There were daylight raids yesterday doing more damage than the night ones. Is this a preliminary to invasion?

We left Helen looking like a Goya, lying on the garden bed, with a black lace mantilla over her pretty white hair and went to tea with the Wests.

I bought some new records in London the other day and this morning I tried them. The Mozart Clarinet Concerto, and a piano sonata played by Schnabel, a Vivaldi concerto. The music was like a balloon whirling us up to a new atmosphere.

The Arandora Star has been torpedoed without warning in the Atlantic. It was taking German and Italian waiters, etc. to be interned in Canada, and about a thousand were drowned. That will make parents with American plans for their children quail for a little.

I wish I had kept a collection of the more imbecile letters in *The Times*, all saying in their different ways, "just see me die, how dashingly I'll do it". Or the balderdash uttered by politicians. Lord M. says, "If we must die let's die *gaily*," and Lord C. that we must do it "On our toes". "Go to it", and "Keep a high heart", and millions of other parrot cries. While we were shooting French sailors to blazes at Oran, other French sailors were careering round London with their arms round the necks of English soldiers, being fêted and stood drinks. Mad hatterdom.

M.A.M. has come for a short visit. She put Helen to shame with her energy and spirit, describing how she and three octogenarians had arrived for a demonstration of how to deal with incendiary bombs, and were greeted by a surprised-looking man who said, "Are *you* the fire-fighters?" She is as brave as a lioness and the prospect of raids on London doesn't make her quail in the least.

*July 6th*

*Gerald* is now in trouble with the police. It seems he was out with the Home Guard a few nights ago, and used his electric torch to inspect the sandbag defences. A short time later several policemen rode up on motor bikes and shouted, "You were signalling to the enemy!" Gerald blew up and they became more reasonable, but he was later told, "We think it only fair to tell you we have reported you to Headquarters as signalling to the enemy". The head of the Aldbourne Home Guard was sympathetic but thought nothing could be done. He quite agreed with Gerald that these were Gestapo methods — "Mind you, I think Fascism in one form or another has got to come." It seems to have come already. Gerald is thinking of resigning from the Home Guard and is very cynical about the hopeless confusion of our home defences.

Eleanor Rathbone in the *New Statesman*: "This is no time to speak of women's rights — except one: to give their lives for their country." R. says Feminists are the only women with a castration-complex. They are mad with jealousy at not being allowed a "weapon".

*July 10th*

For some time now we have had Helen Anrep, M.A.M. and both Wests staying, and considerate though they are I long to get away somehow

49

and somewhere into my own corner, put records on the gramophone, devote more time to Burgo, and enjoy such meagre solitude and independence as is available these days. I had resolved not to be irritated by M.A.M., and am sure she had made similar resolves, as our attitudes to the war are so different. But it hasn't exactly worked out. Today she invaded my privacy to crusade about protecting the nursery. "But I've bought some splinter-proof paint," I said. That wasn't enough; we ought to put wire netting over the windows, or move the beds into another room. "Well, all our rooms have windows," I said. "Oh yes, I suppose so. But don't you think you ought to have some buckets of sand about," and so on. She has been working up Nannie, an easy enough task, and enlisting the Wests and Helen as well. Oh Lord, what a bore it all is. At this stage the "horrors of war" consist in the friction between us ants creeping about and waiting for the "hail of destruction" which doesn't come. After a consultation with R. it was decided that wire should be put.

At dinner the twigs of our different opinions caught fire under the influence of wine. Kitty declared that "Mr. Chamberlain is a much greater danger than Hitler"; M.A.M.: "I always believe in standing up for my views,"; R.: "If anyone thinks he would rather die than suffer Nazi rule let him be the one to do it." Helen wished she could have "educated Milton, shaken Madame du Deffand, or given Raymond a good slapping." Oh for more tolerance!

*July 14th*

Julia and Lawrence arrived to lunch on bicycles. Helen was lying on her boat-like bed on the verandah, and we sat talking to her as she lay like a queen in a bower of blue agapanthus flowers. I thought she was enjoying the homage, but saw she looked tired and fretful. Julia and I walked together to the foot of the Downs while the others played bowls, and we looked back and saw their figures moving on the lawn, and sweet Ham Spray, pink among its greenery. In these dreary old days Julia's company is as reviving as a shot of strychnine. She told me she couldn't work, and was oppressed by not being in her own house, and by the lorries full of soldiers hurtling along the road.

When I went up to bed I opened the window and looked out. The night was soft and dark, the moon half obscured. Then I saw a finger of light make a delicate stroking movement behind the dark shapes of the trees. I went out on the lawn, feeling suddenly excited, and there over the Downs the searchlights were groping and criss-crossing to and fro, sometimes at feverish speed. Where the cloud was thick they made dense pools of light. For a second or two the reality of the German raids broke through my defences, and I thought of aeroplanes not as bird-like

50

objects, but as machines containing foreign-speaking men whose object was to hurl their lethal weapons on to our dear familiar landscape down here below.

*July 17th*

The Wests left for the new farm at Ecchinswell. I think their week here has quietly cemented our friendship. Helen too was all sweetness today and thanked us with tears in her eyes for "all our kindness" to her. I believe she really meant it. But when I took her her breakfast in bed she was looking well and angry. Her letter to Gamel about going to stay there had been answered by a short one from Gerald telling her to "come as soon as she got tired of H.S." and evading her questions about trouble and expense.

*July 19th*

An excursion to Marlow to visit the Myers and James and Alix. Leo [Myers] alluded to his last visit to us at the beginning of the war, and to his being in a queer state of mind. (We thought him practically mad at the time.) He has now dropped his Communism and switched to a conventionally patriotic pro-Churchill position.

At Lord's Wood Alix quickly produced for us *her* new attitude to the war. She has decided that as it is essential to win it we must do everything the Government tells us to. She has tried to give them all her mother's aluminium cooking utensils, she has had her blood tested and is proud but nervous to find herself a Universal Donor, she has put a label on her car saying "Lifts for servicemen" and she never moves without a small sack containing her gas-mask, morphia, splinter-proof glasses, reminding one of the White Knight. At least three times during the afternoon she said, "You see, I've decided we must win the war," and remained grave, in face of the merry laughter this caused. It's odd that so intelligent a woman takes a childish pleasure in carrying out orders.

*July 20th*

We have been told that Hitler has started a Peace Offensive, but no details. It is the first bit of hard news for some weeks. There is a temptation to speculate as to what would happen if we discussed terms, but it's too tantalising, since there's no shadow of doubt we will reject any such suggestion. Now I suppose Churchill will again tell the world that we are going to die on the hills and on the sea, and then we shall proceed to do so.

A letter from Clive with a rather funny description of Margot Asquith asking Virginia to write her obituary for *The Times*. "Virginia took the opportunity of questioning her about her sex life, which turned out to be exactly what one would suppose — virginity up to marriage and monogamy afterwards — 'but I was dreadfully *fast*, my dear.' "

*July 24th*

Raining all day, out of puckered clouds like mackintosh silk. We spent the day with Desmond and Molly at Garrick's Villa — a lovely eighteenth-century house standing in a large garden and looking out over the Thames, a small temple to Shakespeare and a weeping-willow tree. They were living there in space and splendour. Each room had a large bow-window, in which stood a writing-table awaiting literary inspiration, from which could be seen green lawns with an orangery or elegant villa in the distance. Opening what I thought was the door of the lavatory, I found myself face to face with Desmond in a vast study as big and high as a theatre, lined with books and busts. Talked of Boris [Anrep]'s escape from France. Desmond said Boris didn't know what fear was, and when asked to describe the Russian campaign in the first war, he said, "It was just Ball*et*, just Ball*et*, men running forward and then falling down, just Ball*et*." Then we paced into the garden in mackintoshes and umbrellas, and along the road to Bushey Park, through fields of haycocks and a wonderful half-domesticated jungle, with tufts of enormous ferns, streams running under bridges, and a bird sanctuary full of water-lilies. "It's a sanctuary all right, but there are no *birds*," said Desmond.

*July 29th*

News of a terrific air battle over Dover harbour, with fifteen German aeroplanes shot down. Also that Mr. Chamberlain is doing well after his operation. R.: "Has he had his appeasement out?"

*August 5th*

A German aeroplane was brought down at Heath End, only a few miles away, last night. Two German airmen were taken and three dead. Rumour has it that another escaped and his clothes were found in Pen Wood.

To London for a few nights. The chief pleasure of being there is simply seeing people on buses and in the streets. Then to the Leicester

Galleries, an enjoyable spy-film, and to dine with Raymond, who has given up editing the *New Statesman* and joined the Ministry of Information. (R.: "I got on very well with Raymond at the *New Statesman*, and now perhaps I shall go further and fare Worsley.")

Raymond very tired; he says reports from France are extremely contradictory, but give an impression of dazed bewilderment.

The absence of aeroplanes at night made London seem more peaceful than Ham Spray.

*August 9th*

Lunched with Boris and Maroussa. For over two hours we listened to Boris's account of their escape from Paris in every detail. *It was enthralling.* I can hardly say whether or not it was a pleasure listening to it, for the sensation of sucking in brute reality through one's ears was in fact almost painful. It was as long and exciting as a spy-film, and therefore impossible to write down, though I would like to. I will only say that they would not have got on the train had not their wine-merchant happened to be an official of the Gare du Nord as well, and helped them. Maroussa passed off among some railwaymen's widows, and Boris slipped through while his wine-merchant was embracing the Military Policeman on guard, who most fortunately turned out to be an old school friend.

Arrived home to read in the local paper that the escaped German from our wrecked plane has been caught after ten days at large. Listening to the news: "tremendous air battle over the Channel; 53 German planes down and 16 of ours." He has taken my knight and two pawns . . . Every night the searchlights are playing round the sky. Perhaps some change is brewing.

*August 12th*

Gerald writes sadly. Helen had left her blind flapping, and people opposite reported him for "signalling to the enemy". "It seems I can no longer live here, and I think of going to London and trying to get a job."

In the afternoon Burgo and I walked across the park and climbed the Downs. Nearly at the top we sat down and watched the reaper in the biscuit-coloured field below. Suddenly we heard terrific air activity, and planes seemed to be dashing about in all directions, though many were invisible behind the clouds. Then a great grey mushroom of smoke rose up from the direction of Newbury. As we crossed the first field, four large bombers swooped over the Downs, making a deafening noise. They flew over our heads fairly low, and on over Ham Spray. The extraordinary thing was that even when I stared up and saw an unfamiliar mark like a cross on their wings, I *still* didn't realise they were German bombers. But I did think how easily they could have machine-gunned our two little figures, I so conspicuous in my red shirt. Wilde, working in the garden, saw the crosses plainly and knew what they were. I never even mentioned the incident to R., so incredulous is he of unfounded rumours, and it was not until Nannie came back from her day out in Newbury that I knew for certain what a good view we had had of German bombers. She had spent most of the day in an air-raid shelter, and the mushroom of smoke had been from bombs dropped near Newbury. There had been something like an air battle over Inkpen. I felt unreasoning excitement for ten minutes or so. Then I thought with surprise of the old days when Lytton and Carrington were alive, and that now bombs fall on Newbury and German bombers go over the house itself.

*August 14th*

Last night I was making a new blackout curtain when listening to Beethoven. In the middle of the Pastoral Symphony there was a loud but distant CRUMP. I have been unconsciously avoiding imagining the details of air-raids, but this sound brought my unwilling mind a vivid picture of crashing masonry and mangled bodies.

To tea with the Brenans. Gerald is still in a fever about his "signalling to the enemy" and was talking wildly about "having it out with them", "bringing an action for slander" and "writing to Duff Cooper".

A noisy day, in one way and another, and we hear that over eighty enemy aeroplanes were brought down.

*August 17th*

Hot blue day. We bathed, we read, we wrote. In the afternoon the Nicholses arrived. We sat till late drinking sherry on the lawn, as the sky turned pink and the midges came out to bite. Then we gave them a purely home-grown meal — bortsch, roast pigeons, vegetables, figs and peaches. Phyllis, in very fine looks, told us that she was at her mother's house the other day when eleven screaming bombs fell in the grounds. One cottage was knocked to pieces. Then a terrible thing happened: two children whose home it was came back and saw its state, and thought all their family *must* be dead. They rushed off in God knows what dreadful state of mind, and couldn't be found and reassured till next morning.

I imagined that the Nicholses, having got their children safely to America, would feel relieved, and confident that they had done the best thing. Not a bit of it. Even more than parents who have kept their children at home, they worry that they have made the wrong decision, particularly Phil. Phyllis still says she is glad they have gone, though her eyes fill with tears when she speaks of them. "If the war goes on long it will be a disaster for them," says Phil. He is the most besotted of fathers, but besides missing the children badly, he feels they will be brought up as he doesn't want, and suffer from lack of parental love. They left after early breakfast. Alone in the sitting-room, I suddenly felt the war close in again round me, signalising its naked presence by three bombers, which crossed the garden with a roar, and veered off, heeling like battleships into the grey streaky sky.

*August 22nd*

Raymond arrived to stay, waving out of the train window as it came in, and got out curved like a question mark, clutching a pile of books to his chest, sighing and talking. He had been to Charleston and described a heated argument one evening when everyone attacked Clive for saying it would be a good thing to start peace negotiations tomorrow. As he told us this I felt that though he well knew this used to be our own view, he was assuming we must have abandoned such folly, and now toe the line with the rest of them. Anxious not to quarrel, I did not "take up" the challenge, though vaguely irritated by it.

*August 23rd*

The *New Statesman*, read in bed, set both R. and me off in a blaze of indignation at the various attitudes it adopts. There is the *Spanish War addiction* to begin with — the view that the Spanish Civil War was the only one worth fighting in. Those who did so criticise the tactics of all other wars, discregarding the fact that they didn't even win it. Then there is the line that *the War isn't so bad.* It's so good for unemployment, it's so democratic, few people have been killed, in fact it's rather a bracing state of affairs. I find this simply maddening. It is intolerable that those who haven't had much to complain of should belittle the agony, for instance, of those who are in constant grinding anxiety about the airman they love. The quiet *natural-history attitude* of Vita Sackville-West ("Our village in an air-raid") is silly, but less violently annoying. All becomes part of the ancient English rural tradition in some mysterious way. Last, but one that I find more and more painful, is the semi-erotic *excitement about the brave young airmen in danger,* especially when it is felt by highbrows who take care to avoid all danger themselves, or very old people.

Yesterday there was a short barking match between R. and Raymond at tea. Raymond had continued subtly to goad our pacifist position.

R. suddenly almost shouted that it was inconceivable to him that any sensitive person should insist on the importance of the young men of the R.A.F. leading the lives of frightful danger they do when they themselves were *not* risking their lives for the cause they thought so important. The only thing to do if you felt like that was to act like Sir Arnold Wilson and become a rear gunner even if you were over fifty. Raymond took this attack with perfect good nature and hardly tried to defend himself, but I think perhaps he was pleased to have got a rise.

Clive describes Raymond's visit to Charleston (along with Desmond) as "pure joy till the last evening when we got into a hot and unprofitable wrangle about the desirability of a negotiated peace. Of course if people really believe that after a victorious peace the whole world would live happily ever after, there's no sense in arguing. But *why* they should believe it I can't imagine."

*August 25th*

Julia and Lawrence to lunch, at which an old-fashioned conversation on art, etc., sprang up. What a relief after war, war, war. Lawrence had been to tea with the local clergyman, who said *à propos* of her portrait, "Julia Strachey? Any relation of the writer chap who used to live out this way? Fellow looked like a lunatic to me." He had also been to London and had tea with Vanessa, Dorelia and Helen[1], and had been much impressed by "their Norn-like appearance, looking out from the ruins of their past lives."

Poor Raymond grew very depressed as the time drew near to go back to London and work. He told me how much he had looked forward to his little holiday, and now there was nothing but very hard work, air-raids and uncertainty. The train was late so we left him at the station, and I never saw anything more pathetic and forlorn than his figure sitting on the platform, clutching a packet of food and a bunch of flowers. There is too much of the Prep. school atmosphere these days, and most of us wear spiritual grey flannel shorts and snake belts. The station was thronged with returning parents who had been visiting child refugees, and I got home overwhelmed by the sadness rather than the madness of war.

*August 26th*

The news is now entirely concerned with air-raids. Inside every head in England the same questions are revolving: "How many killed? How many injured? How is everyone 'standing up' to the raids?" Oh, the

[1] Bell, John and Anrep.

sordid horror of the news; now it is just one long description of destruction, smashing, mashing and killing. On the way upstairs I saw a monstrous dead blue-bottle lying on its back, and thought it symbolized the world's state. The Germans say we are being unduly optimistic about the mildness of their raids, and that we will change our minds "in the next few days", since they are revising their technique and bombing by night indiscriminately — the famous "war of nerves". Our newspapers tell us how wonderfully unshakeable our morale is.

A long conversation with R. about the French Revolution, Napoleon, Hitler and so forth. I am now in the last volume of Walpole's Letters, and his horror of the violence and savagery across the Channel made me realise what it must have been like having it going on year after year. H.W. was so affected that he felt there must be something radically wrong with the French nation never before suspected, some monster blood in their veins. (Just in fact what people are now saying about the Germans.) But less than a hundred years later they were being taken as the fine flower of an old and dignified civilization.

Joan's Tim came on a week's unexpected leave — the kitchen was in a fizz of hair-curling and excitement.

*August 31st*

I don't seem to have put down that since they began, air-raids on London have been incessant, day and night, though few have got through to the centre. There is bound to be an exodus.

Saxon [Sydney-Turner] arrived for ten days' holiday, looking very white and old. We were both delighted to see him, changed into his silk summer suit, lying out on the garden bed under the weeping ash with a detective story. We had grouse in his honour and a bottle (the last) of Châteauneuf 1923; globe artichokes, grapes, figs and plums, all home-grown.

M.A.M. rang up to say she would like to come down, probably on Monday. We reviewed the winter prospect in bed. We are quite resigned to a permanent full house, no privacy, food in slabs, and being herded together with our fellows. We are so very quiet here that there is no question of anything else.

*September 2nd*

Went off to sleep like a log and was suddenly woken by a loud noise: Slap, slap — slap, SLAP! and the throbbing boom of an aeroplane. My heart started beating very fast until the sound of engines had passed. R. went down the passage to see if Nannie was frightened, and found

Joan and Edie just going in to the nursery, where Nannie was snoring imperturbably.

M.A.M. has come and told us a lot about London life. I'm full of admiration for her courage.

*September 5th*

R. woke bubbling and simmering like a kettle on the boil, because of the pressure of our inmates. He says one can't talk about the war to M.A.M., gets bored of talking about birds with T., and Saxon won't talk about anything. Nor can he and I ever have a private conversation. Then we talked about intimacy. He said he had never hoped to find such intimacy as he has with me. Nor had I. Nor, let me say here and now, had I expected one fraction of the happiness I find in marriage. Why should intimacy be the secret of married happiness? asked R. Because the enemy of married happiness is irritation. But you can't be irritated by yourself, and when another person is so intimate that they are your other self you can't be irritated by them either.

Burgo and I walked to watch the road being tarred towards Ham. A man with a curly mop of bright yellow hair, looking like a Shakespearean clown, let him use his shovel and then asked me when the war would end. I said I wished I could tell him. He: "Not so far off neither, it's the food shortage. If we could only starve every soul in the country, that would be the best thing. You have to be cruel to be kind!"

Roused from sleep in the small hours by the vision of Nannie in our bedroom doorway saying, "There were three quite close. What shall I do?" R. said grumpily: "Go back to bed." I got up and went down the passage. Nannie said, "They *are* busy tonight." It was the refrigerator down below! Went back to bed but couldn't sleep. Heard three bombs half an hour later. Poor old Nannie, I do feel sorry for her. She would love air-raids to be organized like everything else — we should all get up, take our gas-masks and file into a snug dug-out full of rugs and make tea. I expected to find her sheepish next morning, but she only said: "Did you hear those three bombs later?"

*September 8th*

Dead-heading the dahlias, while R. and Burgo collected caterpillars for the ducks and hens off the cabbages. Nothing could have been more peaceful and domestic. Then the one o'clock news brought the news of last night's terrible raids on London, many times worse than anything hitherto. It was still smoking, casualties 400 killed and 1,300 seriously wounded. This ghastly mouthful of reality stuck in one's throat. Lunch was a farce. How could we swallow meat and potatoes as well? We all sat struck dumb, except M.A.M. who tried to look on the bright side and say we could do more damage in our raids than they could. Good God, as if that was a comforting thought! And there's no reason to think they can't go on and on. Nothing to say about the rest of this gloomy day. Didn't want to read, walk or think. What's the point of picking flowers? Is it worth crossing the lawn? Or speaking? What a world to be alive in, if this sub-human existence can be called being alive. After dinner, a loud strange noise in the darkness. The All Clear. Poor Nannie bustled down stairs and fell on her knees with a noise louder than any bomb. I visited M.A.M. in bed. She made me a touching speech saying she was afraid she irritated R. and couldn't bear to do that as she was so fond of him. So is he of her, and she can't possibly go back to London now that the real Blitz has begun.

*September 11th*

A second raid on London almost as bad as the first. I have been wondering what is happening to St. Paul's, and Gerald rang up with the same preoccupation. I suppose it is the Nose of London's familiar face (and everyone knows what noses stand for). It's disgusting to think of that familiar face being destroyed piecemeal. Talked in bed about the awful effects of war on human character – the sinister light of bombs and fires lights up a landscape of isolated hillocks of knobby egotism.

Saxon's departure this afternoon looms up and fills us with despair. He seems utterly unfitted to go back to this horrible life in the front line trenches. He spent most of the day drawing up his Will, and Edie and Wilde were brought in to sign it, looking as if they were in church. M.A.M. still in bed. By way of penance I listened to her optimism for a long time without making a single damping remark.

At tea-time Mrs. Hill of Ham rang up to say four frantic people had arrived in a car from London. Could we take them in? They arrived soon after – Mum, Dad, Gran and Sonny from Wandsworth. We made up beds for them all.

*September 13th*

Our Wandsworth family are moving on to relations today, but they are a foretaste of refugee life. They looked better after a sleep. Lack of sleep was their great trouble, as they had spent every night this week in a stuffy public shelter. Granny, an ex-lady's maid, said she "felt her nerve going". The father of the family was still in a highly nervous state, and rolled his eyes like a shying horse as he described how he thought every bomb was going to hit him. The poor things went off early with much hand-shaking, and the sky cleared both literally and figuratively.

Hungerford was full of refugees looking like east-enders; young girls in shiny black or pink clothes, with faces that ought to be pretty but were somehow stunted-looking, and cigarettes hanging out of their mouths. I felt they thought living in Hungerford would be worse than being bombed. Our Wandsworth family believed that peace *must* come because Londoners couldn't stand this fearful strain and lack of sleep. They were in a way the most pacific people we have lately seen. They had no bitterness against the German people, only sympathy for those we were bombing in Berlin.

*September 14th*

Mrs. Hill on the telephone again! "I've just heard that twenty refugees are arriving in half an hour. Could you have some more?" R., Burgo and I drove down to the village and waited. Then the bus came lumbering in, and children ran to gape and stare. One very small child thudded along screeching out "VACU-*EES!* VACU-*EES!*" As soon as they got out it was clear they were neither children nor docksiders, but respectable-looking middle-aged women and a few children, who stood like sheep beside the bus looking infinitely pathetic. "Who'll take these?" "How many are you?" "Oh well, I can have these two but no more," and the piteous cry, "But we're *together*." It was terrible. I felt we were like sharp-nosed housewives haggling over fillets of fish. In the end we swept off two women about my age and a girl of ten, and then fetched the other two members of their party and installed them with Coombs the cowman. Their faces at once began to relax. Far from being terrified Londoners, they had been evacuated against their will from Bexhill, for fear of invasion, leaving snug little houses and "hubbies".

*September 15th*

My thoughts are involved to the exclusion of everything else with the Bexhill problem. Moved furniture to make their two rooms more habitable, talked to them, tried to get the little girl Jean in touch with Burgo. All began to take shape very well, and my impression of their niceness is confirmed, but will they almost die of boredom? Julia and Lawrence to lunch. Julia brought a letter from Beatrix Lehmann who has just taken her Charlotte Street flat, describing her first night in one of these awful raids. How she and her old dog crept down to the basement and lay there wondering if anyone knew they were there. Of the fiendish noises like express trains rushing straight at your stomach, the Giant in seven-league boots stalking all over London, and the comfortingly cockney voice of the A.R.P. men shovelling up incendiary bombs. Julia and L. had spent a night in London before the really bad raids began, and that was quite bad enough. Neither of them slept a wink.

Bombs and explosions, and who heard what, and what they felt, make up three-quarters of all conversation nowadays. At the same time as thinking how boring it is there's a compulsion to go on, and perhaps it serves a purpose in helping one to digest bit by bit the horror of these new events. What cormorants we are — almost anything will go down in the end. But what surprised me most was to detect in myself a curious feeling of regret at missing some tremendous experience that thousands of people are having.

*September 16th*

Many reports of bombs heard in the night. R. and I heard nothing, but Nannie of course did, M.A.M. also and the Bexhills. Poor Mrs Loker, the mother of the Bexhill family, got out of bed and began to dress in a great state. The London raids are almost the sole subject of thought, conversation and speculation — like a toothache gnawing away at life and spirits. With a sinking heart I feel what remains of me being submerged under the tide of practical arrangements, just as it was last winter, only with infinitely more painful events happening. And apart from the shopping lists, I can brood for hours as how best to fit together the pieces of our Ham Spray jigsaw to make a picture that is most psychologically tolerable.

Lying in my bath this morning, talking to R. and stirring my toes through the rising steam, with the clear watery sun streaming in at the window, I had one of those flashing gleams when the war is annihilated: "Supposing there wasn't a war!" or "*When* there wasn't a war!"

A resolve: to keep as much lucidity and interest as possible from being submerged by housekeeping, refugees and routine. Not to let the steam from the bath fuzz all the windows till I can see no twigs, trees or sky, but only taps and towels. But as I write it down I fear it will not be kept.

*September 21st*

I see that in my family R. and I are considered as dreadful pessimists. Every letter from one of them says "we are all very optimistic here," conscious I know that we at Ham Spray are not. This optimism in their language — a very strange one to me — means that they think we will win the war. I sometimes think so myself, but even so I couldn't possibly call my state of mind "optimistic". It's obviously impossible for them to understand that to us it seems as if in the long run it hardly matters who wins it. That we are pessimistic because the war is horrible in itself, because it is solving no problems and doing no good to anyone, but on the contrary making endless new problems and doing infinite harm to countless people.

A wonderful September morning, rising slowly out of mist; rooks cawing, cobwebs spangled with dewdrops and silky white sheaves of pampas gleaming in the sun. Went blackberrying along the soused hedges.

*September 24th*

Changes: poor old Nannie has gone, tearing herself away from her adored Burgo. Burgo has started day-school in Hungerford.

Perhaps his first day there stimulated his philosophical comment today on a walk along the Downs: "Every stick I see is in the world, isn't it?"

R. went to Aldbourne and came back with the news that Gerald has been in trouble with the police *again*. He spent a whole day at the Marlborough Police Station, and R. got to Bell Court just in time this morning to interview a Scotland Yard man and vouch for Gerald's character. Apparently when Sir Oswald Mosley was in danger of being arrested at the beginning of the war he made a bonfire of his papers, but one or two floated over a wall and came into the hands of the police. On one was written among other notes: "Gerald Brenan, Bell Court, Aldbourne." The Scotland Yard man told R. that if Gerald hadn't been able to explain this he would quietly have been interned for the duration of the war. The explanation was that he had written a letter to the *Telegraph* urging that Sir Oswald be arrested, and was therefore an enemy of the Fascist Party and his name and address noted as such.

Burgo told me there was to be gas-mask drill at school tomorrow, so I tried his on tonight. It seemed dreadfully tight and he said he "didn't like it a bit and couldn't breathe in it". From having longed to put it on he was almost in tears.

M.A.M. came up from the news, her face alight with triumph. One hundred and thirty German planes have been brought down in daylight raids.

*September 29th*

Fast asleep in R.'s arms, I was woken by hearing him say: "H'm." . . . "What?" . . . "Only a bomb." Quite a loud one, he said. There were droning planes, but I turned over and fell asleep again, and then several "Plop-plops". Soon afterwards a loud echoing CR-RASH, far the loudest we've heard so far. We both automatically got out of bed, and R. said, "Shall we go and see how everyone is?" Out of our bedroom window we could see a lot of twinkling lights, like a fair. Watched a little, and then back to bed.

Taking the washing to Mrs. Slater half a mile away we found her still trembling. The lights had been incendiary bombs and a rick had caught fire. The Slater family spent all night in their shelter. "We don't want them any nearer," she said with a sort of half-choked shudder.

Visited the Brenans. The cat was looking out of one window of the sunny façade, and Gamel in a turban out of another. Both Gerald and Gamel say they very much want to go to London, but disclaim curiosity as the motive — goodness knows why. It's a very respectable one.

Gerald told us he is writing a novel, which will be a best-seller. And after that he plans a volume of short stories to show the terrible harm caused by the human virtues — kindness, candour, etc.

R. has taken a lot of trouble to clear away the clouds of suspicion hanging over Gerald. For one thing he got Clive to ask his brother "the Colonel" (who has a lot of influence in Wiltshire) to intercede on his behalf with the authorities. This does seem to have had considerable effect. As the Colonel put it, "Brenan's name was on Mosley's Death List."

Late this evening came Humphrey Slater and Janetta from the Osterley Home Guard School, to have a rest from the bombing. They talked most of the evening about the raids, said Londoners talked about nothing else. Janetta with most remarkable candour and realism said that she felt far more terrified than she would have believed possible, and flung herself on the floor trembling all over. H. said she was really remarkably controlled. Her "tone" about her own fear is the best I've yet struck, though I can't quite analyse why. She longs to get out of London, but is going back in two days' time rather than leave Humphrey alone.

Left Humphrey at Hungerford and went on, with Janetta and Burgo, to lunch at Bell Court off a huge dish of spaghetti. The talk as usual all of London and bombing. In the face of Janetta's candid and sane fear, I found Gerald's endless boastful belittling of the raids in bad taste and rather unlike himself. At last I said I thought he was in no position to judge until he had been in London and seen for himself. He told R. that he thought this was true, and that he wanted to go up.

A conversation about Respect. We drew up a list of people we respected – Darwin, Mill, Hume, Wellington. Janetta said indignantly that she respected no-one. I have great respect for her, as it happens, and would have liked to have added her to my list.

Humphrey and Janetta's descriptions of London have been a shock to M.A.M. She had built up, brick by brick, a view that it wasn't so bad, and everyone was bearing up splendidly. She said anyone could see they were both nervous types. It does seem cruel to break her rosy spectacles, but we cannot possibly wear them ourselves.

While I was bathing Burgo he held forth on Hitler's wickedness. "And Mussolini isn't very nice, is he? And Goering? I wouldn't mind giving Hitler an unripe blackberry."

*October 9th*

To meet Raymond. His description of London life was very convincing. He pooh-poohed the Gerald theory that it's quite all right living there at present. His front door and inner door were both blown in, and some windows broken, by a very large bomb which fell round the corner, leaving his flat and all his lovely books, china and pictures accessible to burglars. While he said the raids were terrifying and the lack of sleep and dreariness of everything unutterably wearing, he said the look of things was "so extraordinary that everyone should try to go to London for a sight of it".

As a subject of conversation the war is alas unavoidable. Because everything else has been forcibly drained of interest, as a surgeon takes blood from a vein, we go on saying the same things over and over.

About 10 o'clock tonight, the thuds of four bombs. The engines went zooming on, and I had as I always do a very vivid picture, four-dimensional and solid, of the aeroplane in flight. "H'm. He ought to have four more," said R., and sure enough, rather louder: BOOMP, BOOMP, then a pause which is always the nastiest bit, with the engines getting louder, and BOOMP BOOMP. One heard the aeroplane turn and go off, and we all breathed again. The awareness that there are bombs to come is extremely unpleasant, but not nightmarish – a distinction hard to define perhaps.

*October 18th*

Departure of the Bexhills, who are being allowed to return to their homes and "hubbies".

Janetta's brother, Rollo Woolley, now training to be a pilot in the R.A.F., arrived at tea-time. The effect of his airforce uniform was electric. Burgo was quite flummoxed by it. M.A.M. softened visibly. I think R. and I were also affected; anyway we like Rollo very much. We

64

asked him a lot about the R.A.F. of course, and he answered all our questions, giving us a picture of young men living in the present or the near future, and absorbed in the technique of learning to fly. R. thinks Rollo fully realises the suicidal nature of his career. I don't know. He has no illusions about the war, is inclined to call it an "Imperialist war with Communists" and "is not sure whether he is a Communist or pro-Nazi, as there's no difference between them". Only about fifty per cent of the trainees finish the course. Some fail only at night flying. The best pilots are not Rugby footballers — it's largely a question of sensitive touch and musicians are especially good at it.

Burgo began dancing round Rollo in a state of hero-worship. M.A.M. wants to provide comforts for him, knit him socks — a strange way it seems to me of blinding oneself to the fact that we are asking this young man to lose his life[1] or be maimed, or at best terribly frightened for the sake of what we want.

A conversation with M.A.M. in her room. I said I had no hopes for the future, though many desires. She said, "I *must* hope or I should blow my brains out." Well, I can't feel there's reasonable grounds for hope and yet I don't blow my brains out. Of course I hope the war will be won by the U.S.A. and Us, though I think ideals will vanish in the final chaos. M.A.M.'s voice was like a drowning man's clutching at a straw, and she buoys herself up with "things are being done . . . people who know tell me . . . I firmly believe."

Poor Saxon wrote very despairingly saying that two of his best friends at the Treasury were killed last night. The Treasury must have been hit, though he doesn't say so.

*October 29th*

Sitting for my portrait to Lawrence, who had been to London, to order a new suit for one thing. When he got there the Fifty Shilling Tailors in Piccadilly was nowhere to be seen. Then he went to the "Studio" office, that too had vanished. But what shattered him most was the sight of Vanessa and Duncan's studio, unrecognizable and pulverized. Only a few pieces of Omega pottery and Vanessa's studio table upside-down — and the ruin of that tin Bridge of Sighs we used to clank across, and everyone must have tender memories of.

*November 4th*

We were sitting round the fire tonight when there was a noise like an old tank or a car passing very slowly overhead, rattling as it went. I

[1] He did.

thought: "Yes, it's a bomb; but it's going over — it won't hit us." Ran up to the nursery, and then came the CRASH. Burgo hadn't stirred (he had been quite seriously ill, but is now better), and I was standing recovering when in came Joan, her hair loose and dishevelled. She looked flustered, and no wonder as she was bicycling up the avenue when she saw and heard the bomb go over. Soon after we had settled by the fire again there was another, and another — CRASH, plop, plop, plop. Good, I thought, I'm getting used to them. R. said, "Well twice may be a coincidence, but if they do it again it'll look as if they were aiming at something." And they did. I see that one does, without trying to, learn something of the sounds of raiding planes and their significance. The nastiest moment is when, after a low flight, the engines shut off and there's total silence.

*November 5th*

Walked out to look at the craters. In the lane at the end of the avenue men were filling in quite a respectable one. They were very jolly. "Only casualty a skylark," said one. One of the last of the "stick" fell in the garden of one of the Ham bungalows, and a little boy, missed by a few feet, was found asleep under the débris. We all enjoyed our sight-seeing expedition but if that little boy had been killed there would have been none of all this joking.

R. and I went to see the Brenans. Gerald, back after his two weeks wardenship in London, looking young and lean. All the time he didn't see one person killed. Each night had its "incidents", houses demolished, people buried or cut by glass, or with all their clothes blown off, shot up into trees, or starred all over with cuts from glass so as to be bright red with blood all over. The amount of blood was the one thing that struck him. Arthur Waley is a stretcher-bearer, and was called in when the Y.M.C.A. off Tottenham Court Road was hit. He said the whole place was swimming in blood and it was dripping down the stairs, yet hardly a person was killed. All were superficial cuts from glass. He believes that most people cannot resist the temptation to exaggerate. The really terrified people leave London or else go down to the tube, others make themselves as safe as possible somewhere where they can sleep. And he says most people do manage to sleep now, and that many people are enjoying finding themselves braver than they knew.

A gale blew all night — it even blew the duck-house over.

*November 14th*

To Oxford for the day. Lunched with David, Rachel away. Leo [Myers] was said by David to have become very "difficult" again. When his daughter came to stay he begged her "not to be too frivolous, as it was unsuitable to current events," and David said, "when that is the one thing we are all trying hard to remain."

Oxford frivolity is very noticeable, but not entirely convincing.

Left David outside Christ Church, took a flying look at Billa [Harrod] and her children and drove on to call on Clare Sheppard. Sydney now says that for the first time in his life he would rather be dead than alive.

What a kaleidoscope of characters.

*November 15th*

All last night the noise of bombers going over was incessant. They seemed to be streaming through the sky, yet there was never that menacing threat towards *us* in the sound of their engines. This sinister noise was so loud that sleep was difficult, and this morning we compared notes, and wondered if the Germans were up to some new horror. At lunchtime came the explanation. M.A.M. came in looking pale from listening to the news, and said there had been a tremendous raid on Coventry all night, and the middle of the town almost obliterated. She had to revise her basis for optimism. "I had forgotten such things *had* to happen."

In the afternoon we drove her to stay with my brother Tom. Then to call on Julia and Lawrence. Talked to Julia about the painfulness of our views being so different from M.A.M.'s, and whether there was any use trying to convince people by argument. There is a letter from Clive in this week's *New Statesman*, putting forward the case for negotiation now, diplomatically and discreetly as I thought, but Julia was depressed by it. While putting Burgo to bed, I heard the stream of aeroplanes starting up again and resented them most bitterly.

*November 20th*

R. looked sad all day, and when I asked him why, he said in an extinguished voice, "I *hate* this war so." I have been hating it more than usual lately too. It's possible to forget it absolutely for a short time, only to remember it again with a dreary pang, like some awful cancer gnawing one's vitals or a spear stuck in one's side.

Up in our bedroom the usual drone of bombers developed a more menacing note. Then there was a fairly thunderous explosion, only one, but I found myself trembling gently all over. For the droners went on droning for half an hour more. How degrading to lie here afraid, and how degrading to have cause to be afraid.

Burgo drew on his blackboard a strange, pointed, sinister-looking shape — he said it was Gravity.

I wake in profound gloom most mornings, with thoughts of death and suicide. It is so impossible to imagine a tolerable world future, and however much one believes in individualism, it's hard to carry out in practice in present circumstances. At the same time I am ashamed of not producing more spirit; but I am in the grip of a depression that surveys the view and cannot see anything anywhere in the public world to like, admire, or look forward to. It's not altogether rational, but though I know the fog will lift, it doesn't console me.

Managed somehow to write my review of Children's Books for the *New Statesman* and felt better.

*November 30th*

Drew the curtains and saw the Downs iced all over with frost, standing in a deep belt of palest pink mist. Over them a baby blue sky with a few tiny pink clouds floating in it. It was completely still and smoke was already rising vertically from the thresher in the field under the Downs. The vegetables had a crisp coating of frost.

We made an excursion to watch the threshers, and nothing I have seen lately has given me more pleasure: steaming horses, carts laden with straw and a buzz of active figures round the sacrificial column of smoke — poking, thrusting, dragging.

Rollo arrived in the afternoon, looking rather more fragile than before. He has passed his pilot's examination and will get his Wings any minute. He touched both R. and me very much by his friendliness and charming manners and I suppose by the pathos of his position.

*December 5th*

The dead-end of the year. I concentrate on the idea of polishing 1940 off, no matter how, hoping that 1941 will bring some new ideas. As for the natural world, there's nothing dead about this December. From the passage window I see every day the swelling buds on the trees outside. Sweet violets are out, the pampas grass white and plumy, and even the hyacinths are poking their noses out of the beds.

The Christmas catalogues appear, much as usual, except for such things as a toby jug, representing Mr. Churchill, round which is written "We will fight on the sea, we will fight in the hills", and for this wonderful historical memento the price is five guineas.

Yesterday in the House of Commons the admirable Mr. Maxton and others brought forward a motion for stating our Peace Terms, with a view to a Conference. In the Peace debate which followed, war-fury raged, and today there are cartoons of bombed men and women with faces like bulldogs threatening to tear Mr. Maxton to pieces.

*December 10th*

At breakfast a conversation about the eighteenth century. How barbarous we seem in comparison to them, with their respect for learning, literature, the arts and rationalism and their dislike of religion. I am just hooking on to the new subject of Voltaire, which may provide reading for some time to come. Since I finished Walpole I've been short of a subject.

Agitating news that our troops have made contact with the Italians on the Libyan front, which R. says means we have begun an offensive. A swoop into the depths and up again at the thought.

*December 12th*

Good news from Libya every day now. We make a quick adjustment to this new state of things, and the dead level of most people's spirits has been raised from the rock bottom where they were resting. There is indeed wild talk of Italy being "knocked out of the war already".

Read more of Voltaire, at first with disappointment, expecting to admire his character as well as his intelligence, so that his trickery and *fourberie* and inordinate vanity were unpleasantly surprising. So were his haverings with the Church. Re-read Lytton on him, and found that (much as Roger does with painters) he made the "point" of Voltaire clear.

The world was blotted out this morning, cold and silent, in white mist and white frost. Then the sun burst through and floated over the Downs like a large luminous button, while streamers of mist rose and fell in the no-man's-land between us and the Downs. I went for a short walk, with Burgo – a little leaping gnome – hanging on to my hand. Such very great beauty in the physical world renews one's zest for life in spite of oneself.

Meanwhile the prospect of Invasion begins to creep to the fore again, and the wireless tells us that an attempt will certainly be made, probably before the spring.

*December 18th*

Edie arrived back late last night from her fortnight's bliss with her "soldier". Today instead of a jolly girl singing round the house, she has

69

become a tragedy queen in the grip of a grand passion, with huge lustrous eyes and her heart miles away. Then at lunchtime it was Joan's turn. The telephone rang and she came back ashy white. Tim was home. So off *she* goes tomorrow. In the middle of all this excitement the poor old house reels along through the waves with its six occupants,[1] like a dirty old trawler, neglected but keeping its head bravely above the waves.

*December 21st*

The Colin Mackenzies arrived in the afternoon. I went to meet them and was for ages stamping on the platform. There they were at last, with tin hats, quantities of luggage and pekingese dog. "Dog Mackenzie" created quite a stir among the children and cats of Ham Spray. Wine, pheasants, etc., in their honour. Colin thinks the Germans ought all to be sterilized, that they aren't like other people — and this statement aroused no anger in me, only detached surprise. Yet he is a very intelligent man. How will this seem in the years after the war, if we survive it? He had no inside information — except that it was all my eye our production being unimpaired by German air-raids. He says it has been very seriously interferred with. Also that food stocks for a year were destroyed at Southampton.

*December 25th*

Christmas Day hardly seemed like a real day — everyone in the house has appalling colds, in spite of which an impetus generated by the three children themselves carried all before it. To children this appears to be no trouble at all, and there is an end, thank heavens, of worked-up adult jollity. Lawrence and Julia came to dinner in a very festive and flowery mood, distributing presents, their style perfect. Lawrence made the most of a squealing bun left by his plate. We ate a fine goose and plum-pudding. Then the Christmas tree had to be lit and the Coombs family from the dairy arrived to see it. As usual it looked amazingly pretty. Lawrence got down on the floor and set off fireworks with the children. Julia peered quizzically at everyone and everything, from the tree itself to Nigel Coombs, who was sucking the end of a balloon and making it squeak.

I don't believe the war was mentioned once all day.

[1] Esme Strachey and her two children spent this winter with us.

Everyone has colds still. Burgo awoke in the night with earache but very talkative in bed with us this morning. He asked a lot about Carrington's portrait of Lytton in our room, because as his own first name is Lytton too I think he identified himself with it. I had told him before who Lytton was, and that he was dead. As he is lying down in the picture he thinks he is dead or dying there. He wanted to know when he died and at what time of day, and why, and in what position, and what became of him after he was dead.

Poor Burgo again tapped on our door, on the verge of tears. "Oh my POOR old ear, it does ache!" he said in heart-rending tones. Put him to bed and took his temperature – 102°. Telephoned the doctor. He came at once. "No cause for penetrating the drum *so far*," he said. So it was back to a nurse's life, sleeping in the nursery. And so ends 1940 on a note of illness.

1941

I start this second year of my war diary stumbling and blundering along, dazed and blindly, hardly noticing, nor much caring about my surroundings.

Raymond's arrival provided the relief of a stimulating adult presence. He perched on the fender, warming himself in his rather woolly brown suit. He says his flat is now uninhabitable; there is a bomb crater which makes it impossible even to get into it except by climbing like a monkey. He lives instead on the seventh floor of a modern block in Piccadilly, with his bed fixed by screws to the floor under a huge plate-glass window — yet he sleeps better than before the war when he could never get off without sleeping-pills.

We made our prophecies for 1941, and opened and read the ones we made last year. Of course no-one had guessed the fall of France. And I wonder what we are all missing out among this year's events!

Bitterly cold again. One of the children came in with some huge lumps of ice and said the pond was bearing. Raymond, who was on his way to meet Paul Hyslop at Bath, began plotting to get his skates from London. All else failing, he decided to go by train all the way to London and fetch them. Such a heroic pursuit of pleasure at the age of forty-five fills me with admiration. He said, "I'm a convinced utilitarian and my entire life is based on the pleasure principle, whereas most of my friends, I notice, seem to conduct theirs on the reverse." He has been absolutely charming and I wish he were staying longer, which one feels about few people if one's honest.

I got from Clive the most melancholy letter he has ever written me. "I don't want to live in London again," he says, "or in Paris or in Rome — indeed I don't particularly want to go on living at all. But if I do life that honour I make no doubt it will be at Charleston." He describes London as "of inconceivable *tristesse*" and says it "has a moral for those who need it, of whom you are not one — that the war won't end till it has ended everything that makes life worth living; that it is a fire, an earthquake, a pestilence, applied to which the words 'win' or 'lose' have no meaning whatever." With every word of which I agree, but it is strange to hear it from Clive of all people, who has always viewed the ideas of suicide and death with horror.

No sun all day, only a dim light reflected from the snow. Burgo helped me burn the Christmas decorations, which we did slowly, enjoying each flare-up and crackle, and the miniature machine-gun fire of the yew branches. After tea we undressed the Christmas tree and packed away all its glitter into the old Spanish tin trunk. It seems only a few weeks ago, not a year, since we put them away last Christmas – so short a time in fact that the tin trunk must have been all that time in the porch outside the front door "on its way" to the garage.

Went to visit the Padels, an Inkpen couple of Pacifists (and I think Communists) to see if they would teach Burgo next term. Mrs. Padel is tall, elderly and shy, with red threads in her cheeks. Mr. Padel has a flashing set of false teeth and a beard, wears knickerbockers and black boyish boots, and looks as if he ought to be skating English style round an orange on a frozen lake. Their room was full of musical instruments and books, a bust of Beethoven, and furnished in lodging-house taste.

Lord Woolton announced a further cut in the meat ration, so that the boats now carrying our meat can carry munitions instead.

Burgo suddenly took against the idea of time passing, and said in a voice of horror: "We can't stop the days coming. Even up in the sky and down in Devonshire and in France they still go on," and after a pause: "I wish I could *stop* living."

Of lunch at Biddesden[1] I remember little, except that Michael [Mac-Carthy] amused us by imitating an anti-aircraft gun at Hampton, which said BOUM in a Cockney voice.

*January 22nd*

To see the Brenans. They had staying with them their Italian anarchist friend, Maria Luisa, wife of the son of King Bomba, the Soho grocer. She is, I think, the most beautiful girl I ever saw, and with this goes great sweetness, a low husky voice and apparent intelligence. She had two red marks on her cheeks which I took for some new style in make-up, but R. was soon wearing them too – they were the stigmata of Gamel's morning kisses. She often uses her lipstick freely before applying these signs of friendship, gently but firmly like a rubber stamp, to every arrival's cheek, and the sight of a whole roomful so decorated is comical in a special and charming way. Gerald and Gamel were in dressing-gowns, bowls of steaming coffee on the table. It was like Spain again, an atmosphere they will now, I dare say, take with them wherever they go. Gamel's vagueness and slow movements give one a delightful feeling that there is no hurry about anything.

Gerald told us that it is rumoured Tobruk has fallen. But it was not till this evening that this was confirmed. A flutter of interest is aroused

[1] Byran Guinness's house.

by these victories, though the apparent brilliance of Wavell's generalship might be expected to do more. There is no excuse to call this a war diary except that it faithfully reproduces the apathy of what I take to be some sort of interim period. Much as I suppose a night-nurse looking after an invalid snatches a quiet moment to fall asleep, I find one sinks, or hurls oneself, into this apathy, deliberately not thinking about the future, supposing nothing, wondering nothing, because one assumes it is "not for long". Yet I keep thinking of Thurber's phrase "then human beings became lower than the lower animals". Food is the most important aspect of the war to us at the moment. But I think most people believe there will be a savage attack on England, probably invasion, within the next few months, and deliberately *don't think about it*, any more than they do of scarred London, like an accident on the other side of the street.

*January 26th*

This frightfully ugly foggy weather still goes on. R. and I to Hungerford on a shopping expedition. The shops display huge mounds of peanuts; beyond our rations there is literally nothing else to buy, except red herrings.

Lovely evening alone with R., with sherry before and sloe gin after our frugal meal of red herrings on toast. Felt faintly hilarious, in spite of the newspapers droning away that we must expect Invasion any day now.

*January 31st*

Music on the gramophone, Mozart G Minor Symphony, etc., brought sense of life returning, or of looking up from the bottom of a well to see that there is at least daylight at the top. During the afternoon there was a moment when I thought the eternal mist was melting, and there seemed a ghostly lightness above the house. The birds were aware of it too, and set up a feeble twittering, but it was soon over.

The nine o'clock news treated us to a touch of last year's grimness. (Like those unwelcome dollops of cold facts we used to get every night.) An American, back in U.S.A. from Europe, says there is no doubt that in some period "between thirty and sixty days" England will be subjected to an appalling attack, which will certainly include the use of "gas on a large scale". These words and the ideas attached to them sent me rocketting down into the suicide-pit. Gas is something the idea of which I cannot stomach, even if we all have the best gas-masks in the world. R. made light of my agitation, and then reasonably explained why he believed it was impossible to use it "on a large scale".

In the course of our conversation I found I had quietly bobbed up from my suicide-pit, and the horror of the evening's broadcast had dispersed.

*February 1st*

The weather has cracked at last, thank heavens! Soon after breakfast a rosy patch appeared in the clouds over the downs.

Oliver [Strachey] and Lucy[1] arrived about six, Oliver a bulky black shape under a broad-brimmed black hat; I found I had not quite remembered Lucy's extraordinary appearance, and felt terrified she should notice how shocked I was by it. She and Oliver had not met for six months, and I fancy he was a bit flabbergasted too; at any rate as she began to tell us about her war job (looking after a hostel of seventy naval tailors) he sat with his head in his hand, and at one point began to snore gently. Later, when pumped for his views on the war, he surprised us by his pessimism. He pooh-poohed invasion and "gas attacks on a large scale", but when someone asked the stale old question, "When is it going to end?" he replied gloomily, "The only way it can end in the next few years is by the Germans winning it." Far the most serious aspect, he told us, was the blockade. It is bound to get much worse in the spring, and what we have to look forward to is years of starvation. Gas or starvation? I couldn't help feeling I would choose the latter any day, but perhaps that's because I can't really imagine it, whereas photographs have helped me imagine gas all too vividly.

*February 3rd*

Snow again, falling lightly. R. starts a panic that we shall be snowed up with Oliver and Lucy. What a thought! Apart from everything else they have brought no rations at all. But they were bustled off on the morning train in a most determined way. Oliver said, "Well, it's been very nice seeing you. One of these days I dare say you'll have me ringing up and inviting myself again." Which was an entirely pleasant prospect. "It's been ripping," said Lucy in her old-fashioned way. It was ripping to see her go.

*February 6th*

Yesterday we met Raymond at the station. In the evening it began snowing heavily with a raging south wind, the flakes flying past the windows horizontally and upwards, rushing, whirling. This morning

[1] Julia's father had an important job in the cypher department of the War Office. Lucy was — or had been — his "girl friend".

78

there are deep drifts with bare patches between, but a hot sun came out and melted the snow to icing-sugar. We went out without coats, our voices echoing in the still air. R. started to make a large snowball, which gradually turned into a figure of Queen Victoria; we decorated her with beads, leaves and shells, and put a gold paper crown on her head.

Our long-term winter visitors departed, and though we saw them go with mixed feelings I was conscious of relief at not having so many individuals in the house.

*February 9th*

The fall of Benghazi has excited and surprised everyone; tonight Churchill made the most confident speech he has ever made and in the most confident tone, although there were the usual references to invasion and gas-attacks. I remember how loathsome his early speeches seemed to me, and wonder if it is I who have changed, or Winston? Have we all given in now and become war-minded, where once we stuck our toes in? Or has he slightly changed his note? I'm sorry to say I think it's the former. Now, when he talks about "*wicked* men" and "*filthy* monsters" I only want to laugh, and I can admire some of his concatenations of words, like today's "Swoop and scoop". Not that this signifies the smallest degree of alteration in my attitude to the whole situation.

There is also a delusive sense of spring in the air. The birds now sing quite cheerfully in the mornings and catkins in the hedges have suddenly shot out like yellow-green concertinas. As we drove off to Ham with the washing, the sun illuminated every detail of mossy tree-trunks. The fishmonger produced some herrings which he said were specially good and came straight from a Scotch port. At Burgo's school we saw a charming little interior: Mrs. Padel reading Rapunzel to the children, the three little girls on the floor by the fire sewing, while Burgo leant lovingly against her chair doing his moss-stitch.

It seems to me that the Invasion's stock is beginning to decline just a little. It's still assumed that there will be an attempt, and that soon, but there isn't much urgency or conviction in the assumption. It's as if we were assuming it "for luck", just as one tries to believe it's sure to rain when one wants it not to.

*February 13th*

A quiet, sweet-smelling morning; a cow moons across the park, followed by a retinue of small black birds. The countryside looks like Peace not War. Went all round the vegetable and flower-beds and the greenhouse, and visited R. in the orchard, which was like an island lapped in fitful sun and balmy air; he spends long hours on end there, muffled in a huge great-coat and scarf, pruning the nut-trees.

We are going to London next week. It will be our first sight of it since the Blitz.

Phyllis Nichols to stay. We took her to visit Lawrence and Julia, and we all sat round their fire drinking sherry and eating shortcake. A discussion about what work is consistent with pacifist views — canteens for instance, either for the military or otherwise. Julia objected to my saying that it was no use being an ostrich and pretending the war didn't exist; also that everyone in this country had to eat. How much should one voice one's views was the next question. All shades of opinion here. Phyllis has lost some of her Saint Sebastian complex, and becomes more cynical and realistic. She says she no longer exactly misses her children, though preoccupied with thoughts about them. Her local pacifists, Max Plowman and Middleton Murry, are trying to form a community on the Brüderhof plan. Murry greatly admires a local couple who are so determined to be self-supporting that they eat hardly anything but radishes. He calls this "an inspiration"!

*February 19th*

I think I was afraid of the shock of seeing blitzed London, and started the day therefore in a deliberately apathetic mood. I wasn't the only apathetic one, however; our carriage held two rows of dumb jogging creatures, with their heads buried in newspapers. No one bothered to look out of the window, and I was the only one who cleared a little patch on the steamy pane, and peered out as we got to the suburbs. Bomb craters were fairly frequent among the houses by the line. First there were broken windows, some filled in with cardboard, and then a smashed roof or wall, or a whole house demolished. It was somehow or other a neutral unemotion-inspiring sight. At Paddington the glass roof was full of holes, and coming out into the street we at once saw several large gaps where houses had once been, like those left when teeth are pulled out. To the dentist in Langham Place. The B.B.C. and the Langham Hotel were fairly badly damaged, but the effect was not very different from building operations in peace-time — mess, and workmen shovelling earth between hoardings. The B.B.C. has been painted a hideous dung colour, and the church and the Langham Hotel each sported a large Union Jack, with an effect that was both pathetic and ludicrous. On the way to the Ivy to meet Clive we noticed that St. Anne's, Soho, had a bomb right through the body, though the spire was still standing.

The Ivy was full of prosperous-looking people as usual, all eating a whacking good meal, meat, plovers and delicious creamy pudding. Raymond told us he had resigned from the Ministry of Information and gone back to the *New Statesman*. He didn't seem at all well and was in his most *distrait* London mood, talking feverishly about new French books as if his life depended upon it.

Boris met us at the Great Western Hotel. (Maroussa[1] had been too nervous to come in to central London.) He told us a bomb had wrecked their Hampstead studio, breaking all the windows and blowing in the doors. When Maroussa shouted "Are you all right, Boris?" he found he couldn't answer. The studio table was on top of him, pressing his chest. So poor Maroussa started running towards him, but the trap-door in the floor where Boris keeps his cartoons had blown open, and she fell in and cut her legs on broken glass.

Nearly missed our train, and had to stand all the way to Reading. The rows and rows of untidy mounds in suburban gardens all along the line presented a disgusting sight; these squalid, mildewed shelters, looking as if pigs or rabbits might inhabit them rather than human beings, are symbols of our fear and degradation.

In one way this glimpse of bombed London was reassuring, and even more so was the sight of untouched farmland in between peaceful villages. Then the gap made by each bomb is curiously narrow, so that the neighbouring houses may be quite undamaged save for broken glass. A clean slice is often made through a block, leaving perhaps a whole lift-shaft and wall untouched next to a heap of rubble. London certainly doesn't seem reeling from the blows she has received. Then presumably nor is Hamburg, Cologne or Berlin. In fact there may be no limit to what towns and their inhabitants can stand, if they can dig themselves into warrens underground. In a strange way this is far from consoling. It looks as if the war couldn't be won by bombing, and if not by bombing, by what?

Tonight the sky was bright with stars and throbbing with aeroplane engines, and there were fairly frequent sounds of bombs and gunfire very far away, like a giant dog settling down in its basket. R. went out to look, and saw a German plane go over, caught in a searchlight. I often notice with surprise a pin-point desire for a really loud bang, or to hear the church bells ringing – for some sort of *finality* in fact.

*February 24th*

R., Burgo, Joan and I set off in the car for Devon, where we are taking over R.'s old family home for a short stay. Up came old Hinton, gardener to three generations of Partridges, a splendid old fellow of over eighty, and gave us a warm welcome. The house has a peculiar

---

[1] Volkova, his 'consort' as he called her.

flavour of Anglo-Indian Victorianism, but the books look inviting – beside Pope, Sterne and Trollope there are a lot of Memoirs and History. R. passed of course into a world of nostalgic memories, where he was partly inaccessible.

*February 25th*

Though we were woken by a very loud explosion last night, and understand there have been quite a lot of raids, I don't think the war will figure much in conversation here. To the Warren beach – a sandy spit of land half closing the estuary of the Exe. I lay on the sand in a daze, while R. and Burgo were digging castles like fiends in hell at the very edge of the sea. Behind me some soldiers were making some mysterious defences out of barbed wire, and cracking feeble jokes as they trooped sheepishly to and fro: "Come *on*, Bill, what d'you think you're doing? Playing at sand pies in the garden?" Peace in front of me, war behind, and overhead they were indistinguishable – there seemed so little difference between the Hurricanes and the seagulls swooping in the blue sky. If anything the seagulls seemed poor imitations of the Hurricanes.

These famous defences of our island fortress appeared pitifully unconvincing, and a poor fight we should put up "on the Beaches" by the look of the few rolls of barbed wire red with rust, which anyone could easily get through with a pair of nail scissors. Where the waves had flattened them they could be stepped over with the greatest of ease.

*March 2nd*

Walked up the hill to see R.'s land, which is let out to a violet-grower. Hinton says they are "some of the earliest fields in England". The gnarled trunks of fruit-trees rose out of the rich red Devon soil, or from fields of daffodils just about to flower; the air was warm and sweet and the sea shone blue beneath us. As for the violets, they were just out and their scent was intoxicating. I ordered a large box to be sent to M.A.M., who is ill in hospital, I'm afraid seriously.

Sirens and All Clear tonight, over and over again *ad nauseam*, as well as the steady zoom of German bombers, a rush of low-flying ones, and the crack-crack of machine-guns. Something that is wholly delightful and even comic is the stealthy passage of the Cornish Riviera Express when an alert is on, as if it were going on tip-toe.

The All Clear was the first sound I heard this morning, later on the voices of the cottagers discussing last night's raids at their front doors. Hinton told us that Teignmouth, a harmless seaside resort, had been bombed, and five people killed.

We agree that we are curiously happy here. Though R. generally refers to his two sisters as Goneril and Regan, I think he is pleased that the old family friends, aunts and cousins have received us all so warmly. One of these, a charming grey-haired woman, asked me "what R. thought of all this awful business", and later, in front of her warlike little old mother, said boldly: "I think we ought to get together and make peace *now*. Of course I wouldn't say that in a bus, but one must say what one thinks *some*times" – surprising in what is an entirely conventional world.

Took the steam ferry-boat to Exmouth. We had looked at its façade for a long time from a distance, like the back drop on a stage: now it was intimate and close. But how sad an impression it made, once we were on shore. The tall late-Victorian hotels stared blankly out to sea with their plate-glass eyes. Inside one could see white-haired old people, silently lunching off long white tablecloths, with tin dish-covers set before them. R. and I left Joan and Burgo on the beach and walked into the town. Here the inhabitants looked even more venerable, walking painfully with crutches or pushed in bath chairs. When we reached the shopping centre the secret of Exmouth's gloom became plain, like some horrid festering wound. The whole centre of the town had been bombed. Large piles of rubble, twisted iron and debris gave it a terribly sad look, and there were broken windows everywhere. On a shutter someone had written: "We are still alive in spite of Hitler." Little Exmouth was a sorrier sight than London, perhaps because it had had no limelight and compensatory glory. Then, out of a pearly grey sky, came a squadron of aeroplanes, flying very high indeed with a menacing hum like a swarm of bees. And an old lady with a long white horse-face waved her stick as she stood on the sea front, and cried: "There they go! Off to drop bombs in France! We don't want any of the other sort here – we've had enough of them."

Two sirens tonight, quantities of aeroplanes, a rattle of gunfire. And I was horrified to realize that we were sitting over our nice warm fire, listening quite calmly to this sound – which was after all the noise of human beings trying to kill other human beings.

Departure day. We piled the car with cockle-shells for our hens, Burgo's favourite stones and shells, gas-masks, provisions and baggage. Hinton came to see us off, bringing a bunch of Devon violets for me; I saw tears in his eyes as he shook hands with R., and they were certainly in mine. We got to Ham Spray by tea-time, and couldn't have had a more glorious day to arrive on. The afternoon stayed golden and mellow until quite late, some daffodils were out, the garden full of vegetables, and quantities of eggs put down in waterglass. But the cats were huffy and refused to forgive us for our absence.

Oh what a pleasure to sleep in the same bed with R., and in spite of the delights of Devon to be back at darling Ham Spray again.

Ernest Bevin has announced that he proposes to call up various sections of the population for war work – girls of 20-21, which includes Joan, have to register next month, and men of 41-45, which just doesn't include R. also. So we're back in the war again, and must listen to the wireless and decide whether to be optimistic or gloomy. Most people seem to feel we are beating Hitler because of our successes against the Italians, whereas the enormous German army hasn't even been engaged for the last nine months.

In Hungerford we ran into Julia and Lawrence, and went back with them to Chilton. They told us a bomb fell on Froxfield while we were away. Julia says the crash was deafening and shook the house like a terrier shaking a rat. She bounced out of her chair shouting "BUGGER!" very loud and very angrily. Lawrence's behaviour was rather odd. He looked at her in amazement and said, "Julia, what on earth's the matter with you?" She saw from his expression (and he admitted it afterwards) that he was pretending for the moment that nothing had happened.

Burgo and I walked across the fields to the cobbler who lives at the foot of the Downs. While Burgo played around the stump of a hollow tree, I sat absorbing the scene, and thinking my own thoughts about these days which slip so quietly by, as if disregarding the war. How little, except for the much simpler life we lead, it affects us at the moment. Or so I sometimes feel; at others, that it has thrown out couch-grass roots to undermine our peace of mind, invisibly creeping and choking the sources of vitality and enjoyment. We live in the present, as if each day might be our last, and to some degree in the past. The future is so nebulous that one barely thinks about it, and those who die, like Ray and M.A.M.[1] seem to have forfeited nothing we have ourselves. Late tonight I thought again about invasion, not in the abstract but as a solid possibility. Such thoughts come in flashes, lighting up the inside of one's head (where all sorts of fears crouch) with an acetylene flare, and then disappear so completely that it's impossible to remember the feel of them.

I found a touching object, a half-finished letter from Burgo to M.A.M.: "Dear Grannie, I hope you'll soon be well. This is you in bed Grannie", and a picture of a cheerful row of people in bed.

*March 26th*

Tossing and turning restlessly in bed, I woke to *Angst*, I don't know what about. Finished the chair-covers I have been patching and then went with R. to look for plover's eggs in the fields beyond the Little Wood. He soon found some, but I'm a poor looker and can't keep my eyes on the earth. Went on by myself to the grass-lined chalk-pit under the Downs, and there I lay on my face looking out sideways across the almost white fields of stubble and the smoke-coloured distance. I could see R. pacing up and down, looking noble and battered, like the general of a defeated army.

Remarks by Burgo today: "Mr. Padel's quite old. I believe he was only three years old when the Congo was discovered." And, "You see, I'm rather strong. Boys are stronger than ladies and you're a rather young lady and I'm an old boy."

*March 29th*

Hills (Heywood and Anne) for the weekend. Poor Heywood looked thin and drawn, his clothes hanging round him. His father has spent a lot of money on buying them a shelter and having it set up in the basement of their London house, so they feel they must sometimes sleep there, to justify the expense.

Heywood and I walked up to the foot of the Downs and sat in the chalkpit. He talked movingly about his horror of the war and dread of raids, his own uncertain position about call-up. He says Anne is much braver than him, and he envies her self-control.

F: "Do you manage to sleep when you spend the night in London?"

H: "Well no; I simply lie and listen to the aeroplanes all the time."

His misery touched me very much, and it seemed completely rational.

Conversation after dinner about War and Peace. Heywood was almost silent. Anne is an ex-pacifist, who thinks, bad as war is, Fascism

---

[1] She had just died after an operation.

is worse. News on the wireless of what really sounds like a naval victory. As we heard the announcement describing the sinking of several Italian ships, all our faces lit up, as with pleasure or excitement. Yet what an appalling thought — those huge iron masses disintegrating and exploding, and hurling hundreds of Italians into the sea. It happened so quickly that one ship simply ceased to exist in a single burst of flame, hit by fifteen shells simultaneously. "Not a pretty sight," said the Admiral commentator.

A tremendous discussion with R. about what should be the limitations preventing one voicing views one believes to be true — *à propos* of Bertie Russell. R. thinks that Bertie should not (as a pacifist who has recanted after fleeing from the war to the security of the U.S.A.) tell all of us who are still "in" it that he finds war less terrible than he expected, and has therefore decided we must go on with it. We fined down his objection (R.'s) to "bad form". I defended both B.R.'s right to change his opinion, and to state it to anyone anywhere, both of which I vehemently believe in.

*April 3rd*

Opening *The Times* this morning I read with astonishment: "We regret to announce that the death of Mrs. Virginia Woolf, missing since last Friday, must now be presumed." From the discreet notice that followed it seems that she is presumed to have drowned herself in the river near Rodmell. An attack of her recurring madness I suppose; the thought of self-destruction is terrible, dramatic and pathetic, and yet (because it is the product of the human will) has an Aristotelian inevitability about it, making it very different from all the other sudden deaths we have to contemplate.

*April 4th*

To London, for a family business conclave, reading Boswell in the train. On the way to meet Hester [Chapman] for lunch at the Ivy I was struck with horror and depression at the sight of the damage in small streets off Tottenham Court Road. The sky was low and dark, and London looked not like a town which had *had* a drubbing, but one actually at war, as of course it is. I thought, "Here I am in the war, and it's hateful," and I shrank into the corner of my taxi, choked with a sort of icy, leaden hatred of it all. No tables left at the Ivy, though Leslie Howard, arriving at the same time, was squeezed in somewhere. We went on to the Café Royal, where, as the windows had been blown in and boarded up, we ate by electric light. Hester was amusing about her life in the shelters with Jewish clothes–merchants, yet couldn't restrain her natural desire to boast. "One feels magnificent the day after a raid, because one has got through it and not shown one is afraid. But of course it is *absolutely* terrifying — I never knew it was possible to be so terrified."

On a bus to Harrods. Great damage all down Piccadilly gave me a series of thwacks and thumps. In the hairdresser's warm *cellule*, I heard nothing but talk on the eternal theme: "There was a whistling and a groaning and I heard my chimney-pot falling. It was a barrage balloon come down on the roof, and there was I in the cupboard with the evacuee. 'Flo,' I said, 'we're finished', just like that . . ."

*April 6th*

I came in late to lunch, and R. who was dishing out the food said, "Well, it's begun, the invasion's started." I looked at him with flat incredulity, supposing he meant the invasion of England, but he went on: "Hitler has marched into Greece and Yugoslavia." My main feeling was *déjà vu*. It was so like Denmark, Norway, Belgium and Holland. Then I said to myself in craven self-defence: I won't think about it; I'm damned if I'm going to follow the dreary old graph of hope and disappointment.

*April 8th*

Sat out on the verandah, trying to write to Clive in answer to his letter about Virginia's death. He says: "For some days, of course, we hoped against hope that she had wandered crazily away and might be discovered in a barn or a village shop. But by now all hope is abandoned . . . It became evident some weeks ago that she was in for another of those long agonizing breakdowns of which she has had several already. The prospect — two years insanity, then to wake up to the sort of world which two years of war will have made, was such that I can't feel sure that she was unwise. Leonard, as you may suppose, is very calm and sensible. Vanessa is, apparently at least, less affected than Duncan, Quentin and I had looked for and feared. I dreaded some such physical collapse as befell her after Julian was killed. For the rest of us the loss is appalling, but like all unhappiness that comes of 'missing', I suspect we shall realize it only bit by bit."

*April 12th*

Spring began suddenly this morning. R. and Burgo went out to hunt for plovers' eggs, and I wandered out later to join them. The warm air softly embraced me as I walked; this and the trees bursting with purple-brown buds combined together to thaw the frozen corners of my brain.

"Ah, here's the spring!" and then along comes Hitler's spring offensive, and a house built of the flimsiest cards, and not even believed in, comes toppling down. Yet I feel both more detached and more fatalistic than I did last year. Indeed no time has been harder to bear, it seems to me, than the Norwegian campaign. I contrive to live much more within our magic Ham Spray circle, R., Burgo, me, the cats, the garden. Yet there lies beneath my pleasure in all that — and it *is* real pleasure — an implicit acceptance of the fact that we probably possess it all only for a little time, that it is a life with no future, that we are sailing along in a boat which has a hole in the bottom.

Wrote letters, sitting on the verandah most of the morning — the sky perfectly blue: peace visible, tangible and audible; the cows lying down in the field; Burgo and R.'s voices by the bonfire under the glossy leaves of the Portuguese laurel, the bees buzzing in the grape hyacinths; far off the hum of a tractor. No aeroplanes. Positive happiness invaded me, and though I know that it is achieved at the cost of ostrichism I cling to it and do not want to lose it. I supppose if I held beliefs of an idealistic sort about the perfectability of man and the innate goodness of the Universe it would be different. As I don't, this actual, momentary, individual happiness is the best I hope for. The processes of nature go on regardless of war and cataclysm; their resources against their own cataclysms of storm and frost seem boundless. Where has that principle got to in the case of human beings, who are, after all, a part of nature?

*April 19th*

In Hungerford this morning we saw the battered remains of a German aeroplane being hauled into place by a crane. It had obviously been carted round half the counties of England in an effort to whip up interest in War Weapons week or the Spitfire collection. It was like a jaded old music-hall star who has been relegated to the provinces, or a wasp whose wings have been pulled off by a child. A gloomy sight — being gloomily inspected by a small crowd, mainly of children.

In the afternoon Roy and Billa [Harrod] arrived. Roy takes it for granted that our one aim is to support the war effort, to which end he is keen on suppressing all poultry-keeping, because the poultry-food takes up too much room on the ships. He has worked it all out by calculus, ignoring the practical facts of hen-life, about which he knows nothing. As he is on the Economic Advisory Committee which controls our food and fates, we were rather astonished to find that he was unaware that hens don't lay the same number of eggs all the year round!

A very pleasant evening, however, Billa telling amusing stories, sewing and gossiping. Roy tried to persuade us that we were all happier than we had been in the piping times of peace. I suggested that it was shocking if true; that we ought at best to be able to put up with such beastliness, and in the process of doing so, or even learning to enjoy it, we were probably becoming more bestial ourselves. Talking of "standing" the war, R. said, "I can *stand* Peace all right."

*April 20th*

Raymond and Eardley [Knollys] came to lunch on their way back from the West Country, on errands for the National Trust. They were stopped twice under suspicion of being spies, once by soldiers, once by police. The officer had never heard of the National Trust, and asked Raymond, "Are you in this racket too?" At Bristol a woman saw them photographing a building and rushed to the police, describing them as "an obvious Italian with a blond German-looking man".

Heywood came down for the night, to see about getting taken on at Tidcombe as a market gardener. R. drove him over and did his best for him but the interview was disappointing. I asked Julia over to cheer Heywood up. She looked very comic and delightful sitting on the sofa, spectacles on nose, running her hands through her hair and producing complete chaos there, talking all the time about *Madame Bovary*. Extremely thick stockings and eccentric boots completed the picture.

Julia told me that Lawrence was thinking of returning to London as he can't paint without the stimulus of other pictures. "So I shall look for a female friend to share a house with, as I haven't got husband or wife?" (*Sic.*) F.: "What about your writing?" Julia: "Oh my hateful writing. I tell myself I can live for my work but I can't."

*April 26th*

Yesterday Angelica and Clive arrived on a three days' visit. R. and I had both felt anxious about Angelica, whom we barely knew, but she arrived wearing a charming and friendly expression, and struggling with a small Victorian hat, which the wind was trying to blow off her head. Her face is strikingly lovely, with great grey eyes and bistre-coloured skin, and her figure beautiful and distinguished. We are already delighted with our visitors. The weather is fiendishly cold, yet they entertain themselves and us too. In a sunny half-hour I had a talk to Angelica about books and writing, as we sat on the verandah. Then she came in when I was playing the piano, and I got her to sing to my accompaniments. In the evening she brought out a patchwork quilt, which put mine and Billa's to shame; hers was a work of art, she had put so much thought into it and produced such delicate combinations of pattern and colour. What a delightful and gifted creature she is! R. and I agree that she and Clive are our nicest visitors for ages. They have brought a strong

89

whiff of Charleston's civilisation, with its aesthetic projects and cease-less activity.

Early departure of the Bells. Just before four o'clock Janetta rang up to say she was at Hungerford Station. Humphrey is in camp as a private soldier, and "it is horrible trying to live alone". Rollo may join her here, as he has leave. We were overjoyed at seeing her again. She told us about the big Wednesday air-raid. She was dining with Ivan Moffat in Fitzroy Square. When the raid began, Eve Kirk, who is an efficient air-raid warden, put on her tin hat and went off, and Ivan Moffat went on the roof to fire-watch. Cecil Beaton stood at the window exclaiming: "It's *too* fascinating, *too* extraordinary."

Rollo arrived for dinner in his Pilot Officer's uniform. He looks bigger and stronger, and there's a peculiar sweetness in his expression. Janetta blossomed in his company and talked about her marriage, which to her "was an unimportant ceremony and will remain so until I want a divorce".

Tonight we had a conversation about the war. Rollo believes, in a *simpliste* youthful way, in "greater organization as a means to greater freedom". He thinks the Nazi regime comes as near this as anything else. I was just wondering if he would follow this to its logical conclusion by thinking the war not worth fighting, when he said so himself. Indeed his position is an unusual one. He is fascinated by flying and by the glamour of danger, and excited by his own position as a fighter pilot and the world's reaction to it; but he thinks the war a mad one which should never have been begun. Not sure whether he is a Communist or a Nazi, he is unusually clear-headed in seeing their resemblance. Janetta feels the war must be won, to protect the intellectuals for one thing. We all, including Rollo, asked her if she was sure the price was not too much to pay, and she disliked being put between these nutcrackers, and said the war might not — or she hoped it might not — involve great slaughter.

Bunny writes that Angelica was delighted with Ham Spray and its inhabitants. "Why didn't you tell me what enormous charm Ralph has?" she said. "I told her it was better to find out such things for one-self," says Bunny.

Janetta is leaving today to get the house ready for Humphrey who returns tomorrow.

After dark I went out on the lawn. R. shouted, "Don't go out that way! Remember the Japanese policeman!" (so-called because of his
90

oriental appearance) "and *do* look out for the black-out!" But I was already outside, breathing in the sweet-smelling night air; there was half a moon sailing through the clear sky and no aeroplanes. I felt I didn't care a fig for the Japanese policeman, nor the war either – just for a moment. And wondered for the millionth time how human beings came to make such nights hideous with their hellish explosions.

*May 8th*

The event of today was a visit to Ned Grove at his Hampshire farmhouse. It had a rather Japanese appearance and he said he had made it himself, with one man to help him. No signs of visual taste, but the kitchen gloriously equipped with pounds of yellow butter, and great sides of bacon. In front of the house stood a block of concrete, like a boot-box on end, decorated with bas-reliefs of Pan and nymphs. "What's the history of this?" asked R. N.G. laughed with a note of embarrassment. "The originals of most of the casts are in the British Museum," he said. Indoors were shelves of books on Black Magic and the Witch Cult, a negro altar and a large wooden bowl full of ashes. We realised that the suburban-looking object must be an altar to Pan. In his bedroom were signs of packing, tropical clothes and guns, and he told us he was leaving for Africa at the request of the War Office. "I was in Africa after the last war, and for two years I was King of a native tribe, but I'm afraid I'll go to different people this time." While we ate home-made home-ground bread with masses of yellow butter he put a record of African music on the gramophone. "They were made for *Sanders of the River.* When I saw the film I was amazed to recognize My People, and their songs and dances. Korda gave me the records." R. says *he* must have been the original Sanders.

*May 11th*

When Joan brought in the green tea this evening after dinner, she gasped and said, "Mrs. Partridge, I want to leave and do war work, as Tim's being sent abroad." I went with her into the kitchen, where she told me that he was going in about three weeks' time, and she felt she couldn't bear it unless she was hard at work all day, so she had been to an aeroplane factory in Newbury to see if they would take her on. I didn't know how to show her how sorry I was without upsetting her more, her white face and breathless voice were so pitiful. I came back to the sitting-room so struck by Joan's tragedy that I felt on the verge of tears, and neither R. nor I could read or think of anything else for some time. Here was something absolutely good (Joan's relation with Tim) and it has been struck, and is crumbling away so rapidly that she has to try and

91

drown her misery in the rumble and crash of machinery. And of course it is the happiness of not one but hundreds of Joans and hundreds of Gunner Robinsons, thousands, millions I should say – of all nationalities – that is to be sacrificed in this awful pandemonium. R. went to talk to her. We were both too upset to read.

The ducklings were put out this morning in a run on the lawn and we spent some time watching them. Our life gets more domestic and agricultural and when Joan goes it may get more so. If only I could cook!

On the wireless we heard that Westminster Abbey, the British Museum and the Houses of Parliament were all damaged in last night's Blitz.

B. suggests writing to Hitler: "Nasty Hitler! Stop this horrible war and go right away altogether." "And then," he said slyly, "I should sign it 'Love from John'."

*May 20th*

R. and I rode on our bikes to tea with Julia and Lawrence, to see Hester [Chapman] who is visiting them from London for a day or two. After gliding through the fresh spring greenery and buttercup fields, with water purling under bridges, it was quite a shock to find oneself looking into Hester's heavily made-up face, with eyelashes clogged with navy blue paint. We had our tea beside the river, sitting under an awning.

For someone living in the Blitz, who finds herself among four country-dwellers, Hester's tone was perfect. She discussed how to keep rabbits as if it were the most important thing in the world, but when she did start on her shelter stories they were fascinating. She described how one night as she lay huddled and terrified on a mattress in the shelter, listening to a series of appalling crashes and whizzes, she heard two voices discussing German airmen – "They say they're heavily made-up, *you* know, red *nails, lip-stick* – I mean when men do *that* . .". CRASH – BANG – WHIZZ from above. And a more outspoken voice put in loudly: "Why, everyone knows Hitler himself is a Pansy!" CRASH. BOOM. BANG!

*May 29th*

To Raymond's cottage for the weekend, driving through green luscious fields, saturated with rain and thick with buttercups.

Found Raymond alone in the sitting-room, which was overflowing as usual with books, pictures, spectacles, china knick-knacks and medicines. Beyond the tiny green lawn the even darker green river slid silently and rapidly past, and beyond that again was the dense jungle of Magpie

92

Island. This Thames backwater seems further from the war than any-where we have yet been, with its heavy silence except for the birds singing in the trees, and its moist warm riverside atmosphere. Eardley came back in the evening. Raymond told us he was terribly crushed by the death of Frank Coombs in an air-raid, and this was apparent in his face.

Delicious supper, asparagus, wine, chocolates. Talked till nearly one.

*May 30th*

Came down to find a log fire burning. At breakfast a refreshingly unwar-like conversation about painting.

The sun came out early, and turned everything dazzling blue, yellow and green. Raymond and Eardley brought out a carpet from a friend's bombed flat; we spread it out at the top of the garden, measured, cut and swept it, in bursts of practicality interspersed with long lazy pauses, when we sat on it in the sun and conversed.

The papers brought the news that clothes are to be rationed from now on. I was impressed by Raymond taking it so philosophically, and set-ting aside with no sign of a pang his passion for buying ties, shirts and "woollies".

We drifted off in the punt round Magpie Island. Again the amazing peace, no sound but the water lapping against the sides and a bird orches-tra from the trees. It was such an old-fashioned sensation gliding through the opaque water with tangled weeds trailing from the banks, that I wasn't at all surprised to hear a distant voice singing, "Oh you beautiful doll — you great big beautiful doll!" Home to a dream of a lunch — lampreys in a marvellous sauce, foie gras and champagne, and then we had to say goodbye and go to fetch Alix and James from Lord's Wood. In spite of the summery heat, James had on two or three waistcoats and Alix a felt hat with ear-flaps to keep out the draught. Ham Spray garden, when we reached it, was bathed in beautiful sunlight, and Burgo had arranged a row of deck-chairs for us facing the Downs.

In our evening conversation Alix reaffirmed her support of the war, "as I have decided Hitlerism is worse than war". Yet she is enormously impressed by the formidableness of Hitler, and not entirely in a hostile way, in fact I am inclined to think she holds the most Nazi views I have come across.

*June 3rd*

James' charm is irresistible, and I would like to show him the warmth of my feelings towards him in some way, but how to do so is the question, for he appears to live in an enclosed world of his own. Alix grows more absorbed in the eccentric details of her life, her various dodges to protect herself from cold and discomfort, midget efforts towards luxury — like eating lots of mustard because it's very expensive just now. She fills her days with journeys to change her library book, or buy some trifling object, in fact lives much like any old lady ending her days at Torquay. Yet in spite of all, her formidable intellectual character rises like a rock out of the welter of these slightly pathetic activities.

Julia and Lawrence to lunch. The sun came through the mist and we sat and lay on the lawn, bemused by its sudden heat. Julia lay with closed eyes under a green sunshade; Lawrence pulled his chair between R. and James, who were talking about hieroglyphics. The insect world was another topic, and someone said that a wasp, when it sees a fellow wasp is short of food, will bite the tail off and give it to its head to eat. This is supposed to show the superiority of humans, but Alix said she thought it showed quite the reverse — the superior intelligence of insects.

Every evening Alix draws up a stool to the fire and launches some theory or other, crouched there like a witch. James, in his armchair, hardly looks up from studying his hieroglyphics through a magnifying-glass, so it is generally left to R. or me to take the other side. Tonight it was standardization versus individualism. Alix is delighted, highly eccentric individual though she is, at the increase of standardization, and is down on local customs, village shops, and variations in cooking. Her dream is a world of chain stores, where every town in England cooks fish in the way a board of experts has decided to be the best; a world of tins, cafeterias and efficient bus services. She sees no point in variety or change, and holds that there is no sight more debased than a house-wife going off to shop with a list and a string bag. Oddly enough the housewife coming back from the lending library or cinema with her head full of fantasies seemed to her a nobler spectacle! Agriculture is a degrading activity, and we should have imported everything we wanted for the war right from the start, tinned it and buried it, thus leaving all available man-power free for the services and munition-making. In spite of our stupidity in *not* doing this she thinks we may well gain a crushing victory. James thought a compromise peace might be better. It was left to us Partridges to stand up for individualism, and say it might even revive after the war. It's strange what pleasure Alix gives by her faithful-ness to her own character.

*June 6th*

Quentin [Bell] joined our party today. He and Alix had a conversation about colonizing the blacks, Alix maintaining that there was much to be said for the French method of relentless hygiene, hypodermics and drugs, and also relentless interference with their more barbarous religions

94

and customs; I expected to hear her say any minute: "Of course I think it would *really* be better to exterminate the lot."

When we listened to the news tonight James said in an agitated voice: "Yes, I think we've invaded Syria." "Why," I said, "there was no mention of Syria whatever." "Yes, that's just why I think so." (Like Sherlock Holmes's dog in the night-time.)

*June 7th*

James looked excited at the breakfast table. "I was quite right, you see. We have gone into Syria." He spent the afternoon raking the ether for more news, but all he got was Cairo saying, "Cheerio, B.B.C."

Talking to Quentin about the war I told him how I envied him his passionate interest in it. He wouldn't have been born at any other time for anything, he finds it so enthralling. I tried to convey the sense of constant disgust I feel weighing on me whenever I think of it, and he looked at me in surprise and said: "Oh I see, you are a *real* Pacifist." Why are people so loth to recognise the fact, I wonder. I find no difficulty in recognising their bellicosity.

Yesterday at lunch Quentin and Alix, who have many points of agreement, were saying that it was inconsistent for Pacifists to pay their Income Tax, I said, "Well, I think it's inconsistent of those who support the war in theory not to do so in practice. I don't understand why you, Alix, are not in a factory making submarines." She turned slightly pink and said, "Well, my line about that is that I shall be called upon when wanted."

People write to the papers endlessly about clothes rationing, struggling to press themselves forwards in the guise of exceptions. Surely as expectant mothers they can have extra coupons for maternity gowns? Surely as mothers of sons killed in the war they can have them for mourning? Or, if not, can they at least have some special armlet to indicate their bereavement?

A few days ago the Japanese policeman arrived and told us that by order of the Government all domestic pigeons were to be executed. He didn't exactly know why, but it was something to do with invasion. So ours were killed and eaten in a pie, but one snow-white one managed to escape and now wheels about against the green landscape. We feel we can hardly bear to condemn it to death also.

Lawrence drove over to have a second go at painting my portrait. I enjoy his conversation, though painfully aware of all the duties I'm neglecting. He told me he and Julia had been worn out by Hester's visit. She kept them up till three every night trying to batter down their Pacifism with her loyal support of the war.

"She's just a natural alligator," he said.

95

Somewhere in the middle of the night we were woken by crunching sounds on the gravel, and the engines of motor bicycles and lorries, also heavy steps and male voices. "It must be the invasion," was my first thought. Then, realizing it probably wasn't, I still felt that if it had been I should only have sunk back to sleep just as passionately. Later there was knocking on the doors. R. looked out and said, "The army is everywhere, lorry-loads of it." By breakfast-time a sense of drama had possessed the house and its inmates. Our house was, in fact, no longer our own. Processions of soldiers drew water from the tap; others went to the lavatory or to telephone. In the kitchen were pleased, self-conscious faces.

The day became hot, the red poppies so big and bright you couldn't look at them. While I was planting snapdragons along the drive a Scotch army cook came up and said, "Missus, could you sell me a few spring onions to give a taste to a stew?"

Burgo was mad with excitement. When he got back from school, he and I walked down the avenue; from end to end it was full of armoured cars — huge rhinoceros-like objects, striped and spotted like wild animals — drawn up between the tree trunks. In them and under them and beside them, in bunches and rows and heaps, lay strong, red-faced sweating young soldiers, mostly asleep in the attitudes of statues. I was struck by their look of health and toughness, sometimes of beauty, but their machines, I was just reflecting, were the ugliest things the human mind could conceive, when Burgo gasped out, "*Aren't* they lovely?" As we reached the gate we met Edie just turning into the avenue, flashing a crack at two sentries and walking with swinging skirts and a tossing head and sideways-darting eyes, looking very dashing and splendid, like a Spanish girl.

The Army left with only half the noise they made arriving. The invasion was over.

Ring on the telephone. "Er — is that Major Partridge? Hold on, Major. Have you by any chance seen an armoured car about anywhere? We seem to have lost one." "I'll go and look," I heard R. say, as though it had been a pair of spectacles.

To London for the day. This marvellously hot June weather made it seem like peacetime. The heat somehow dissolves the strained awareness of war, and I even caught myself joining up the gaps left by bombs with my mind's eye. Sometimes I even saw beauty in the sunlit devastation. Bought macaroni and parmesan in Soho, and then to my tailor, who appeared to have been blown up into a higher storey, each floor on his staircase revealing the outer air through yawning holes.

On to the Leicester Galleries to see Vanessa's pictures, and to lunch with Clive off cold salmon, asparagus and zabaglione. Clive said he spent last night at the Shy Bride's[1] house at Ascot, pillow-fighting in the garden with young Americans from the Embassy. H.G. Wells was there, and in a fervour of anti-Catholicism had bored everyone by insisting that we ought to bomb Rome, till at last one exasperated American burst out: "Very well then, BUMB it!"

On the way to meet Boris and Maroussa for tea at the Cafè Anglais, I walked through Gerrard Street, moved by a sentimental impulse to look at the old book-shop[2], but I could hardly recognise it. There must have been several bombs, some taking slices from the great tenement buildings backing onto Charing Cross Road, where the cascades of rubble reached so high it seemed impossible that dozens of people should not still be buried under them. Other bombs had penetrated a theatre, leaving a semicircle of broken seats going right up to the crazy, Chinese-looking roof. This staggering scene boomed through my head and out again, like a funeral bell.

Maroussa's nerve is still gone. She had not been as far as Leicester Square, even in daylight, since the Blitz started, and when I begged them to come to Ham Spray she said: "What about the Invasion?" for that is her obsession at the moment. I could see she was in a state of permanent dread, her words often faltering in the middle of a sentence. She said: "I cannot read now, I just sit and sit before the fire till my arm and my thigh is burnt brown by it."

Travelled home in an infernally hot train crowded with soldiers, sailors and ATS: the only available seat was in the corridor on a suitcase opposite the lavatory, from which a stench of urine poured, and edged in by hot soldiers in their thick uniforms, mopping their foreheads and complaining of thirst. One carried a pile of poetry books.

*June 22nd*

In the middle of another grilling morning, only distinguished from the others by a violent sirocco, Lawrence rang up and said, "What do you think of the news?" "What is it? We've not heard." "Oh, they've invaded Russia! — a tremendous attack all along the frontier. Poor little

---

[1] Mary Baker, an American heiress.
[2] Birrell and Garnett, where I had worked for some years.

*things!*" His voice ended in a high squeak. I rushed to tell the others, feeling I was the bearer of good news. Perhaps I was, as presumably it means that our own turn is to be postponed for a little. R. was cock-a-hoop, as he has long foretold this and even had a bet with me about it. We speculated at intervals all day as to how long it would take the Germans to polish off Russia, and what would be the line of the Government, the *New Statesman* and the Communist Party.

Hester has come on to us from Julia and Lawrence, bringing with her arguments about how much we are missing by living in the country instead of the Blitz. At least her attack is nominally against Julia for leaving London – missing so much and so much, the beauty of the fires, the observation of human beings under stress. She is very amusing and makes herself agreeable to Burgo – this afternoon she gave a spendid rendering of the death of the Prince Imperial for his benefit, allowing her not inconsiderable bulk to crash to the ground by the swimming-pool when struck by an imaginary assegai.

She had spent a long time – "a good two hours" she claimed – over her toilet, and very surprising it was. Under a mountain of fluffy curls her face was made up in red, white and navy blue, with monster Woolworth pearls in her ears, startling the bathers by the pool; and for dinner she appeared in a black lace evening dress with a train, cut up and down as far as possible.

*June 23rd*

It was some time after waking that I remembered with a start that Russia had been invaded. Last night Winston C. made one of his most brilliant speeches; it will fairly take the wind out of the sails of the *New Statesman* grousers.

These hot balmy transparent days make the time rattle through one's fingers like a fishing-line off a reel. Yet underneath, beating away monotonously, is the pulse with which one is aware of the war, and at this moment, of course, particularly of Russia.

Dora Morris and Eddy Sackville-West arrived to tea, stepping out of their car like two elegant Edwardians. Dora carried a Japanese parasol and wore a turban and pearls, Eddy was in a pale grey suit and floating tie. Tea under the ilex tree. When for some reason I asked Eddy if he ever went to the cinema, he answered with a pained expression: "No, I never go – it's against my conscience to go to any form of entertainment now-a-days," and though I would have loved to know how his conscience formulated such a principle I sheered off from embarrassment.

R. had a letter from Gerald, describing a visit from his father and new step-mother and then going on to the War: "Every German woman and child killed is a contribution to the future safety and happiness of Europe, for the worst thing about the Germans is the fact that there are 75 millions of them. When we have won the war the licensed days of taking human life will be over and we shall have to treat them as our friends. Today, death to every German. This will shock you. I see your pained clergyman's expression." There follows, taking himself I dare say as much by surprise as it did us, a violent attack on us pacifists. "Those I know seem to me people who for some reason or other are bad at arithmetic. They can't add up even simple sums. Poor creatures, I think, and when I see that they feel sad because they are cut off by their beliefs from other people, that it is often a strain to be natural and at ease, I feel sorrier than ever. And then — this is bound to happen in the end — my curiosity makes me write a letter which is likely to annoy them." *The old humbug!* What a cheek he has!

Helped R. sort a huge box of salvaged raisins into those suitable for the chickens and those for us. They had been bombed while on the railway and partly burnt. We plunged our hands into the dark, sticky mass and separated them out with our fingers, the blonds for us, the brunettes for the hens. There was a lot of coal among them, slates, splintered wood and even glass.

A conversation with R. about Agitators — whom he is always down on for creating unhappiness where content exisited before. But I feel it may sometimes be a case of exchanging immediate happiness for truth, and between these two values how is one to decide? A hedonist needn't necessarily envy Voltaire's (?) pig in its sty. The agitator could say that by destroying the blind happiness of ignorance he was introducing a more far-reaching and lasting happiness to be got from knowledge.

During the afternoon Isobel [Strachey] arrived from Oxford, also Barbara [Bagenal] and Saxon. Isobel is now a Government servant, translating from Spanish and Portuguese at Blenheim. She is like the *cigale ayant chanté*, she has spent all her dress coupons on frivolous useless things like a white cotton plus-four suit, covered in West Indian emblems. Barbara has brought with her (for health reasons I understand) a Bulgarian fungus, looking like a cauliflower, in a pot; it has to be fed with milk to keep it alive, and she came into the kitchen to ask for its afternoon drink. I looked at it with aversion, and thought I saw waving tentacles.

Saxon sits under a tree in his white silk suit, fast asleep, with a volume of Horace on his knee.

*July 3rd*

Frenzy reigns in the kitchen, where a substance called "beestings" has been brought in from the dairy. It is the first yield of a cow that has calved, and we struggled to make it into a pudding, as it is supposed to be highly nourishing. The house is chock-a-block with visitors (three more arrived today) and I am making desperate efforts to learn to cook. Tonight I cooked supper, put Burgo to bed and spent a long time after that planting out and watering the asters. Before supper we all walked down the avenue to see the haymakers, and a baling-machine making its curious gestures. As we lifted our feet through the stubble Burgo said, "We're like sewing-machines."

*July 9th*

The heat all day was oppressive and frightening, and we hourly expect it to burst in thunder. Watered the garden again after dinner; the moon, a great circle of sour cream against the grey sky, looked menacing but did not as formerly call up the idea of air-raids — for we have had complete immunity from all night sounds, sirens and evening aeroplanes ever since the Russian campaign began. Nor have there been raids in other parts of the country. Even the food aspect of the war has temporarily faded before the groaning plenty of our kitchen garden, from which beans and strawberries now come in profusion. R. and I have done all the fruit and vegetable bottling ourselves, and thirty bottles make a handsome row on the larder shelf. I wake early, thinking of jam and bottles, and this practical life makes me happy in a new sort of way. We occupy our minds building a solid fortress-like existence to withstand the batterings of war, but I wonder if in doing so we are getting more self-centred and losing our power to be interested in other people.

*July 12th*

The heat-wave is breaking up at last. Raymond (who is a sort of witch-doctor always bringing rain) arrived this afternoon, and with him the deluge. Took him to the Mill House, to tea with Julia and Lawrence, who had 'Aunty Loo'[1] staying with them. I had scarcely seen her since Julia and I were often together as children at Ford Place, with Uncle Logan hovering inscrutably in the background. She had then seemed to us relentless and insensitive, though with a certain dry, eccentric charm, and I was surprised to find her today a handsome, distinguished figure, with her grey hair and clothes. As we were leaving she drew me aside and said: "Don't you think Julia's happier than she's ever been? And I *adore* Lawrence!"

*July 17th*

Our days continue extraordinarily busy with fruit-picking, topping and tailing and bottling. Yesterday R. took twenty-seven pounds of gooseberries into Hungerford. Everyone is longing for fruit, and no-one has any. It is most gratifying to see eyes light up at the sight of our produce. I was under the net this morning, picking strawberries, when Julia arrived on her bicycle for the day, looking like a music-hall version of a French artist, in velveteen trousers, with long hair on her shoulders and a bow under her chin. She said Aunty Loo had lost her head utterly towards the end of her visit, and the greedy relentless egoist had come out. She had stripped their landlady's garden of flowers without even asking, and when Julia protested she said: "I know it's awful of me, but I'm like that."

*July 26th*

Burgo sat gravely reading the *New Statesman*. "Oh *this* doesn't sound good news at all: 'The British Empire is poorly'." Molly and Desmond arrived this evening, both maimed in their different ways. Molly had run out of batteries for her electrical aid to deafness, and Desmond had left his anti-wheeze machine at Bath. He looked pale and ill, and taking his temperature before dinner he found it nearly 100°

*July 27th*

I managed to equip Molly with a battery borrowed from Mr. Coombs, the cowman. She looked much relieved and repaid my trouble by being brilliantly funny. After lunch we were picking over the blackcurrants on the lawn, Molly pitching them all over the place with gestures illustrating her fantasies, when a shining Rolls appeared in the drive, and out got a little squirrel of a woman called Mrs. McKenna, who had brought Desmond's anti-asthma machine half across England for him in spite of

---

[1] Alys Russell, first wife of Bertrand Russell.

petrol rationing. So both were fitted up at the cost of considerable trouble to others paid for in Irish charm.

Julia and Lawrence, who arrived later, had been to the Brenans, and said that Gerald talked rather self-consciously about his recent letter to R., wanting to know how it had been received. "Oh, I think they were very amused by it," said Lawrence. (Julia had in fact made us one of those children's board games, on which one square said "Letter from Gerald: go back ten!"). But this was not what Gerald hoped to hear. "I'm sure Ralph was very annoyed," he said.

At dinner R. asked Molly if she could order him some wine he wanted from the Army and Navy Stores. "Oh *yes*," said Molly, "of course I'll order it for you. I'll do *any*thing for you. Really it's terrible the way I never do anything for people and always have things done for me."

Desmond: "Oh no. Much better face the fact, as I did at the age of seventeen, that you are *incapable*. Incapable people always have things done for them." His charm and blarney are terrific, as is his power of sensitive, sympathetic understanding, but Molly's wit and originality even beat his to my mind. This evening she and I talked about the war — she describing with the greatest acuteness War frenzy, War optimism and all its other distortions, in an unbiased and piercing manner. She spoke with a certain irritation of Desmond's optimism and frantic desire for revenge on Germany. Not only does he admit to feeling all Germans ought to be exterminated (after the complete victory he is sure we shall gain) but it's clear that he somehow doesn't assimilate the fact that they *can't* and *won't* be. Molly thought of this as peculiar to Desmond, but I think really it is the typical attitude of Liberal, enlightened and cultured middle-aged people, most of them so gentle and humane in private life that they wouldn't hurt a fly. Then we got on to Courage, and Molly shook her head at me frowning: "Must have *fine* men you know, not poor weaklings," with the expression of one who says, "Drop it, bad dog!"

Courage is like many other qualities — the two extremes are undesirable, and the mean desirable. Everyone dislikes cowardice, but they don't always see that reckless and extravagant courage disregards other very important values, such as human relations, life itself. In peacetime instead of the dazzling selfless courage of the Pilot, we get the ruthlessness of the undergraduate in his racing car, whose contempt for other people's lives clearly has a gangster element in it. And why — I can never understand — is it always thought so noble to disregard the value of your own life?

Desmond and R. returned from the wireless room, and Desmond put on some spectacles to look at our photograph albums.

Molly: "Oh *Des!* Those *specs*. Do take them off."

102

Desmond: "Why? They're very nice. They only cost sixpence. I got them at Woolworth's."

F.: "Can you see through them?"

Desmond: "After a *fashion*."

R.: (calling Molly): "Your bath's ready, Molly."

Molly (starting up in bed): "A bomb in the garden?"

To tea at the Padels. Their two sons, both schoolmasters, were home on leave. One plays the 'cello and one the violin, and they played us a Beethoven trio after tea. I was much moved by the sight of this admirable family setting to with such a will and producing music of so high a standard. I should like Burgo to go on being taught by the Padels as long as possible. But will it be possible? Mrs. Padel said she heard the children talking about angels one day. Burgo said there were no such things, nor fairies, nor heaven – "if there was, the aeroplanes would bump into it". The little girls were very shocked, and next day their mother came round and said that they had been much upset by being told at school that there was no heaven, angels or God, and what was the meaning of it?

A disrupted and chaotic day. Lawrence came for a last go at my portrait, but I think we are to buy another picture instead. R. was charging about the country to arrange for our beehives to be stripped of their honey.

When I put some jazz on the gramophone for a change, R. said, "It's very soothing and emollient – probably because it makes nonsense of everything, even the war and the poor old Russians at Smolensk."

I had written to Clive telling him that three people had told me he was no longer a pacifist, but "perhaps there was no meaning in the word at present". He agreed and then makes the following declaration of faith: "If Hitler proposes peace this autumn I am all for accepting ... I infinitely preferred the uncomfortable conditions of 1938 to the intolerable conditions of 1941. I would prefer to pay my taxes with a roof over my head and both legs on. I am quite sure, whatever happens, war will never make the world a pleasanter place to live in."

Four days' stay with the Nicholses in Essex. The handsome house is set curiously low at the end of a broad avenue, and below runs the river Stour between a forest of tall reeds with blue leaves and purple tassels. A certain sadness pervaded the house, and grew upon me, or perhaps it belonged to the lives of the Phils themselves. The absence of their children is evidently agony to them; they were always talking about them and one evening when Phyllis brought out their photos to show me she trembled so violently that the sofa on which we were both sitting shook beneath us. It was raining cats and dogs as we left Lawford.

On the way home we came through London, driving in a taxi past St. Paul's Cathedral, which stands up stupendously big and grand out of the largest area of devastation I've yet seen. Other parts of the City are levelled to the ground, but I was struck by the beautiful spaciousness and the light let in more than anything else.

Three days ago we came by train to Haverfordwest, and thence to a farmhouse three miles from Solva.

All responsibility for house and food magically gone; huge meals are set before us, with home-cured bacon, eggs and plenty of butter. There is *no war* here. We have not seen a single newspaper since we came, and all we can hear of the wireless is in snatches through the kitchen door. This evening a familiar sing-song, though wordless, showed that Winston was making a speech. I opened the door and listened for a bit, but was shocked by the futility, hollowness and unreality of the ideas he was expressing, shown up as they were by the amazing beauty of the natural surroundings we have lived among in these last three days, and which I was consciously aware of on the other side of the thin walls boxing in his voice — the fields rolling right to the edge of savage cliffs, promontories covered with heather and tufted plants, white farms among clusters of nearly black trees, streams tinkling between a jungle of wild flowers, buzzards and seagulls overhead instead of aeroplanes. The only sign of war is a cluster of barrage-balloons over Milford Haven — which, as we came home from a picnic, were shining a dazzling silver, like holes in the sky letting light through from behind.

Bathed at Solva, and ate our picnic on a stony beach. Fat mothers and evacuee children had spread their towels on the rocks and exposed their dimpled knees and the varicose veins on their legs, while their voices
104

droned monotonously on about knitting and rationing and babies.

This evening we heard a series of soft thuds and aeroplane engines, and peering through the blackout I saw the shafts of searchlights sweeping across the sky; soon afterwards great flashes splashed upwards, which I knew must be falling bombs, but all to the accompaniment of gentle noises like the patting of kitten's paws, and the ever-crossing, weaving pattern of the searchlights. Then streams of giant copper-coloured sparks rose into the night sky, like sparks from a monstrous bonfire. "They've hit something," I thought, watching what looked like a firework display.

*September 3rd*

Three glorious days, sun-bathing and going naked into the cold sea. We have several times seen those extraordinary orange-legged birds, choughs, here. On our last day R. said: "I have a sort of feeling that I shall see that seal again. It was on a day just like this that I saw him twenty years ago." And almost as he finished speaking, like a good omen, up there rose a round gleaming head in the middle of the bay – the seal himself!

*September 17th*

Leningrad has not fallen, though every day I go to the wireless I expect to hear the news of it. Neither has Kiev nor Odessa, and the Russian winter is supposed to begin a month from now.

R. said later: "What animal lives we lead." F.: "Yes, perhaps it's time we tried to pull up our mental socks and do a little thinking." R.: "That's the worst of war. One doesn't *want* to do any thinking."

Yesterday on the way to Biddesden we saw Italian prisoners at work on the harvest at the top of Tidcombe Hill. It was a glorious afternoon and from where they were there was a view over half Wiltshire. We caught a glimpse of handsome dark and youthful faces, and extravagant rows of white teeth, as they smiled and waved to us. Each had a crimson disc sewn on his back and an armed soldier was watching them. As we were describing them to the Guinnesses at tea, Michael MacCarthy screwed up his face and said, "Don't let's be *sentimental* about the Italian prisoners," which in fact I don't think we were being. They seemed to have no connection with the war, that was one thing that gave our spirits a lift. We talk a good deal about the futility of worry. Well, all I can say is if one can't stop worrying one must just endure it, futile and also exhausting though it is. Anyway, time goes on passing inevitably, and will in the end carry one into the grave where worrying stops.

It seems ages since we got back from Wales, and I wrote about worry. Equanimity has returned, even happiness. Ham Spray is a cornucopia from which flow fruit, vegetables and dahlias. Drove round with presents of plums, including thirty pounds to the old Padels. Alas, Mrs. Padel feels she must give up the "school" and wants me to teach Burgo myself. That I would gladly do, but I want the company of other children for him. That a mother should teach her own child is one of Mrs. Padel's blind beliefs; she is against schools, meat-eating, Mrs. Molesworth and water-closets.

The Padels have been trying to persuade me to take up the violin again, and though I could never have dreamed of the possibility without their instigation, I feel very tempted – but sheepish. Mr. Padel swears I could play chamber music in six months. What a thought!

Julia and L. to tea. Julia and I went for a walk while aeroplanes practised machine-gunnery overhead, and as we clambered through a gap in a hedge a shower of bullets, or bullet-cases, fell through the trees all round us, rattling angrily against the branches. Julia looked up indignantly and shook her umbrella at them, like an old lady in *Punch*.

We talked about our separation from the Brenans, Gerald's apparent reluctance to make it up after his uncalled-for "stinker", and the strong feeling I have that he doesn't want to see us at all.

*Another* stinker from Gerald to Ralph this morning – the result no doubt of Julia's having told him that we thought he no longer wanted to see us. And I must say he has fairly riled me just as of course he wanted to. He begins by saying condescendingly that of course he is still fond of us. "It's not pacifism I dislike . . . but your particular brand of calling yourself a pacifist and at the same time sympathising with the aggressor rather than with the attacked[1] is very disagreeable to me . . . I think your ideas need sorting. We are none of us rational people, but when we fail to give a certain colour of plausibility and reason to our ideas we find we lose contact with other people and isolate ourselves. You would feel better if you had some work to do. And if you served a turn as fireman or ARP warden you would feel better still . . . However you can be certain that I am not going to quarrel with you or take against you over your opinions . . . indeed I don't regard them as deliberate opinions at all but just as fragments of lava thrown out by your volcano. We all have volcanoes, we are all liable to eruption.

[1] Quite untrue.

This war is a strain on everyone and whilst it lasts life is a perpetual struggle for calm and sanity. Nothing therefore I say here is said *de haut en bas* ... If you have strong feelings about people who resist aggression, remember that I have equally strong opinions about the pacifist-isolationists, who I consider by their short-sightedness and folly have helped to produce this war."

What right has Gerald to send us, unprovoked, these prosy lectures? Since his first letter we have done our best to ignore it, continued to take them presents of fruit and vegetables, and got my brother Tom to offer him the very job at Oxford he has always wanted (which of course he refused), quite apart from the occasion some time ago when R. went to his rescue with the Marlborough police and Scotland Yard. Well, there's nothing to be done but keep away for the present, and hope – in vain, I fear – that he will somehow regret his behaviour. R. and I cannot help toying with various teasing replies, though we know full well that the only possible answer is silence. The truth is, however, that I for one shall miss their company, and resent being cut off from it. I also find it rather absurd that the only person to pillory us in any way for our Pacifist views is Gerald, almost R.'s oldest friend. His reference to doing dangerous work is what amounts to a boast on Gerald's part, because of his celebrated London fortnight in the Blitz – and yet it's not like him to boast. Nor is there a trace of his old characteristic irony and self-depreciation in the whole letter.

A fresh and lovely morning. Went on from school to Kintbury station, whence R. saw me off to London. We paced up and down the platform, raised above the vegetable beds, their dark earth moistened by the river Kennet sliding sluggishly by. The next minute I was in the train, sitting bolt upright in a stuffy kennel, hemmed in by sweating sick-looking human beings, and composing myself to become part of this unit and rattle with them into the unsavoury darkness.

Lunch with Janetta at the Ivy. She was looking very pretty and unusually elegant; our lunch was smoked salmon, cold grouse, chocolate mousse and Nuits-Saint-Georges. Clive and Desmond were at a near table; we heard Clive's crackling laughter. He made us join them at the end of the meal, and hear Desmond tell two stories about Tolstoy and Turgenev. One was about Turgenev staying with the Tolstoys and being earnestly told by Tolstoy *on no account* to empty his po; a little later he was told the opposite by the Countess.

Travelled home with two Free Frenchmen, who remarked on the beauty of the scenes we passed through. In the rosy sunset glow, with purple shadows, even the gasometers and bungalows had a charm. Then it got dark and I stood in the corridor, watching the moon tearing through the strips of silver water beside the line.

Off on my bicycle to the Padels to consider the question of re-starting the violin[1], for the seeds they sowed have taken root. Mr. Padel was waiting for me, and handed me a violin with a sweet and mellow tone. His manner could not have been better designed to cure me of my sheepishness. I took it up and stuck a few strange wobbling notes. Before I left we were playing exercises together.

Clive and Isobel to stay. Talk all afternoon, sitting in the sun in deck-chairs, while R. thundered by mowing the lawn. Clive told us how Hore Belisha had proposed to the Shy Bride. His brains and her dollars could achieve anything, certainly the premiership.

In a dim light, with a dying fire and wrinkled carpet, the conversation tonight wound itself through interesting personal matters, figures of the past, and old times in general, and on to Christianity and the antagonism it aroused in each of us – least of all to Clive and most to me. I felt uneasy when it dawned on me that my belief in the supremacy of reason was perhaps itself as much a religion – that's to say an unfounded faith – as Christianity or Communism.

A foundation of melancholy underlies these days – Russia, Gerald, the sadness of autumn. In me it takes the form of subhuman apathy, in R. of irritability and saying: "I don't like my fellow-men", the implication behind which is usually that one doesn't like oneself.

Italian prisoners are now working in the potato fields in Ham; Burgo and I walked to see them and listen to their soaring, trilling voices singing in Italian against a background of English mud and a grey sky. Three soldiers were guarding them. They had nothing against the prisoners except that they got more cigarettes than they did themselves.

To tea with some Inkpen ladies, whose snobbish county smugness and unimaginative self-confidence depressed me. They appear to question nothing, neither the war and the way it is conducted, nor the inferiority of everyone else to themselves, and of course of all Germans to all English people. The thought of these women and their beastly form of patriotism and their stupidity and the brave way they tackle their hens and jam and the servant shortage is somehow profoundly indigestible. I am alarmed by the insidious way we are getting drawn into their company. We *must* get out of it all.

Listened to the wireless all evening, well aware that the war is passing through one of the most acute crises it has yet produced. During the

---

[1] I had started learning at nine and dropped it at thirteen.

News I gradually became aware of a faint voice, speaking in far-off sepulchral tones like Hamlet's ghost: "Tell us the TRUTH!" Then "ROT!" it boomed out, and quite a lot more about the Jews and the Americans having "sold us down the river". When the news ended, the Voice made quite a long speech beginning rather mysteriously: "Winston Churchill will never be Duke of Marlborough." The English announcer then said primly: "If you have been hearing interruptions, it is the enemy." The "enemy" – how fantastic it sounds! But the Voice gave us a great deal of pleasure, so strange a manifestation was it.

*October 14th*

To combat the anxiety produced by the Russian situation I forced myself to do mechanical tasks, like painting beehives and sweeping the verandah.

In to Hungerford, but there was no food to buy except salted cod, no offal. As we drove home talking about our cupboard of reserve tins, R. said: "We'd better keep them for the invasion. I firmly believe there will be one", in such a matter-of-fact voice that the Hungerford-Ham road with its familiar ranks of telegraph poles looked all at once menacing and unreal. But I suppose I don't, at this moment anyway, believe in invasion.

Started reading Pepys this evening. Bad news on the wireless – "A deterioration in the position of the Russian front." This is the beginning of the end, I thought, and visualized us pathetic human beings like crabs trying to crawl out of the pot of boiling water that is about to finish them off. And then came the Voice again, distantly booming: "Kick Churchill *out*! We want Revolution! Churchill must go-o-o!" And last of all: "Britain is *doo*med! Britain is DOOMed! God save our King – from the Jews!" This last word came out in a protracted hiss, and we were quite cheered up by realizing that the Germans could be so imbecile as to imagine that such remarks could have any effect.

*October 23rd*

This morning Burgo hurried in with the news that the rats had eaten a hole in the passage carpet "big enough to put your waist through". True enough. They had gnawed two very large holes in the floorboards and dragged the carpet through them, presumably to make nests with.

The Germans have shot fifty Frenchmen in cold blood as a reprisal for the shooting of two of their own officers. They say they will shoot fifty more unless the man who killed the officers gives himself up. I was surprized when R. said in a voice of great emotion: "There's one thing too horrible to talk about – the shooting of the fifty French hostages."

109

In the conversation that followed I understood that, apart from everything else, he was entering into the state of mind of the German soldiers who had to shoot these fifty innocent and irrelevant individuals, and that this action performed completely in cold blood has a horror for the person made to do it which distinguishes it sharply even from the action of a man who picks off a sniper with his rifle in the heat of battle. R. has told me everything that happened to him in the First War, with the greatest detail and vividness; but there is one he cannot describe without his voice breaking; when he was the captain ordered to take a squad of men to shoot one of our deserters, and had to give the signal to fire. It's for this reason that the last act of *Tosca* is almost unbearable to him, and by infection to me also.

*October 29th*

To Hungerford to buy rat poison and meet Saxon's train. My clearest memory of today was R. telling Saxon and me the story of the charges of the Light and Heavy Brigades, from Kinglake which he is reading. He told them wonderfully well, and (try as he might) Saxon had to keep going off into explosive puffs of laughter, though he was red in the face from trying to suppress them.

*October 30th*

R. and I to London for the day. Hungerford platform was peopled by prosperous elderly ladies in fur coats, snarling greetings to each other with their too-red lips curling over strong yellow teeth. Obviously no doubts of their superior status crosses their minds, but why? What have they done to be so categorized?

To Harrods, where we tried to get a new zip for R.'s windcheater. "Impossible?" said the assistant. "Nothing's impossible: not even winning the war. Yet we don't seem to be doing it — not in *my* estimation at any rate." Lunching with Clive at the Ivy we were delighted to see Robertson Hare, funniest of actors, at another table. Near the end of lunch a little girl of about four suddenly set up a despairing wail and was bustled out, choking back her sobs. Clive was delightfully sympathetic. "Yes, she's quite right. We're horrible, greedy, noisy, wild beasts all of us. I'm on her side and I should like to tell her so."

About to start on the third year of the war, I wonder what shift in emphasis has occurred. Boringly enough the answer must be that shortages — food, petrol, clothes — now occupy the foreground.

To lunch with Julia and Lawrence to meet the Pritchetts, only for the second time and liked them both enormously. V.S.P. has been investigating the arrangements for dealing with bombed Londoners, interviewing them and visiting the rest-centres. All these centres are arranged to segregate Men and Women, but the candid organizers admitted there was no question of keeping to this when the Blitz was on. One said, "I realized it was hopeless ever since a man came rushing in to the Women's part, half mad and screaming for his sister. He had just seen his mother killed before his eyes, and when he found his sister he got into bed with her there and then and had sexual intercourse with her." Pritchett said he was very much struck by the organizers' genuine kindness and understanding, but it often didn't go with great powers of organization. One woman blitzed her own house to get compensation, but was detected because she couldn't bear to break her best tea-set.

There was a hard frost last night and all the grass was white with it. The pond on the way to school was frozen over, and the solitary duck belonging to it was walking about looking puzzled and indignant, while an old man feebly tried to break the ice with his stick.

The rats which ate our carpet have paid us back for poisioning them. One of them has died under the sitting-room floor. The question is, must we have up the floorboards or can we stick out the appalling smell?

Bunny and Dermod [MacCarthy] to stay the weekend. Bunny seems like a man starved of conversation, having had none for months. He often exclaims that he had forgotten such an existence as ours could continue. We did nothing but talk all day.

Richard [Garnett] has gone into the R.A.F. rescue squad, who go out in little boats to save the lives of airmen brought down in the sea. Bunny frankly desires to keep his sons out of danger, yet he is behind the war effort in every other way. R. and I have discussed for hours whether it made it better or worse that, wanting the sons of others to risk their lives, you should try and put your own in safety. We disagreed — he thought it worse. At least I think I disagreed, but cannot quite decide. The primary fact is that wanting other people's sons to be killed to get the sort of life you want and believe desirable is horrible. Given this, I think it's better to be human about your own sons' danger than the reverse.

Julia and Lawrence to lunch. Bunny fixed on Julia the concentrated searchlight of his attention and admiration, and from the moment she came into the room had his head perpetually swivelled in her direction with a look of bursting delight on his face. When she had gone he seized a cushion and hugged it saying: "Oh Julia, Julia, what a wonderful woman she is! I'd forgotten she existed." Julia took his admiration very well, and so I must say did Lawrence.

Old Mrs. Garnett is failing in health, and when Bunny was there last week she suddenly began talking complete gibberish in the middle of an interesting conversation about relations between Russia and China. He was alarmed and took her up to bed, and at the top of the stairs she suddenly recovered her speech and broke out into indignation, saying that really if she was to lose the faculty of speech as well as sight and strength it was a bit too much. I should think so indeed. Dermod says there's no doubt that the health of the nation has improved if anything since the war began.[1]

Tonight Winston made a most confident speech, offering us no blood or tears whatever, but announcing that we have now achieved at least parity in numbers with the Luftwaffe. This was a great surprise, and it also really looks as if a deadlock was settling in in Russia. He rattled the sword very noisily in the direction of Japan. Should they declare war on the U.S.A., he said, "England would be in it within the hour." Thunders of applause from the Mansion House or wherever the speech was made.

Hope is an awkward customer to carry about with one, and makes life more agitating and restless than despair or fatalistic resignation (in which so much of the war has passed). And it *has* popped up, even if for a short stay.

*November 12th*

Hester had rung up to ask to come for two nights. She is much thinner and if her teeth weren't all over lipstick would look rather fine. But she lives in her own Ruritania, backed up by belief in "loyalty", "our little set", or "me and my friends". It is difficult to realise that some people not only talk but *feel* in clichés. We asked Julia and Lawrence over to entertain her, but after they had gone Hester said how bitterly she felt Julia's departure from fashion, make-up, etc. R. unthinkingly made an unforgivable remark: "A woman over forty," I think he said, "should never try to make herself sexually attractive." While Hester reeled from this body-blow I tried to pull the chestnuts out of the fire by bringing in Dorelia and Vanessa, not at all relevantly, and the evening was spoilt I fear.

[1] He was a doctor, a children's specialist.

112

Pouring with rain all day. Didn't go out at all, but spent it with Burgo or practising my fiddle. R. said how happy he was, so did Burgo and so did I. When I wake these days, in spite of the war and our uneventful life, it is to a pleasurable anticipation of minute things — the books I'm going to read, the letters the post will bring, the look of the outside world.

This evening twiddling the wireless vaguely, I heard the familiar voice of Lord Haw-Haw. This time he was making half-hearted jokes about getting the mice out of our gas-masks and the cauliflowers out of sandbags in preparation for the next German onslaught. Such imbecility ought to be consoling, but instead I feel exasperated, as by the performance of a lunatic trying to pass off as sane.

After a busy ordinary morning the paper came, and I saw in it that we have launched our expected attack in Libya. Read it, crouched on the carpet on all fours, with a breathless feeling. There is no attempt to minimise its importance.

Raymond and Eardley arrived last night. A lovely glistening morning: we took the visitors for a walk. Three tractors were ploughing the sloping field this side of Prosperous Lane, making endless long coffee-coloured stripes. The lane itself was thick with berries of all descriptions, hips, spindles, haws, large clusters of black privet; it looked rich and gaudy, and made me think of the Treasury at Constantinople and all the jewels there. The plain was full of delicate light and shade.

Dora Morris came to tea. She told us how Julia had given her blood for transfusion, doing all she was told very carefully, resting and taking her recuperative pills. She thought it was to be used for civilians, but after it had been taken the nurse said: "Well, you have the satisfaction of knowing it is going straight out to the front line in Libya." Julia, who always gets a bit confused about the implications of her pacifist beliefs, said, "I was so horrified I had a good mind to ask for it back."

Endless delightful talk with our visitors and comical paper games this evening, which made us all laugh a lot.

Dragged myself out of sleep like a boot out of mud, for I was going to London for the day. I felt it a wrench leaving R. and Burgo even for so short a time. Yesterday had been R.'s 47th birthday, and Burgo was in an endearing state of excitement over this event, giving him a gold

113

safety-pin and insisting on crackers and jelly for tea. ("I do want darling old Ralph to enjoy his birthday.")

In the train, three soldiers, all strangers to each other were eagerly discussing the Libyan campaign. A fourth figure, an elderly Civil Servant, said he had fought there in the last war, and "The climate was the best I ever knew in my life." A dark young soldier envisaged the possible taking of Moscow by the Germans. A Scotchman next to me with pale fanatical eyes thought this impossible." "The B-rrr-eetish would never allow it." I was much impressed by their friendliness and lack of barriers and desire to communicate.

Lunch with Clive at the Ivy. He was not in a very good mood. He now declared he's indifferent to everything except the loss of the civilized existence he has always enjoyed. He thought war-weariness in England was so great that when Hitler launched his Peace Offensive a large number would be in favour of accepting his terms. I'm afraid he's wrong there. He told me Adrian [Stephen][1] had been staying at Charleston. He has a job after his own heart, namely trying to frighten the shell-shocked heroes of Dunkirk by turning on machines which make the noises of a dive-bomber. If that doesn't work he repeats the process in utter darkness.

*November 28th*

Drove to Oxford, where R. and I dined at the George. Watching the airmen and their girls, R. and I discussed whether it was possible to be in love when one is risking one's life in a war. R. said no, it was not, only in lust. Yet one of the airmen gazing with froglike eyes at his unsensual-looking blonde was, I believe, in love with her in a way. Lust was certainly the bond between another stocky red-haired fellow and his sophisticated little friend, to whom he was talking shop all the time.

*December 2nd*

Most of the morning in the music-room writing my review of children's books. I felt very virtuous and cheerful when it was finished. Out with Burgo collecting food for the rabbits in a cold, soupy mist. They provide us with quite a lot of solid meat — it's a pity they really taste so disgusting whatever we do to them.

On turning on the news we received a blow. There has been a reverse of some sort in Libya. Then Winston outlined his proposals for getting greater man- and woman-power for the War Effort. Men between 40

[1] A doctor and psycho-analyst, he was attached to the "rehabilitation" department of the army.

114

and 51 are to register for military service of a modified sort. That includes R. We talked about his position. He has obviously been thinking about it a lot, more than he's let on, and seeing this coming. I got the feeling he found it a difficult subject to talk about, perhaps because his views are not consolidated. He said: "I rather feel I must testify as a conscientious objector. It's a bore, and one can't guess how it will affect our local life. But I think I must, for reasons of self-respect, not that I believe in 'sticking my head out for no reason'. But I don't think they'll chop it off."

Burgo very agitated when he went to bed, saying he was "thinking of horrible things". Pressed to say what, he said it was about Macbeth and Lady Macbeth and "all the killings". A few days ago I told him the story, and read him a little of the play. He didn't seem to mind then, and was delighted by the idea of Birnam Wood coming to Dunsinane. I tried to explain that thoughts were only thoughts and one could think of horrible things and remain intact − but I do not think he believed it. Nor is it really true, alas.

Oh dear, oh dear. Went to bed depressed, feeling the walls closing in on our personal life. R. says his conscience would not prevent him doing an agricultural or defence job. Supposing they make him?

*December 3rd*

Catharine [Carrington] came over to lunch. She and Noel had been to see Gerald. She was plainly trying to be discreet about what had passed between them on the subject of our estrangement, and then said: "He thinks you're pacifists." The extraordinary thing was that, old friend as she is, she didn't seem to have any idea that we are, or hardly to realise that there were such people or that it was a possible position to hold. While I was out with Burgo, R. preached her a pacifist sermon, he told me later, which left her gasping and quite unable to think of a single argument. She told R. that Gerald had said R. had become too effeminate and uxorious, and it was my influence that had made him a Pacifist and it didn't suit him at all. We seem to be in a cleft stick − either people are bored by being treated too frequently to our ideas on the subject, or they don't believe they exist.

*December 6th*

Julia rang up to say that Oliver was being sent to Canada for six months, and in a great flutter, buying clothes to dine at Government House. He says he never sees Lucy now. "And do you pine away for her?" Julia asked him. "Not in the least. Never give her a thought." Julia said she

115

was feeling "rather grey" and what about the new call-up, and what about R.?

The thought of the probable inclusion of Japan and U.S.A. in the war depresses me, though R. says he feels "an immense detachment towards it", I think of it as if a mortal cancer was spreading further through the body politic; and it's impossible not to be aware with a part of one's mind that absolutely everything is whirling and rocketing and crashing around us, and that here we are in the middle of an earsplitting earthquake in which all our values are disappearing. Not only are these objects, this furniture — the spiritual tables and chairs of our existence — fast vanishing, but most people seem to forget they ever existed. The *New Statesman* makes no bones about using the words "individual" and "voluntary" as terms of abuse.

*December 7th*

All the events of today have been blotted out by the evening's news. Japan has opened war on the U.S.A. with a bang, by an almighty raid on the American Naval and Air Base at Pearl Harbour. No ultimatum, no warning; the damage done has been ghastly and casualties extremely heavy. Nothing could have been more unprovoked and utterly beastly, nor could anything have thrown America more effectively into a condition of war fever. R. and I react differently to the news. He is greatly excited and stimulated, and I think feels it is good news, because it may lead "to a war of quick decision". I feel as if I had a load of undigested food on my stomach. The disease is spreading, and the possibility of pacifying this vast inflammation must surely become more remote. After we went up to bed, "What does a Honolulu pacifist do now?" I asked R., feeling that this appalling event would put an almost impossible strain on his principles. Then we argued about whether or not events going on now were more painful than those in the past. R. thought not; I wasn't sure, but I do know that I think of war entirely in terms of individual human feelings — fear, anxiety, pain, and this awful, permanent disgust. And if these exist *now* and are capable of being resolved or relieved, how not be consumed by impotent desire to do so?

*December 8th*

Began to think about the Japs as soon as we woke. The uncertainty and lack of news make us broody and irritable. R. keeps referring to my suppositious "Honolulu pacifist". As to his own position about the call-up, he remains unperturbed and says there is no need to make decisions before he has to.

116

A lovely frosty morning, dead still. I biked down to Mrs. Slater's to thank her for her plum-pudding, but she wasn't there, only Phyllis bathing an enormous and splendid female baby in a tiny basin. Stopped and talked to her in the hot kitchen while the fat soapy baby sat bolt upright and gazed at us.

In the evening I fetched Burgo from tea at Inkpen. It was exquisitely lovely walking home in the dusk, with the stars incredibly large and bright. Burgo was very excited by the aspect of Venus, and couldn't believe he was looking at a planet such as he had read about. As we walked up the avenue the sky had lost nearly all its rosy colour, and the witch-elms stretched their branches in the utter stillness, each making its familiar, amiable gesture. Burgo declared he would "almost die if anything happened to them".

Sebastian [Sprott] came to stay. We haven't seem him since the beginning of the war. He looked and seemed ten years younger, twinkling and serene.

*December 20th*

Took Sebastian over to see Julia and Lawrence, but lovable character as he is, I thought he was a bit rusty in the art of conversation. He likes telling stories, and listens to them with equal concentration. But general ideas? There are a few, like psycho-analysis, he will discuss. He thinks about the war as little as possible, and by this means remains quietly contented with his strangely limited life at Nottingham University. For one of the most endearing things about him is that he is the least ambitious man in the world. His extremely affectionate nature, accepting his friends as he finds them, and (though he sees them rarely) taking up the thread exactly where he left off, is another.

Tonight he told us about a Swiss professor whose life's work was the study of humour and the analysis of jokes. "I will tell you a choke," he said to his students. "An elephant was walking one day in the jungle when he met a mouse. 'You're very *small*," said the elephant. 'Yes,' said the mouse, 'I've been ill lately'." He then proceeded to analyse this delightful "choke" into three parts:— Disappointment: (you expect to get information about the elephant and none is forthcoming). Contrast: (between huge elephant and tiny mouse). *Schadenfreude,* or pleasure in another's misfortune: in this case "the social quandary the mouse was in".

*December 23rd*

The news, both from Russia and Libya so good that in spite of the Japs I was just thinking to myself the War *might* — who knows — be over in the spring, when the announcer said: "Since this broadcast began an announcement has been put out from Germany that Hitler has assumed sole command of the Army." A row between Hitler and the Army? One could hardly have hoped for it so soon.

I am now doing all the housework, which fills me with a glow of virtue and makes me enormously warm.

Holly-picking. This year the trees are thick with berries. As we turned into the avenue with our load, two pairs of cart-horses, each with a man on his back, came lumbering up, silhouetted against the golden afternoon sky. I said how beautiful they looked, and Burgo said, "Yes! willing, tired, forlorn", which was a perfect description of them.

*December 28th*

The fag-end of the year. I am very conscious that that's exactly what it is, like a stained, burnt-out cigarette hanging between my lips. R. has been very low spirited – partly because he hates Christmas. He has spent hours sitting in his chair by the fire reading book after book – Bury, Mill, Malthus, all writers bearing on the development of ideas. I envy him, and listen to the ideas they inspire, and discuss them with him. Today we had one of those arguments that go right back to the root of things – Ethics in this case. I fished out my old Hedonism and found it intact and not moth-eaten from having been stowed away in my mental cupboard. Or so it seemed to me. I was particularly impressed by the fact that it is the only theory which explains, and even makes inevitable, the absolute impossibility human beings find in deciding moral questions – because the hedonistic calculus demands what is impossible: following the results of every action in terms of happiness to a final conclusion. So that the hedonist's behaviour must by definition be founded on guesswork, even when that is informed and inspired.

Well, after a faint flash of hope and excitement over Hitler's taking over the Army, we sink back and contemplate the deary waste of war: from the Eastern front where the German soldiers freeze and die of wounds which ought not to be fatal (this is supposed to give us exquisite pleasure judging from the voice of the B.B.C. announcer) to the Australians, who shriek that we have let them down in their hour of peril, and who only look to America for help. To Winston who has somehow got across the Atlantic, where he is "doing his stuff" and basking in the applause of American journalists and not feeling a pang (I can't help thinking) over all the mistakes, the death and disaster, he is responsible for; and boasting and threatening, and speaking in rolling phrases of what we are going to do to the enemy in 1942, 1943, 1944 and 1945, God help us all!

Julia has come on a week's visit. She feels the cold terribly, and huddles in countless jerseys and her coat of false fur, over the fire. It has indeed become piercingly cold, and everything looks dead, drained of colour and life, while the vitality of us human beings is enough, but only *just* enough, to keep us alive.

Opened last year's prophecies, read them out and made new ones. R. alone had scored a success, by foretelling that Japan, Russia and U.S.A. would all be in the war. I was surprised to find myself writing down that the war would be over by January 1943. It seems to me it is a logical possibility. Why then don't I feel more cheerful?

1942

A letter from Gamel to me today, saying "couldn't we meet?" I wonder if she knows the nature of Gerald's letters to us. It takes a good deal to make her overcome her aversion to writing. I have written back saying we would love to see her and Miranda, but that there is no question of our visiting them since Gerald says he finds our company intolerable. We will see what happens next.

Julia had temporarily relapsed into complete sluggishness, either sitting over the fire reading detective stories or going up to snooze on her bed. Now she has revived and become her normal fascinating self, all speculation and fantasy. Today she described how Oliver's renderings of opera arias, especially Mozart's and the airy gestures accompanying them, had put her off them for life. Then a talk about male sex-appeal. She defined the exact way a coat should cling to the masculine form. "It should *mould* the shoulders and back, and then *fall* away from the hips — like a boat leaving harbour", she ended rather unexpectedly.

At breakfast I was amused to find a letter from *Gerald* to me. I had half-guessed that if I wrote to Gamel he would be the one to answer. It was couched in a mild and reasonable strain. Catharine had told him that R. thought he regarded him as an enemy — but this was not true at all. It was only that after much thought he had decided it was better for them not to meet. Wouldn't *I*, however, come over and see them, if "I didn't regard him as unmeetable?" I wondered how this would strike R: he smiled somewhat cynically and said, "Gerald always pulls out the *Vox humana* stop in the end."

The truth is that Gerald doesn't possess the ordinary affections most people have; his various relationships are seen in purely literary terms. He often speaks of trusty Gamel who has plodded along beside him for so long with a detachment that freezes the blood as if she were some kind of domestic pet. One cannot, or anyway does not, feel friendly to someone one can't bear to meet, and it is absurd to pretend it. R. analyses the situation with his usual detachment thus: "In our long relationship I have always been fonder of Gerald than Gerald of me; now at last I have had enough of it, and feel all the bitterness of 'a woman scorned'." Because of Gerald's affair with Carrington, because of his curiously jealous sense that R. was a better soldier in the first war than he was, perhaps because he identifies him with his father, R. has long been the object of a campaign of rivalry to Gerald, and when campaigning there is no-one like him for laying subtle and elaborate plots to humiliate his enemy and make him look in the wrong in the eyes of the world, as I can testify from experience. In this letter he wants to do several things — forestall all possibility of Gamel visiting us by asking me over instead; get me over, thus scoring a triumph over R. (by condescending to receive me and not him, and so dividing us); and appear well in the eyes of our friends by telling them he has made this conciliatory suggestion. Then he, Gamel and I all look like reasonable people, and R. alone remains outcast, "the unmeetable". I have read Gerald's letter over several times, and I believe this interpretation to be perfectly correct. I will not in any case go, and I think probably the best thing will be to ignore his letter. But it is a masterly production.

Lawrence fetched Julia away. We birds are alone again.

*January 10th*

Today's invasion of Garnetts came as a relief, turning our interest to another direction.

Angelica looked pale and ill. William is at the stage when it's as much as his life is worth to let any expression cross his face, and he remains silent and impassive until some gust of amusement creates an explosion from within. This almost universal condition of adolescence is the one Saxon has stuck in for life. In contrast, Burgo, with his gestures and antics and wildly changeable expressions of face, seems like some extraordinary little foreigner. Bunny has turned into a complete civil servant, thin suit, black hat. He said he found it essential to buy the symbolical umbrella (the best make, always perfectly rolled and taken out in all weathers) and that since he did so he has been treated with much greater respect.

*January 20th*

Looked out to see four or five inches of good soft snow; and no possibility of getting out to shop in Hungerford or take Burgo to school until we had set to, and with tremendous labour dug a passage out for the car. I stood in the fishmonger's shop with a dumb group of patient figures in mackintoshes, with white, pink-trimmed faces. The "Dutch gentleman" (as he is called for some unknown reason) threw a great fish's head on the grey and white marble slab, and its huge eyes wobbled like jellies.

I have been very energetic these days in physical ways that I can take no interest in, like scrubbing the whole of the nursery floor, and thinking how awful life will be when we have no daily help at all.

Now that we are faced with having to do everything ourselves it doesn't seem so bad. Burgo, too, has become sweeter and happier. Last night he said: "I shall be exceedingly sad when you and Ralph die. I shall come and see you when I'm married." I asked him what sort of wife he would choose. He said: "A nice *young* woman, with dark hair and pretty flowered dresses."

I kept to today's plan of going to London to buy a fiddle from Marjorie Hayward at the Royal College of Music. She was short, with grey frizzed hair. I carried off the violin so quickly that she shouted after me: "Is the case done up?" I had only carried it a little way when a Jewish-looking gentleman stopped me and asked, "do you want to sell your violin, Madam?" I'm fiercely aware of being a violin-owner. Afterwards I looked in on the Hills in their bookshop. Heywood came in just as I was leaving. He may be called up in six weeks' times, and I'm afraid joining the army may nearly be the death of him. In the train home a Kintbury woman got into conversation with me, and I couldn't resist trying out a little propaganda on her, as an experiment as it were. I know now just how much the woman in the street will take. She reacts favourably when one says it gives one no pleasure to hear of ships full of Italians or Germans being drowned, will agree that they are probably harmless young men like our own soldiers and sailors, but doesn't like to hear any good of the Italian prisoners working in our fields. "It's not right that they should have better food than our own men." (Nor is it, if true.) God was brought in frequently. "If it wasn't that I know God will see that the right side wins, I can't see how it's to happen."

This afternoon there arrived our new "help", Alice Cooper, Freddie her little boy, and her soldier husband on a week's leave. Alice is a peculiar shape, broad in the beam, with a good-natured flat face and brown stumps for teeth. Having dreaded the invasion beforehand, I didn't mind it when it came. R. says a sob rose in his throat at the thought of this human flotsam and jetsam drifting into our house. He says he's always finding sobs rising, for instance when he heard a pilot describing on the wireless how he got his damaged plane home. This strong human sympathy he has, combined with his sharply ironical and critical side, both delights me and puts me to shame.

*February 2nd*

I don't know how to describe my state of mind. it is so ambivalent –
sadness and a sort of content inextricably mixed. The solid background
of our days is being restored by splendid Alice, and I now feel stirrings
of life, which is not a purely pleasant sensation, but rather more like a
leg or arm coming round after it has gone to sleep. It is as if the texture
of our existence were a material which had been worked at and shredded
by fingers until it became gossamer-thin, but in a patchy way, painfully
lacking pattern. It just hangs together, no more; you can see right
through it in places.

A visit to Julia and Lawrence "to give ourselves a tonic", R. said.
Getting home cheerful, he then opened the paper and fell into despair.
The Libyan situation and the Pacific are both equally catastrophic, the
Japs are everywhere. One can well imagine the Germans saying: "Surely
the English can't survive all this. They *must* crack soon."

"Well, we've got through one month of 1942," said R. "One month
nearer the end of the war. We've only got to survive."

The limp, frozen-up leaves of the winter honeysuckle, seen out of
the dining-room window, appear all too symbolical of the state of human
beings after two and a half years of war.

*February 13th*

I have no desire whatever to write anything in this diary, and my
only reason for doing so is to show that I am still alive, and not unhappy I might even say. But I have never in my life been less aware of
my surroundings, got less pleasure from the visible world, nor felt more
completely insulated from thrills of excitement. Our life is all interior.
Household things and my relation to R. and B. are the whole focus of
my vision; anything outside is a bad photograph – a blur of whitish
greys.

Tonight, feeling that my favourite records had been neglected, I
put on a whole series and enjoyed them. I don't want to become deaf
as well as blind.

*February 20th*

R. and I to London for the day. An intelligent little boy of about
eight suddenly approached R. in the train and said, "Shall I show you
my stamp-collection?" R. looked at it and said if he would give him his
name he would send him some stamps. "Klaus Wusselburg", was the
answer. (I noticed his mother had an Austrian accent.) He looked eagerly out under his red school cap with bright eyes at the suburbs of Lon-

don, now approaching. "I want to see some bombed houses. But what I'd *really* like to see is dead people."

Old scarred London – I barely glanced at its wounds. Not because of feeling indifferent to them – quite the reverse. They are just as unpleasant, but contemplation of them is somehow stale. To Mr. Parfitt, my tailor. What a strange view of the human body he has, solely in relation to the points of sensitivity where a seam might cause discomfort or a collar rub. Or that most dreaded of disasters—"seating" happen to a skirt. His little room with its rolls of tweed and half-made clothes is the temple of his religion. He got on a stool to bring down and show me, like a sacred relic, an old box thick with dust in which were some treasured pieces of pre-war white flannel, smooth as cream and with a tinge of ice-blue.

*February 25th*

The greatest pleasure I have these days is watching Burgo grow into an independent being; he is mad about R. at the moment. When I went in to bath him this evening, he looked at me in a dignified way and said: "What shall we talk about, Horse of Troy?" Now that he is freed from Nannie's bunchy presence and possessions, he expresses his personality even by the queer concatenation of objects in his bedroom – a squeaking bun, his squashed blue velvet slippers and a policeman's black notebook full of strange scrawled memoranda.

At lunchtime Alice came breathlessly into the nursery looking for Freddie. Mr. Cooper had just arrived on embarkation leave. We are painfully oppressed by the Cooper drama. The poor man has quite lost his former jauntiness, and instead of briskly polishing up the silver he sits brooding aimlessly over the paper. Who knows what thoughts fill his head? I think of the family like helpless twigs swept along by a torrent. R. said, "I know what's the matter with Mr. Cooper. He's *afraid*. It all comes back to me." He is to go back to camp, but believes he will be sailing in a short while, and his outfit is tropical.

The news continues as depressing as possible. Men up to forty-six are to be called up, and R. is forty-seven. Women born in 1901 are to register this summer, and I was born in 1900.

*March 11th*

I wrote a line to Gamel the other day suggesting our lunching together at the Three Swans in Hungerford. She wired back at once, and today I drove through pouring rain to meet her. We sat in the long, dark, upstairs dining-room, our voices ringing out with seemingly bell-like clarity, and at times I wondered if our cynical views of the war

127

might not cause offence. For Gamel really agrees with us. Gerald, so she says, believes that some good will come out of it. "I wish I could agree with him," she said, "but I can't. I think in his case it's a form of compensation for minding it so terribly." We didn't touch on Gerald's attitude to R. though I half longed to. Now I regret that I didn't, and feel it would have been more human. At the time I didn't want to embarrass her; it needs just the right key to unlock her door and I wasn't sure what it was.

We hear that there is to be no more petrol "for pleasure". From June the basic ration is to be abolished completely, and only those with special allowances for special needs may run cars at all. I find the idea rather exciting, I can't imagine why. Masochism, or inverted claustrophobia? Then in a clergyman's voice the announcer told us that Mr. Eden had today revealed to the House the hideous atrocities perpetrated by the Japs in Hong-Kong, women raped, civilians bayoneted, etc. The Government had wished to spare the relatives the agony of knowing these things, and so had kept them back until now. Why not spare them that agony a little longer? It is a sinister sign of poor morale, a shot of cocaine to ginger up the dying dog, and serves no other conceivable purpose whatever.

*March 13th*

R. said sadly that he missed human contacts and relations with friends, which were gradually being strangled by the war, and with them communication which was almost the most important thing in life. I agree most heartily, but was surprised because he often shrinks from the idea of having people to stay, and is never the one to suggest it. In my surprise was an element of shame at my own obtuseness in not seeing that this was what he felt; I hope it doesn't mean a failure of communication between him and me, but there is a terrible lack, alas! of things to communicate.

Quiet reading, as usual after supper. R. read some books on Pigs, for we are expecting "two good little pigs" from Biddesden shortly. I peeped into them; they opened up a new and bizarre world of "typical Porkers" and "ideal Baconers". And will anyone believe in twenty years' time that the wireless makes pronouncements about "Cats doing work of national importance"?

*March 14th*

Looking in at the kitchen window with some message, I saw that Alice had a stricken expression. R. told me a telephone message had come saying that her husband was sailing tonight. She had hoped to get a last glimpse of him today, and had been sitting in the kitchen turning over the bus time-tables. Oh, the pathos of it. When I went in to tell her how sorry I was I burst into tears almost before I could get the words out, and she turned with a simple and dignified movement, put her head on my shoulder and wept too.

Michael MacCarthy to lunch bringing us two little pigs, dear little grunters with soulful eyes. We all feel immensely proud to be pig-owners. He also brought us a leg of mutton — an unheard-of piece of generosity which had the most mellowing effect on him. His face always expresses his mood transparently, and today it was genial and alert, with wide-open eyes. I've seen him when the company bored him, with his eyes half closed and a comical look of sour distaste on his face. More rationing — clothes, coal, electricity — and hints of more to come. Perhaps next winter we really shall go short.

*March 23rd*

Freddie Cooper has the Itch!!

*March 26th*

I am writing now too long after it happened to be able to describe my pleasure in Janetta's visit. The slight veil that swathed her during her subjection to Humphrey has floated away, and I am confirmed in my view that she is one of the most intelligent, beautiful and sensitive young creatures I know.

We sat out in the hot sun most of Janetta's stay, walked to the wood for primroses and picnicked in the bracken. Then we saw her off, waving and hoping she would soon come again, as we have so often done before.

*April 2nd*

To a concert in Newbury, with Mr. Padel in his floppy tweed hat. Handel Concerto Grosso, Mozart Divertimento, Brandenburg No. 3. How long it is since I was at a concert. I had forgotten the visual (apart from the audible) pleasures; the intent expressions of the players as they filed in and settled round their instruments, the satin brown of violins and 'cellos, hands quivering on their necks like humming-bird moths tirelessly extracting honey.

*April 6th*

Alice's father, a very handsome old gentleman of great charm, came to see her, bringing me a magnificent bunch of Calla lilies (one of the

129

flowers that move me most). He told me he was once a huntsman in the Craven, and described hunting in Savernake Forest, and how the hounds used to mistake young fawns rustling in the bracken for foxes, leap on them and kill them.

Burgo took me to the little copse on the way to Ham. We found it tunnelled into narrow paths opening into miniature clearings carpeted with green — moschatels, bluebell leaves, spotted arums and a few very freshly opened white anemones. As I sat on a log I made a resolve to try and enjoy everything possible for a change — a resolve born out of the sudden unexpected beauty of that midget, almost suburban wood taking me unawares as I sat there on my log.

I feel particularly sorry for R. because his hopes about the war have been constantly frustrated, because he is so magnificently realistic, and also because he has fewer practical tasks to distract him. My conscience is pricked with fear that I don't provide him with enough support. Absorbed in household chores, and basking in his continuous sweetness to me, perhaps I have become lazy towards him in an unpardonable way. And towards myself too. Ever since childhood I have been so terrified of disappointment that I have done as little hoping as possible; and now in a strange way I've given up the war *as a bad job*. I have even lost, with hope, the desire for a crushing victory over the Axis, and returned to the view that a dreary stalemate from which no one profited would be the best possible outcome. Then everyone would be forced to realise the futility and wickedness of war.

This evening another moment of natural beauty made me realise what a cataract I have grown over the surface of my consciousness. The sun came through the clouds just as it was setting, and shot its long yellow rays sideways across the park, making the velvety texture of the Downs and ploughed fields brilliantly clear. The buds on the beeches were copper-coloured, their trunks verdigris green, and one pigeon perched like a bird in a fable on the dead branches of the oak. A rainbow arched over the Downs, and soon the clouds and rain came back and away flew the pigeon.

*April 7th*

The "New Bread", the only sort we are to have henceforth, made its first appearance yesterday. It is a pale grey-brown, mealy in consistency, and smells of barns. The cats adore it.

Dermod came for the weekend. He has left Great Ormond Street Hospital and is to be called-up as a naval doctor next week. He said it was the first time he had really taken stock of the war, and he was appalled. Also that Freddie still has a thriving Itch — alas!

130

Boris and Maroussa arrived for one night. Maroussa has never left London since they got there from Paris, and she still seems desperately nervous. Boris looks very grey both physically and mentally, and though as always the best company in the world he seems low in spirits. He has a job at Reuters, listening to and translating Russian broadcasts. When he first went to the B.B.C. for an audition they passed him as perfect but said they had no use for a Russion expert. Exactly two days later Russia entered the war; they wired frantically for Boris and sent an enormous fast car to fetch him to listen to Molotov's speech, which otherwise there was no-one to understand. Maroussa is obsessed with fear of starvation, gets into a panic, stuffs bread, feels faint and stuffs more, giving herself a sequence of indigestion and faintness. She never stops complaining about rationing, and hates Lord Woolton with a bitter personal hatred as the cause of all her troubles. All this is the result of shattered nerves, yet she won't leave Boris alone in London, and sticks the Blitz out with great courage.

Boris and R. paced the lawn talking, while Maroussa and I discussed rations and coupons on the verandah. Boris is so afraid of losing his interpreter's ability that he keeps hurrying into the music-room and switching on short wave news from Moscow.

Burgo in his bath tonight pointing to his balls: "What are inside them?" F.: "Nothing at the moment. When you're grown up there'll be seeds for making babies." B. (giggling wildly): "I shall sell mine in paper bags at fourpence each. And on one bag I'll write GIRLS and on the other one BOYS."

A letter from Jan [Woolley][1] from Lisbon, where she has just arrived from German-occupied France, after a long, slow, crowded journey "with no money and no shoes. I'm so thin that I rattle in the bath, and my bones have actually come through my skin in some places." At the best of times she looked like a Raemaekers cartoon representing Famine, so it's no wonder everyone is anxious to ship her home in the first possible plane. May she come here? she asks. R. has sent off a warm welcome. She might be surprised at the envy her letter excited with its smell of foreign travel, its storks and judas-trees.

When the war enters a new phase it takes some time for us to realise it has done so. The latest is a series of nightly raids on towns of historic

[1] Mother of Janetta and Rollo and wife of a celebrated V.C. of the First War.

or architectural importance. So far Exeter, Bath and Norwich have copped it. The papers describe them as "Baedeker raids". Alice asked me: "Have you seen about these new Baedeker bombers the Germans are using?" Later she said: "Well, it was Hitler's fifty-third birthday the other day, and I suppose baby Adolf will soon have his first." F.: "What *do* you mean, Alice?" A.: "Oh yes, didn't you know? Unity Mitford. I heard about it from a friend of mine who worked for her. And in the papers too they said, 'Miss Unity Mitford is as well as can be expected.'"

*April 30th*

At 10 tonight Alice rocketted along the passage and knocked sharply on the door. "Mr. Partridge, come at once, the dairy's on fire!" R. dashed out to see what he could do, leaving me to ring up the fire brigade. Alice said, "Mrs. Coombs is in a dreadful state. She says there's calves in there." I could indeed hear a melancholy lowing, and pictured the poor creatures trapped and burning. I walked along to the nursery window and looked out — the whole room was lit up by the leaping red light of the flames as they made their indomitable progress, for the dairy roof was thatched and being rapidly devoured. They made a deep roaring, the wind was blowing them our way and it seemed they must catch our woodshed and piggery and so reach the house. Ham Spray itself was in danger, I thought — my heart beat fast, and I felt a tremendous affection for our threatened house, as though it were a person. When I got close to the fire some little calves were being let out of the big barn, whose great vaulted roof had a bar of fire running along its edge. Inside it a brand new threshing-machine was standing. Somehow or other I found myself, along with the landgirls, one or two youths and Alice, vainly trying to push this iron mammoth out. Above us was smoke and fire, and one landgirl looked up and said, "Mind the roof doesn't come down." Soon afterwards the fire brigade clattered up, with R. somehow in control, plunged their pumps into the farm pond and surprisingly soon had a jet of water on the flames. I never for one moment expected them to put out this ferocious fire, but this is just what they did. And a feeling of flatness settled on the villagers who had collected to enjoy the fun and exchange comments: "We thought it was one of Major Partridge's bonfires." "My wife was so worried, she though it must be Ham Spray." "Hope the Jerries don't come over", (this had been one of my first thoughts) and, "Let out the old Bull!" Someone did and he capered into a field of cows.

Out to look at the scene of the fire. The dairy was nothing but charred beams and black ashes, in the midst of which a black cat was lapping a saucer of milk.

Three churns of milk were practically boiled in the blaze and Mr. Coombs gave them to us for our pigs. Wilde ladled some off the top for them, not realising it was pure cream. The poor creatures are now suffering from violent bilious attacks and won't look at food!

During the fire Mr. Mills told us that Joan was to be married to Gunner Robinson yesterday. R. offered to drive anyone to church, and was busy most of the afternoon, with white ribbons on the car, driving up and down the lane with a beaming face. We were therefore put into quite a flutter when news of another wedding dropped out of the telephone today. It was Bunny, asking us if we would come to London "for a very special occasion – to be witnesses to my wedding to Angelica". We were flattered at being asked, even so late in the day. Would Vanessa, Duncan and Clive be there, we wondered.

First we went to Cameo Corner for wedding-presents: a pair of Queen Anne earrings for Angelica and a seal for Bunny. At the Ivy we found only William beside the pair themselves. I think our presents were a success; Angelica was wearing a romantic black hat and veil, and looked lovely in the earrings, which she put on at once. The ceremony took place in a registry office in the city, and we went afterwards to the flat in Clifford's Inn where Bunny and Angelica have been living for some time. "Now perhaps at last the neighbours will respect me," Angelica said. We came away with no further clue to Charleston's reaction to, or even knowledge of the event.

Raymond and Jan Woolley arrived at tea-time. We pumped Jan about conditions in France. "Very little indeed to eat: no coffee, no tea, no milk, very little 'grease'; only vegetables, a small ration of bread and of meat. There was nothing to drink or smoke in the cafés, but people went there all the same. I used to take a fan and fan myself, so as to have something to do. The French were hostile to all foreigners for eating up their food, and there was no love for the English, though many references to 'when you come'."

We sat out under our flowering cherry-tree in idyllic weather eating our tea off a wicker table; Burgo was brown as a nut in nothing but

133

a bathing-suit, and all round us two families of fluffy chicks ran about looking for worms.

Penroses to supper. Alec had been to the Brenans, and told us he had tried to persuade Gerald to "bury the hatchet". Gerald: "The hatchet is none of my making." "Oh, *isn't* it?" said Gamel, and Gerald laughed and sent us his love.

*May 14th*

Raymond writes that he met Clive who told him that Charleston was not warned of Bunny and Angelica's wedding. They say that it is not the wedding itself they object to but the Byronesque pose of secrecy, making it look as though Angelica were being abducted from unwilling parents – which is not very far from the truth.

Janetta rang up asking if she could bring her new friend Kenneth for the weekend. We had Desmond and Moll coming, so beds had to be made up in the nursery.

Desmond and Molly gave a fine display of MacCarthyism – the utmost charm and the utmost lack of consideration. No information about the time of their arrival until Molly rang up after lunch on Saturday and burst out, "How do you *do*?" She then failed to hear anything I said, and went to fetch a foreign maid, who heard but couldn't understand. She arrived very worried because she had lost her bag, and much telephoning had to be done about it. Whether their rations were in it or not I don't know, but in any case they brought none – not a speck of butter or sugar, which didn't prevent them from taking sugar in every cup they swallowed. Next Molly lost her spectacles, and after Julia and I had spent a long time pacing the garden looking for them Molly was discovered in bed, having found them, but worn out by the struggle. They left by an impossibly early train, and insisted on R. waking up and calling them much earlier than was necessary, so that they shouldn't keep waking up themselves.

So much for the bother they caused. The pleasure is of course boundless, and we had lots of what Desmond calls "good talk". I remember there was a discussion about India and that Molly said, "Queen Victoria was the only person who could manage the Indians. She was a great paper-weight on a heap of fluttering papers." For Sunday lunch we were a party of nine, with the addition of Lawrence and Julia. It was hard work and I felt physically and mentally exhausted when it was over, but greatly enjoyed it at the time.

I forgot to say that for the last few days the Russian front has once more come horribly to life.

Articles in the paper have for some time been describing a new method of training our soldiers to attack – by spattering them with blood, shouting obscenities in their ears, taking them to slaughter-houses and repeating, "Hate! Kill! Hurt!" You would think it the most typical of unfounded rumours anyone could imagine. I still simply can't really believe it. Yet that it *was* true seems to have been conclusively proved by the fact that an order of the day was published yesterday saying that it must now stop.

The latest correspondence in *The Times* comes from octogenarians, who declare in one quavering voice that they complain of nothing, want nothing, and are (they know) nothing but a nuisance and feel the best thing they could do is to die: they can only help the war effort by their absence. The new ration-books have just been issued by three brisk officious females in Ham village hall. We troop like sheep, humbly, into an atmosphere that seems to be telling us that we civilians and children are "nothing but a nuisance" too, mere numbers on cards, and lucky to get any food allotted to us whatever.

R., commenting on our both pouncing on the same small source of worry: "I don't know whether great minds think alike or not, but husband and wife certainly *worry* alike." He works hard all day with his families of chickens, ducklings and rabbits, as well as in garden and greenhouse. Then he says he lies worrying for at least an hour after I have dropped asleep, and starts again in the morning. "About the house, garden, money – and to tell the truth I worry a great deal about the war. I have no confidence at all in the way it's being conducted."

Rang up Julia about something or other, and she said enigmatically: "We too have our problems." F.: "Oh, what are they?" J.: "Not such as can be discussed on the telephone." F.: "Can't you give one small clue to them?" Julia (after a pause): "I could not love thee dear so much loved I not honour more." From which I deduced that Lawrence was being called-up for some sort of war service.

When we saw them today this proved to be the case. Lawrence has received notice that he will be called on to do full-time Civil Defence, in spite of his exemption. He replied that he had no conscientious objection to that whatever and was only waiting to be told what to do. He seems very calm, almost relieved, and nothing could be more consistent than his position. But Julia is anxious about his health, which she has always viewed with an exaggeratedly alarmist eye.

The Nicholses for the night. It may be the fact that she is pregnant that made Phyllis much more passive than usual. None of the old desire to testify — the Saint Sebastian complex. Where is the Phyllis who refused gas-masks for her children? I much prefer her present realistic attitude — which endorsed Lawrence's attitude about Civil Defence among other things. Phil embroidered a theory that we should need an aristocracy after the war. What sort of aristocracy? — money appeared to be the criterion, and it didn't matter who got it, since riches automatically brought disinterestedness and responsibility. Could anything be more untrue?

After tea we drove off in a daze of heat to spend two nights at Raymond's Thames-side cottage.

Raymond was lying reading in his punt at the edge of the small rough lawn which slopes down from the pretty miniature house with its trefoil window: behind him was a white screen of the massed-up flowers of the guelder rose on the far side of the river — their reflection as clear as themselves until Raymond, leaping up, broke the surface into a thousand ripples. After an exquisitely-cooked dinner we sat out for a while, devoured by midges, and then strolled through the drowsy Tennysonian park of the big house.

I don't know who suggested that R. and I should sleep out, but our tiny bedroom was infernally hot, so we took our blankets on to two garden beds drawn up side by side under a yew tree at the very edge of the water. Slept intermittently, but almost glad to be awake, so delicious was it breathing in the fresh night air and listening to innumerable rustles, twittering and the gentle slip-slop of the river. It was a delicious extension of the day's pleasure, a bonus. Most of this morning I sat out in the punt alone; the fact that I was not on dry land, but only attached to it by a string, made it easier to think with detachment. But separation from the lawn was nothing to the separation from Ham Spray and its perpetual background of swarming, fizzing, buzzing preoccupations and responsibilities. In my punt I read, wrote and above all *thought*, with a rare feeling of enjoyment, while tiny kingfisher-blue dragonflies floated round me or settled on the olive-green water. Lord, how long it is since I attempted to orientate myself. It seems to me I have been blind, deaf and almost inanimate for months.

136

Raymond gave me a book by an intelligent and candid fighter-pilot to read, and it aroused many speculations, and also talk, about danger, fear, heroism, mutilation, and the reactions of those not actually involved to all these things.

Raymond said: "I feel passionately that not a single German should be fed by the Red Cross until every Greek, Pole and Czech has been satisfied. Don't you agree?" Of course he was trailing his coat, and of course we stepped on it, saying what really mattered was who needed the food most. Probably the Greeks would come first. Then he testified to his lifelong hatred of the German people, and said he devoutly wished they could all be exterminated. "Yes," I said, "but don't forget they *can't* be." Both Raymond and Eardley think in terms of revenge, and base their post-war plans on it. I believe all this that the intelligentsia say about the German people will not be credited in a few years' time.

*June 8th*

Ham Spray again. Oh dear, very quietly but quickly the eiderdown of this rustic, practical life has risen round our necks smothering us. My head seethes with practical considerations. Which day to kill rabbits, should we bottle some beans, ought B. to have taken a jacket to school with him? The pleasure of floating between water, fronds, dragonflies and thoughts is only a delicious but fading memory. What to do about it? Is it a useless struggle?

Conversation in the bathroom:

Burgo: "I don't think I want to have any children."

F.: "Why? Are they too much nuisance, do you think?"

B.: "No, not that, but getting them born would be such a bother."

F.: "Their mother has most of the bother of that."

B.: "Yes, but this seed business – I'm afraid I shouldn't know how to manage it."

*June 9th*

To London to spend the night with the Nicholses. For R. and me, who go so seldom to theatres, the whole evening was a treat and "went" as it is called, splendidly. A Leslie Henson revue followed by supper at Prunier's and light-hearted conversation. On the way home we stopped at a nightclub. I saw the motley mixture of humanity there in a peculiarly flattering light – a genial Jew in fireman's uniform, a German-looking girl and her sugar-daddy, a mother dancing with her soldier son on leave, a drunk diplomat. So I interpreted them, and also as warm-blooded, gay, full of human feelings and hopes. Yet there will be times

137

when those same beings appear as herds of sordid animals, who cram their stomachs, sweat, shit and die. What performs the miraculous change? Sometimes good jazz will do it, or classical music, or drinking in congenial company, or natural beauty.

I can almost sympathise with Hester's view. Perhaps there *is* a risk of losing one's curiosity, the sense of the strangeness of existence and the intensity of experience, surrounded by grass and munching animals as we are at Ham Spray and spending most of our evenings sucking facts from a book as if through a straw.

*June 13-14th*

We were in bed about 11.30 when the telephone rang. R. went down and I heard him say in a serious voice: "Is he badly hurt?" I sat up in bed, stiff all over with horror. R. came upstairs to say that that delightful old ex-huntsman father of Alice's had been seriously hurt in a motor crash and was in Reading hospital. What was to be done? The hospital wanted to know if Alice could go at once, or if they should ring us up if he died in the night. I lay trembling violently at the thought of this guillotine-blade hanging over poor Alice, and the realisation that *we* had to decide when it should fall. I was appalled at my own sense of shock and inefficiency, and the knowledge that I would have been incapable of breaking the news. R. — who always rises to such emergencies — was wonderfully kind, courageous and practical. He decided he must tell her at once, and use our last drop of petrol in driving her to the hospital. I knew he would be as calm and supporting as it was possible for anyone to be. He gave her some neat whiskey and even brought me a glass . . . It was 3 a.m. when he returned to the bedroom with the one word, "Died". Then he told me the whole story. The arrival at the hospital had been horrible, Alice was so sure he would be dead, as he was; but even in her misery she was able to think, "I've been nothing but a trouble to you since I came", and thank him warmly for his kindness. Her world takes death very differently from ours. They rush to see the corpse and kiss it, and in that embrace perhaps they accept the fact of death more completely than someone more sophisticated would. All the way home she discussed her plans for the funeral, forgetting nothing, even that he would have clothes coupons which she might be able to use. It is a perfect form of catharsis.

After talking to her this morning I have no doubt she has been cruelly struck; yet I think of R.'s emotional reaction to Lytton's and Carrington's death, and Vanessa's to Julian's and wonder how and why it is so different.

The News gets worse and worse. Rommel has pulled a fast one and we are in full retreat towards Egypt. I hate listening to this weary ding-dong in Libya, yet it is impossible to switch off. Nothing could be more fickle than morale — it leaps like a May-fly.

The Padels have got a 'cellist and we are to try quartets next Tuesday. I have been playing a Haydn and a Mozart on records. The gates of paradise seem to be opening — only to shut with a bang no doubt, leaving me mangled and discomfited.

Alice came back from her father's inquest wearing the haunted expression of someone who has seen an important ghost. She described with melancholy gusto the terrible list of injuries read out by the doctor. "My friend said to me, 'It must have been mincemeat'."
Burgo said: "I'm very sad. He was such a nice cheerful man."

Like a sudden explosion in our stagnant lives, Clive came to stay, and Kitty and Anthony to dinner. After they had gone we sat out with Clive in a bath of warm night air on the verandah, while the light slowly drained away from the panorama of the Downs, and the great white owl in the aspen hissed whenever our voices got too loud. We talked about Bunny and Angelica's marriage. Clive became suddenly unbuttoned, as if released from a vow, and for the first time dropped all pretence that Angelica was his daughter. He said Duncan was full of resentment, while his picture of Vanessa was rather tragic. She was bitterly hurt, yet longed to make it up. Bunny had gone down some weeks before the marriage to announce that it would take place, and the meeting was painful in the extreme. Vanessa couldn't really accept it, and when Angelica telephoned later to say it would be next day she complained of the shortness of the notice. R. said she hadn't a leg to stand on, and no more she had, but I see her as painfully caught in the pincer movement of Duncan's resentment and Bunny's victory. Angelica goes down to Charleston for weekends, and the question is, shall Bunny be asked? Vanessa is for trying it. "I'm devoted to old Bunny," says Clive, and is secretly enjoying reminding them of the days when both Vanessa and Duncan were always telling him what a fascinating character Bunny was.

Very hot still. Sat in the shade of the beech-tree, having endless conversations with Clive. We ranged over the inexhaustible subject of what

139

was of ultimate value. Happiness, said I. Clive said: "We set too much store by human life *per se*." The vast majority of lives, according to him, are of practically no value, the criterion — as far as I could make out — was whether or not a person could enjoy contemplating St. Paul's. He wouldn't *quite* say it was whether they like what he liked himself, but very nearly.

He says Maynard [Keynes] is delighted with his title, and so is Lydia. They came to brave the scorn of Charleston. "O-ah!" said Lydia. "We come to be mocked!" And no doubt they were, for Charleston cherishes what seems to me a totally irrational prejudice against titles earned by merit. Any rationalist has a right to object to the other sort. Leonard [Woolf] was far the most scathing apparently. Maynard is very optimistic about the war, sharing this attitude with the Prime Minister, with whom he is very thick. "Well — we must make the war last another year," he says however, "because we haven't got our plans for the peace ready."

*June 26th*

Clive left us. This afternoon my first quartet session took place. The heat wave continues, and I arrived melting, partly with agitation. I never guessed when I wrote "gates of paradise" that that is exactly what it would seem like — another sphere altogether. If this is to be a regular feature of life it is going to make a great difference to it. How lucky that we invested in bicycles; I carry my violin in a rucksack on my back, rousing hoots of derision from the village children.

When I got home, Alix and James were stalking beside R. on the lawn — James wearing a large straw hat; they have come for a week. These are days of intense heat, strawberry-picking, horseflies, bathing — and bad bad news from Libya. There is other fruit to be picked, and vegetables, which we take in to be sold in Hungerford or distribute in the village. It is all quite hard work, what with our visitors, but they are a constant stimulus, keeping us amused, surprised and delighted by their originality and outstanding intelligence. They are like two trains that persist in their cross-country courses, ignoring all railway lines. A conversation with Alix today about "other people". "I find it extraordinary to feel curious about the people one shares a bus with. My one thought is how to avoid talking to them", was one of her utterances; yet she is always thinking, and surely other people supply the raw material?

Julia and Lawrence to supper, Julia looking lovely and blooming in a pink linen frock with a blowsy pink rose and silver jewellery; she made us laugh all the evening with her scintillating stories about the
140

sexual approaches of American officers to the upper-class ladies of Chilton Folyat.

*June 27th*

Noises of summer fill the air, lowing of cows, thudding of their hooves as they charge by with tails in the air, maddened by the botfly, buzz of bees, hum of tractors. I read *Gulliver's Travels* aloud to Burgo under the shade of the beech-tree. James sits in his runcible hat studying his hieroglyphics. Behind the weeping ash glimpses are to be seen of Alix's alarmingly skinny form, sunning herself.

She told us about her mother's meanness about lavatory paper. "She won't buy any, but carries off the *Radio Times*. Once I found she had taken the current number, and I was so angry that I spent a whole afternoon pasting it together again. And my mother *actually* apologized. I nearly burst into tears."

They left today and Bunny and Angelica came. One evening we had music and Angelica sang for hours on end to my accompaniment. Then she stood in the bay window while the great white owl flew to and fro through the darkness, clutching small animals in its claws. She sang a beautiful song called Bedlam unaccompanied, and when she'd finished she grew suddenly charmingly excited like a child after a treat.

Bunny talked to me about his job in the Air Ministry; he said German morale was frightfully bad in spite of all their victories. "Do you think so?" "I don't think so, I *know* it. All the secret reports come to me."

*July 11th*

Today women born in 1900 had to register for National Service. Took B. with me and went into Hungerford to do so. Other forty-twos seemed to be mountainously large or weakly nervous and uncontrollably talkative. ("Are you married?" "Married? I should say I am, very much so", etc., etc.) I was asked the same, any children under fourteen and how many I "catered" for. I was sent away with a slip of paper, saying that if I was called for an interview I should be legally obliged to take the work I was directed to. People, people. Kitty [West] and her baby have come to stay for a week's rest cure. Roger Fulford over from Oxford to lunch. I know he admires R. but am far from sure he approves of me. He doesn't like "the sex", as he likes to call women, to be at all free in their conversation. Then I ask myself how he can reconcile his theoretical belief in God and the Royal Family with his practical interest in smut and scallywags. Also I felt he had no right to rub his hands over Burgo's atheistical remarks if he really sets store by Christianity. In *theory* he disapproves of malicious characters like Maurice Bowra, and "all dons' wives who flirt with the undergraduates and permit loose talk particularly about unnatural vice in the greatest possible physical detail".

The other day we ran into Julia in Hungerford and walked with her to the "British Restaurant" where cheap meals are served to all and sundry. As it wasn't open we sat on a bench outside, surrounded by villas with gardens full of Dorothy Perkins. Inside a large spacious polished hall we had coffee, while the music of Haydn and a poster of Churchill's confident boozy face embraced us in a democratic aura. I gave way to the spell. It is the temple of Universality; individuality has to be disinfected out like a germ.

*August 7th*

R. points out that I'm trying to take my tempo too fast. Very true, and today I struggled to reform and as a result felt much calmer. Jan [Woolley] left us today after a very successful visit of several days. She went off with her hair belling out under a little round blue cap, looking like a young man in an Italian fresco. As she turned to wave one saw her fine eyes set in a deeply-wrinkled face; they have lost none of their beauty with age and even gain by the contrast. We both liked having her here very much, and feel increasingly at ease with her.

We listen to the bad news with barely a qualm. A mood of fatalism is I think very common just now, and everyone is sick at heart with waiting for the Second Front.

*August 17th*

Marjorie Strachey for the weekend. Dearly as we both love her and enjoy her rumbustious and eccentric character, I was slightly afraid of a skirmish. We haven't seen her since the war began. She had evidently heard of our views and was I think surprised not to find us more provocative. Much talk about education, but not a lot about the war; then when we were sitting on the sunny lawn on the last day of her visit she suddenly said: "All conscientious objectors ought to be dropped by parachute in Germany since they wish to be ruled by the Nazis." R. said, "Well, thank goodness the Government is more liberal-minded." Does she ever remember that both Lytton and James and most of their closest friends were C.O.s in the last war, and would she have wanted them to be treated likewise?

There is agitating news of a large-scale raid on Dieppe, by Commando and Naval forces, with vast losses on both sides. It sounds important − a rehearsal for the second front perhaps? Raymond has come

142

to stay for a week, working all mornings on an essay on Duncan. R. is in low spirits. I have the sense of fumbling, blundering through a long black tunnel. Peaches and grapes ripen almost too fast to eat.

*August 20th*

Equilibrium restored. Raymond is the best possible company, going to the library every morning and stepping out at lunch-time, a butterfly from its chrysalis.

More and more visitors – what a breathless whirl! – the Hills to stay, both Nicholses to lunch and tea, and then late on Saturday night we heard that someone had sent us an American sergeant called John Yeon. We rushed round rather hysterically, making up a bed in the nursery, pushing debris out of sight, and saying how unlike a proper house he would find Ham Spray, though Raymond indulged in a few fantasies of a different sort, about how much he would enjoy finding himself among "the intelligentsia and an Earl's daughter". John Yeon turned out to be tall, dark and handsome, with a tragic, humourless mouth which suddenly flashed into gaiety when he smiled, in fact very attractive in an austere, geometrical way. I don't think he made much of anything, except the view of the Downs – which he convincingly admired, and my saying what a relief it would be if we could shake off the Empire for good and all.

The war news has been unspeakable all week, and there were even a few old-fashioned thuds during dinner. I went out onto the verandah and looked at the dim line of the Downs under a sky of grey felt which seemed to press down on them. It was warm and deathly still, except for the wild raucous shriek of bird or beast from the distant woods, the steady hiss of the owls in the aspen, the wheezing cough of a cow, and a far-off, unsinister "pom-pom" of anti-aircraft guns I imagine, making up a whole which was mysterious and somehow soothing.

*August 31st*

All our recent visitors have left – and we remain alone with our reflections. There is, we conclude, very little pleasure in hospitality to those who disapprove of us, and don't want us to have the very things we are trying to share with them. Eating with relish our home-grown honey and fruit, they will with equal relish imply that we shouldn't be allowed to have it. "Where do you get this petrol? You won't have *that* much longer." Yet they enjoy being met at the station. Or there's Marjorie's view that pacifists have no right even to live in their native land, eat in its restaurants, travel in its railways, an argument which might as well be applied to Conservatives living under a Labour Govern-ment. R. points out with his usual logic that we are English, Ham Spray is our home, and we have a perfect right to live here, although we don't support the official line. On the other hand he does not believe in for-cing our views on other people, and again I think he is right; yet I like expressing my opinions and find it tiring not to. As I clean basins, sweep stairs and dust tables, I often find my thoughts congealing into pacifist configurations, and wondering how so many intelligent people fail to accept the supporting arguments. Yet at present that is unmis-takably the fact.

Frances Penrose came to a picnic lunch in the garden. There are a lot of American troops stationed near her, and it seems that one of their officers gave a lecture to a collection of local English ladies about how to treat the blacks. They must beware of any friendly impulse to-wards them, never let them into their houses, and above all never treat them as human beings, because they were not. Frances said the faces of the ladies were a study in delighted horror, as they heard that none of their daughters' virginities were safe and that all the blacks carried knives. "How are the poor blacks to be entertained?" asked one brave lady. "Oh you needn't worry about *that*. They are always happy, and make their own entertainment by singing and laughing."

*September 9th*

R. and I to London for the day, lunching as usual with Clive and Raymond at the Ivy. Both in their scatty London moods, and Raymond's attention quite unable to focus on what other people were saying – it is at times a flighty insect. The streets looked very drab under a grey sky and Scotch mist. Utility and Austerity have made their mark on the perambulating crowds; there are no smart girls, no style or swing, just a confusion of uniforms, slacks, bare legs and gypsy hand-kerchiefs. In Daniel Neal's a number of quite monstrously ugly parents (so it seemed to my jaundiced eye) were choosing dull grey clothes for boys of all sizes, the smaller ones capering round with cries and squeals. The siren went at this point, but no-one paid the least attention.

*September 10th*

Burgo and I went to a circus at Hungerford, too rare a treat to miss. A green awning cast a livid light as of extreme illness, not to say approach-ing death, on the faces of the audience and the mainly octogenarian performers, lending them a macabre beauty. We sat on rocking benches above the heaped excreta of horses, which gave off a hot smell. At one end, on seats draped with red plush, sat the children of the upper

144

classes, with their mummies and nannies. The children were clean and brushed, white as worms, and their clothes spotless and well ironed; their little legs hung down limply in clean white socks. When they stood up they looked as though they were almost too weak to stand at all. The mummies and nannies pursed their mouths at the clown's obscene antics. The side benches were filled by the children of the proletariat, strong, active, brown and uproarious. It was the class war in concrete form and I saw it with proletarian eyes. The war has greatly emphasized this war between the classes, while paradoxically enough reducing the difference between them. Whereas the lower orders used to accept, God knows why, the idea that ladies should spend their time ordering meals and jealously preserving their beauty, now (when they flap about inefficiently with dusters) the cry is: Why the hell shouldn't they do more? Of course this only applies to the quiet domestic scene; danger and fear break the barriers instantly.

*September 16th*

Wonderful day – all meals in the garden, and many people to bathe in our pool. Catharine[Carrington] came straight from the Brenans, bringing us Gerald's love! "He added, 'I think we'd better not meet until the war is over'."

Ned Grove bicycled over from his Japanese house in drill shorts, with masses of butter – a large, healthy man, with a rugged face, deep voice and monocle. Swift-moving conversation all evening. Ned G., besides being a man of the world, is a clear thinker, used to probing directly into an argument. The group mind, the materialistic hypothesis, co-consciousness – Ned G. is a plausible pleader in spite of the unpalatableness (to us) of many of his mystical views. With unusual candour, to which I take off my hat, he admitted that his own thoughts about the war were invalid because the subject aroused so much emotion.

*September 27th*

Sebastian [Sprott] has been here for three delightful days. Though we only see him about once a year we take up the threads at once; he is the easiest and most affectionate of friends. One of the oldest too, and I think rather nostalgically of the days when we went to the same philosophy lectures at Cambridge and he was the only one of the class who dared question McTaggart's assertions about Hegel, as he rolled round the room looking like an outsize baby. His position towards the war, slightly uneasy last year, is now frankly escapist. R. says "he ignores it as much as possible, saying it is an uncivilized and incomprehensible outrage to the intelligence".

Yet it – the war – has been horribly interesting, with the Germans throwing all they have into the effort to take Stalingrad before winter sets in. It has miraculously *not* fallen, though there is street fighting in part of it.

*October 5th*

Alice has left us, and under the new régime I do all the cooking. I am managing – no more can be said, and R. has been infinitely kind about my efforts. He says, "For a woman not to be able to cook is like impotence to a man."

Saxon is spending a fortnight's holiday here – very sweet, very obstinate and more talkative than usual. He wrote to ask what he should bring in the way of food. I wrote back, "nothing but your meat coupons". These are the only thing he has *not* brought. The first sight one catches of him in the morning is a stately figure in a once-good but now indescribably dilapidated dressing-gown over pyjamas to match, parading very slowly towards the bathroom with his false teeth in a tumbler of water held somehow rather defiantly in front of him. Unable to greet one in speech, he gives an emphatic nod. He comes down to breakfast in a prehistoric black suit (no doubt made by a first-rate tailor) and a royal blue shirt – or in summer an extremely well-cut white silk Palm Beach one frayed at the edges. Black button boots, a volume of Pindar in the original under his arm, slow but elegant movements and a face beautifully cut out of old ivory, long periods of complete silence broken by moments of sudden animation with a faint rose-petal flush appearing on his pale cheeks – all these are important elements, but nothing can add a final touch to the portrait of this lovable, exasperating, and (I'm convinced) deeply affectionate man.

*October 14th*

This evening R. opened in Saxon's honour a bottle of Corton Charlemagne 1928. Subdued expectation was on all our faces. Saxon sighed respectfully; then, after a pause: "A NOBLE wine." R.: "If anyone wants to know what Body is – this is it." It was not only delicious but potent, and gradually I felt infused and vibrating, as a violin string vibrates with a note. The whole world grew rich and mellow. Saxon became reminiscent: "When did you last have a bottle of this?" R.: "When you were last here, Saxon." Saxon: "Hm. I feel highly flattered."

The conversation slipped off unexpectedly into cricket, or had got there when I became fully conscious again. "That was Richardson I believe, but I suppose one would rather be Lockwood . . . and do you know who bowled him out? *A.O. Jones* . . . They said he finished his stroke before the ball ever reached his bat." I sat bemused and happy, still vibrating, but not understanding a word.

I have far too little time to talk to R. these days and there's one thing I particularly want to discuss. A day or two ago he received papers saying he was liable to be called-up for the Home Guard or some form of Military Service. He didn't mention them for at least ten minutes, and then gave no clue as to which way his cat would jump, and even sounded a little embarrassed.

I worry about cooking a good enough dinner for Saxon and for the wines R. brings up from the cellar for him. At night I lie awake and go through the motions of cooking in my head.

Julia and Lawrence to lunch – a tonic visit. Julia gave an amusing description of Aunty Loo and Logan Pearsall-Smith each waiting for the other to die. They have lived together for at least thirty years but really dislike one another intensely, and hiss at each other like two cats who have decided for some reason to share the same kitchen.

*October 21st*

Saxon left us. I never felt more truly sorry to see him go.

This was the great day when our pig and Wilde's were to be executed, and tension spread through the house like an infection when it was known that Jack Lovelock the butcher had arrived. We were all obsessed by the thought of the imminent death of our pigs. Out of a sort of prudery perhaps I had not been near them for weeks, yet now I caught myself saying "You and Pig," to R. when I meant "You and Wilde." What a relief when the dull report of the humane killer was heard from the barn. Everyone but me went out to view the bodies and described how vast they looked, suspended from the roof and with blood dripping from them. Burgo said, "They're as big as barges." Pailfuls of strange marine-looking objects, pink and frilly, kept being carried into the larder. They seemed clean and not at all disgusting. "If *that's* all fresh entrails look like," I found myself thinking, "things aren't too bad." Wilde laughed his head off as his pig, draped in sacking, was tied to the carrier of the car and went off looking like a case of murder. Inside the car were my niece Jill dressed as a Wren, Burgo, bunches of dahlias, and the two pig owners. The sides of our pig from which bacon is to be made were laid out full length in the bath in our bathroom which they are now to occupy.

That night we sat up till midnight making the brawn. Head, heart, trotters, et cetera, were all boiled in a cauldron till they became a grey,

147

gelatinous mass, and then seated round the kitchen table with our visitors, like the witches in *Macbeth*, we hand-picked it and chopped it, removing first an eye and then a tooth, or detaching the fat from an ear. After the first horror it was quite fascinating.

*October 27th*

Raining, raining most lugubriously. Fairly loud bomb explosions during the afternoor

R. "rendered down" the lard of our pig – a heroic act, for it made a sickly-sweet, hot, oily smell of such fearfulness that it drove me out of the kitchen. But it invaded every room in the house in time.

This very busy practical existence makes for unanalytic acceptance of what comes along, and not for much thinking about the war, but I believe at this point I would have ceased to do so in any case. I feel about it – the war – as if it were a permanent accompaniment to life, an unpleasant one like rheumatism or the knowledge that death must come, and one that I avoid attending to as much as possible. Fatalism has increased, and so has the desire to put off making decisions as long as possible in case something or other turns up. R.'s call-up is an instance in point. While washing up the other day he directly asked my opinion about it. I had felt certain scruples about giving it, having an instinct that I should in no way try to influence him, but back any decision he made. As I answered his questions I began to see clearly for the first time that I hoped he would refuse, not because I fail to realise that it may well lead to local awkwardness, nor because the matter has much significance; indeed it would be far less trouble to accept. But because it seems somehow not *digne* to act in a way that doesn't correspond to principles that are seriously held. And on a lighter level the Home Guard has always appeared totally useless and ludicrous, with its pikes and hats decorated with leaves. Moreover, once R. had handed himself over he would be in the sausage-machine, with no more right to choose his own manner of life than the meat in the mincer.

From his manner I could see that he had been giving a lot of careful and fairly painful thought to the matter, but he finally and with admirable sang-froid filled up his form as a Conscientious Objector and posted it off. Well, this morning another form has come, in which reasons for objection are to be entered, and there is the implication of a tribunal. The net has closed with disconcerting rapidity.

*October 31st*

We are steadily eating our pig. So much meat is quite upsetting after months of deprivation; we have no appetite for bread and cake, feel

148

overfed much of the time, and dream uneasily at night. But I never tasted better pork.

We ask all our friends to help eat it, and they seem to enjoy it; in the light of present sensations I see everyone is slightly hungry all the time. Today we had Judy Hubback, who is obviously having to make a constant effort to swallow her terror for David, [1] who is in the thick of the battle raging at El Alamein. As she left she showed signs of wanting to unbutton her feelings. She said, "I've knuckled under now", and the grimness of what she has to bear — which is in fact the "horror of war" I find it most easy to imagine — rose up like a chilling fog around us. "It's a nightmare" — I couldn't think what else to say. Then she said, "If I were religious I should believe that if David was killed I should see him in the next world, but as I'm not, I can't."

R. wrote his C.O. testimony, short, to the point, unprovocative and *admirable*.

*November 7th*

All else blotted out today by the news that American forces have landed at several points on the North African coast, and do not seem to be meeting great opposition. Rommel still goes back, and fast. It is becoming difficult to resist the sensation that the *tide is turning*. Is it the Second Front? What will the Germans do next? We lay in bed discussing it tonight. "There's no doubt what they'll do," R. said. "They will go into unoccupied France."

*November 11th*

He was perfectly right. They have. They've been pretty prompt I must say, and my spirits sag at this evidence of their aplomb.

We have had a lovely visit from Janetta, though she was suffering badly from morning-sickness. She dreads "that catlike inward grin I've so often seen spreading", dreads not doing the best for her child; the one thing she doesn't dread is its birth, and she wants to have it without anaesthetic, which R. thinks unreasonable. Though surrounded by communist-minded young, she still is (and I think always will be) an individualist, and her packed life has made her more tolerant without melting a quite stern critical attitude. Individualism, criticism and tolerance seem to me the most vital human characteristics. She left us this afternoon, and we are very loth to lose her.

Today the church bells were rung all over England to celebrate the victory over Rommel; they will not ring again until peace or invasion.

[1] Her husband

149

Prospects of peace suddenly loom closer. Next year perhaps? The agitation of the news has brought back the hateful waiting-room atmosphere; so far as mental or intellectual life exists the fire is nearly out, spiritual dust lies on everything and I sit gazing in front of me, wondering "What next?"

*November 26th*

A wave of quiet domestic happiness absorbs our lives; I don't know whether it is due to the rising tide of hope about the war or not. R. is angelically kind about all my bungling efforts at cooking, and especially kind to Burgo too, who is going through a phase of fantasy. The other day, walking on the Downs, he added his own inventions to what I was telling him about Bunyan's Hill of Difficulty – such as "The Patch of Exhaustion" and "The Yard of Confusedness". Tonight, coming up from the village in the dark, he began on a monologue about imaginary figures, "rather like Greek Gods, called the Night Witches or Night Men: there's Soft Creeper, who is a very strange shape like curling smoke, only dark red in colour. Then there's Wind Sweeper and Quiet Stone, and Fast Runner, who is shaped rather like a cow only longer and runs very swiftly. And then there are the Day Men, like Cats' Sweetness, who makes cats soft to stroke, and Bright Glistener, who tries to think how to stop the war and the black-out and the bombing."

*November 27th*

Dramatic news. As anyone might have guessed would one day happen, the Germans pounced on Toulon harbour at dawn, where the residue of the French fleet were anchored. As soon as they had dropped mines in the harbour mouth the order was given to scuttle, and every ship is now at the bottom of the sea, the captains going down with their ships, the surviving crews interned by the Nazis.

This event is a signal for Casabianca emotions – *la gloire, l'honneur* and all the rest. But my writing ironically does not mean I am not profoundly moved myself.

*December 17th*

I was at the sink washing up the breakfast things. Enter R., saying: "There, you see how it is. I shan't be here for Professor Frisco", (the Hungerford postman, and conjurer ordered for Burgo's Christmas party). He was holding a summons to attend a tribunal at Bristol on the same day. We only talked a little about it during the day, which was very odd in view of our usual high level of communication. I suppose he

150

will talk about it as much as he wants to. I did ask him if he was worried about it and he replied, "No. Not consciously." I do worry, though. Feeling tired after lunch I lay on my bed reading Henry James. Then the story came to an end and at once I began thinking about R.'s tribunal and my heart went thump thump thump. My worry has no very articulate content. I don't even know what to be afraid of, yet I'm still glad he decided to testify.

Dick Rendel [1] came last weekend for his first visit since the war. He is excellent company, tolerant, sensitive and understanding. It has been a delight to him to get into uniform again, red tabs and all, and he is always polishing his buttons. Among other things he told us about the landings from Dunkirk at Dover where he was stationed. His men had to receive the boat-loads and sort out the living from the dead and push them into trains. They were so dazed that if you could get one man into the train the others would follow like sheep. The numbers of dead and badly wounded were appalling — in most of the boats everything was awash with blood. One boat-load of six hundred contained only thirty men who were conscious, and he doubted if any of them survived. In the midst of all this horror (merely to hear about it was like buffets from a boxer's glove), Dick saw men making a cage on the beach. "What's that for?" he asked. "The Dogs." "What dogs?" "Why, the dogs from France, the strays the soldiers are bringing back." "What will happen to them?" "They'll all be sent to quarantine, after being carefully marked with their rescuer's name and number." After the landings Dover lived in constant dread of invasion, for which preparations were negligible. They were shelled and bombed. One day when the alarm went they looked up to see the sky black with German aeroplanes — hundreds of them. "Well, here it is, now we're done for," he thought. But to his amazement they all passed over Dover without dropping a bomb. It was the beginning of the Battle of Britain.

Dick also told us about the board he is now on, for testing would-be officers. Adrian Stephen is also on it, as psycho-analytical expert. He is extremely popular as well as eccentric, usually wearing battle-dress over an ordinary suit, which shows through the loops where he has failed to button it, and a forage cap put on back to front. He speaks of the soldiers as "my patients".

*December 29th*

Christmas is over at last. We were over twenty to see Professor Frisco's conjuring display. His personality was most sympathetic, and the things

[1] My brother-in-law and Lytton Strachey's nephew. He had been a regular soldier and was now a Colonel.

he produced from his hat or tambourines were ravishingly pretty — huge bright handkerchiefs folding to nothing, palm trees of coloured feathers. The tea-table was piled with cakes and jellies and the tree had a proper present for each child. It was much enjoyed, and Burgo thanked me formally: "I *do* really congratulate you." But of course the whole occasion was made for me unreal and dreamlike by the fact that R. set off to his tribunal at early dawn and didn't return till the guests had departed. I couldn't get over the queerness of our experiencing such very different days.

As he came up the stairs he said, "No luck at all." He told me he had gone there full of belief in British justice, and the conviction that since his pacifism *is* sincere the judges were sure to discover the fact. I was rather surprised that he hadn't anticipated, as I had, the hostile and angry light in which they would view him. We have had ample proof (for instance Gerald's violent reaction) of what emotion is aroused by disagreement on this subject. Anxious not to get angry, he had remained uncharacteristically meek while they lectured him about the Treaty of Versailles, told him as sympathetically as they were able that he was a war-weary veteran of the last war, and made no attempt to question him about his views whatever. The proceedings lasted ten minutes; the Tribunal's findings were "we are not satisfied that there is a conscientious objection within the meaning of the act in this case," and "that the applicant's name be removed from the Register of Conscientious Objectors". He came away thoroughly frustrated. The facts came out at once, his emotional reaction only gradually, and of course he spent a wretched night thinking of all the things he ought to have said. How I wish we had discussed it more, and rehearsed the statements that he must get out whatever questions the judges asked. We had buried our heads in the sand, like ostriches. He is going to write to Craig Macfarlane to ask if it is possible to appeal, and whether it would be a good thing to get letters testifying to the sincerity of his views.

1943

A thorough discussion of R.'s tribunal with Julia and Lawrence. Lawrence pointed out that one trouble is R.'s appearance being so completely healthy and normal, and unlike the judges' cranky picture of a C.O. He was full of sound advice, presenting the problem as one of strategy. R.'s beliefs *are* coherent and sound; the difficulty is to present them to the tribunal in such a way that they can put him into one of their preconceived categories, and convince them — not that he is a thinking man — but a believing one. It was a great relief to talk to sympathisers for a change.

Sorting out chrysanthemums on the verandah in wintry sun, the two cats bunched up beside me with folded paws, gazing owlishly towards the Downs, I feel the stirring of one or two thoughts, like maggots in cheese.

Later, watching woodmen throwing branches on a bonfire in the Little Wood, I thought about Freud's distinction between "active" and "passive", and how the desire for activity isn't always the wish to exercise power, but may be to make something of one's experiences, so that instead of letting them beat on consciousness like waves against a rock, one subjects them to some process of cookery or chemical change. The woodmen sent up a cloud of lively red sparks, but in a few seconds they dropped to earth as grey ash, reminding me of the way what seem like bright ideas look five minutes after they have dawned.

A postcard from Janetta and a letter from Jan both bring the same news — that Rollo is missing in North Africa, and that Geoff [Woolley] [1] who is also out there evidently believes he has been killed. I felt no surprise; Rollo always seemed to have a doomed air, as if he knew himself not to be long for this earth. Gradually a sense of crushing grief descended on me. We are to go to London tomorrow and had arranged to lunch with Janetta one day and Jan the next. I am a coward about facing human pain, just as I hurry away from street accidents, and the misery they must both be feeling must be near the peak of human suffering.

Death was so much in my mind that I talked to Burgo about it, while I lay on his bed feeling suddenly exhausted. The result: when I ran over to the cowman's cottage with a telephone message, he "thought I was dead" and burst into tears.

[1] Rollo and Janetta's father.

Up to London for the night, with suitcases full of eggs for our friends. I really dreaded meeting Jan, but the instant I saw her sitting in the hot lounge of the Rembrandt Hotel with a glass of sherry and Geoff's letters in front of her I realised that her courage was equal to the situation. She began to talk at once about the letters, the possibilities, what could be inferred. There was never a tear and no more tremor than usual in her long thin hands. An old gentleman came up and very indignantly asked us to observe the Silence Rule during the broadcasting of the news. We talked on. Geoff's letters were maddening: instead of definite details about the exact wording of the report, he wrote crazily about feeling Rollo near him, and the stars, and God, and how kind everyone was being to him. So much for his Christianity. Next day we lunched with Janetta at the Ivy; her courage was as remarkable as Jan's, but different.

At the present time, when violence reigns supreme, anyone who believes in reason rather than force is bound to feel frustrated and painfully out of tune with their surroundings. As I go through the motions of cleaning baths and peeling potatoes I often think about this subject, and nothing shakes my absolute conviction that progress can never be achieved by force or violence, only by reason and persuasion. Intelligence not dynamite, words not bombs are the only means to convince people, slight as that possibility generally is. And anyway I'm not at all sure I believe in progress.

The two old Padels bicycled up this afternoon to express their sympathy with R.'s tribunal troubles. It has evidently been reported in the local papers, so now at last most of our neighbours know us for what we are, and on the whole it's comforting to be able to appear in our true colours. R. has collected a bunch of testimonials to the sincerity of his pacifism – Clive and Phil Nichols, and promises of others.

I have got into the way of blotting out what I'm actually doing – sweeping or cleaning the bath – and pursuing the thread of some general idea. Today I thought how our lives were becoming indistinguishable from those of the petite bourgeoisie, and how necessary it was not to follow them into respectability and conventionality – but to keep the good old flag of Bohemia flying and realise that what "the world" thinks of one matters not at all.

A letter from Anne Hill. A week ago there were suddenly a couple of bad raids on London, one by day in which a school was hit and forty children killed. The night raid was very noisy and began on Heywood's day off, just as they were dining out before he caught his train back. What does he do? Naturally and humanly, he sees his pregnant wife home, and so misses his train. You would think it might be overlooked, but no: he was confined to barracks for several days and given particularly disgusting jobs to do. He says that in the field where they do bayonet practice there are large notices saying "Remember Singapore. How would YOU feel if a yellow man raped YOUR mother, sister, wife?" His group are mostly on the elderly side, and include a highly-educated Indian who is unmercifully ragged. A feeble and neurotic ex-chemist was heard to say during parade: "Sergeant, may I fall out? I'm nothing but a bag of nerves!"

*January 29th*

Proverb by Julia, here to lunch today with Lawrence: "There's many a woman bears a child in sorrow and many a hen lays an egg in pain." This was part of a plea for kindness to hens; most of the conversation was more interesting; now that gossip has ceased to exist, ideas get more of an innings.

Later came Judy Hubback and her little girl. As we sat in the sun on the verandah, drinking rum and milk, she told me she had been feeling quite mad this last week. I told her that in her position I thought she would be mad if she did *not* sometimes feel mad.

Julia rang up in great agitation. As a "mobile woman" she has received a summons to appear at Hungerford tomorrow, with a view to being directed into industry or agriculture.

*February 4th*

Julia to lunch after her crucial interview, arriving on her bicycle, pre-occupied and tousled, her fringe awry and a pensive expression on her face. She had lain awake all the night before, picturing herself in prison as a C.O., which she might have spared herself had she mastered the fact that women of her age cannot be actually conscripted. When she said she was writing a book, the interviewer herself suggested six months' postponement. "What sort of a book?" she asked. "A novel. But not an *ordinary* novel — it's a novel with a *message*." She has worked out quite logically that her conscience does not forbid agriculture or civil defence.

A spidery note from Mr. Higgs the bacon curer announced that our ham and bacon would "D.V." be ready today. So we drove to Newbury to collect it — the last time we shall have the petrol or the excuse. The

157

frail little old man unlocked the oak doors allowing a glimpse of great smoked pigs hanging in rows, then trundled out our sheeted corpse, and came to thank Burgo with tears in his eyes for having written him a letter of sympathy on hearing that a burglar had broken in, knocked him down and robbed the till. "I shall keep that letter," he said. We drove away, Burgo rosily blushing, and R. reciting a litany describing all the rich MEAT we now possessed. A rich, smoky aroma filled the car, and "D.V." we shall eat our first slice of bacon tomorrow.

The last remnants of the German army at Stalingrad have given in to the Russians. When first they were encircled and in danger, this seemed too good a piece of news to hope for. Now it has happened and one begins at once feverishly looking forward to the next phase in this drama, even while clouted on the head by the horrifying details of the capitulation — the enormous casualties, hideous cold, soldiers eating their horses and a posse of generals cornered like rats in a trap, unkempt, unshaven and unnerved.

*February 9th*

Sounds of a bicycle crunching on the gravel, and in dashed Lawrence, sweat on his forehead and a look of frenzy. A new calamity. Oliver has had a sudden violent heart attack and Julia was this morning summoned to his bedside. She had gone off in such a hurry that she had no time to find out what her own feelings were about the disaster (evidently the worst was expected) much less could Lawrence divine them. He didn't know what to be at, had a desire to munch but nothing to bite on. We feel responsible for him in Julia's absence. When he asked me over to listen to records I went somewhat unwillingly, but I'm very glad I did, for they were Benjamin Britten's *Michelangelo Sonnets,* and I felt I was hearing a work of genius for the first time. We sat listening in Lawrence's tiny sitting-room, with the window open wide and rain falling softly on the tufts of violets outside. We played the records right through twice, but can one trust these certitudes?

*February 11th*

As I stood bung-eyed at the stove, over the breakfast frying-pan, in came Wilde for the chicken pail and burst out, "Newbury was bombed yesterday." "No! Was there much damage? Anyone killed?" "Yes, quite a few. A school and a church were hit." It turned out to be exactly true, and some eighteen people were killed. If this had happened earlier in the war people would have stopped sending their children in to school at Newbury. Now it's as if being bombed by the Germans was one of the normal hazards of life, like being run over by a motor car,

158

and there was no use trying to avoid it. Probably it's more realistic than the earlier reaction.

*February 13th*

A letter from Julia giving a hopeful account of Oliver. He has to lie absolutely still for a fortnight without lifting a finger, literally on pain of death, but it looks as if he would pull through. Julia has a surprisingly strong sense of duty, and though she really rather dislikes Oliver than otherwise, her duty to a sick parent takes precedence over duty to Lawrence, so she has agreed to stay there six weeks and nurse him.

Heywood came over from camp at Aylesbury in his little forage cap. The worst time for him was waiting to be called up, and he seemed more relaxed now, yet he loathes the army. He described the friendly, hearty young men he lives among, some fresh from school, and how he tries to read in his bunk through the din and horseplay, bangs and bumps. The conversation is on the model of "this fucker's going to fucking Wales tomorrow".

Just before tea the telephone rang. It was a telegram saying, "Jan died this afternoon." I couldn't really take it in. R. rang Janetta up. She had had a sudden relapse after 'flu, and been sent to hospital. "When I took her there I suddenly saw she was dying," Janetta said. "The hospital couldn't understand why she had died and said she should have had every chance, but seemed to have no resistance at all." There had been no more news about Rollo, and she had clearly lost the will to survive.

*February 19th*

Lawrence came over on his bicycle to say that Julia would be home for the night tomorrow. We talked of many things: amongst others, conversation. He described the charm of Old Bloomsbury conversation as lying in its being obsessional in some way, coloured by the speaker's mood or moment of vision. Certainly conversations can take the place of events. Here we've been all winter, cooped up like hens in a hen-run, yet I have the feeling the time has been studded with events (sometimes sad but never dull) because of all the endless conversations with R. which make the daily material of our life.

Raymond, Janetta and Kenneth from Friday to Monday. I was nervous because of the standard of cooking I knew our visitors would require and which my talents aren't equal to, and lay awake on Friday night humiliated by my shortcomings. All through the weekend the stress was on *Food* – what we were going to eat next, or what a good meal we had just eaten, and I couldn't help feeling that sometimes too much attention is paid to this admittedly very important subject. However they went off saying they had never had such delicious *food* — so I hope they enjoyed themselves.

*March 3rd*

R. digs hard in the garden. The spectre of his approaching appeal tribunal haunts us both, and this time we mustn't make the mistake of avoiding thinking about it.

In the evening I went alone to supper with Judy Hubback. I wondered if there was any special reason for her asking me, but there didn't appear to be — our conversation ranged straightforwardly over education, sex, Communism. She said that she and David never complain in their letters as much as they would like to, because they don't want to upset each other. "So I don't tell him how lonely I am." He writes that Cairo is full of deserters, and soldiers desperately trying to have a good time, and tarts who have V.D. so badly they can't walk, but have to be taken about in carts. Then she began on the village, and the queen among the gentry, Mrs. Hill. She said, "You're in her bad books, you know." "I rather thought so. What about?" "Well, I said one day, 'I'm not free that day as I'm teaching Burgo', and she almost fell over backwards and said, 'I simply can't believe it! *You*, a serving soldier's wife teaching the child of a Conscientious Objector! I'm going to have nothing more to do with them myself. I used to go up there sometimes, but now I'm going to boycott them absolutely.'"

*March 5th*

After tea a military car drove up and an exceedingly gentlemanly Major in the Guards stepped out and asked if there was anywhere some of his men could sleep for a night or two while on manoeuvres. R. offered them the nursery to sleep in and the music room for their office and Headquarters. The Major vanished, and it wasn't till the middle of the night that we were aroused by the tramping of boots and the sound of lorries revolving in the drive. R. tumbled out of bed to receive them, while I gave way to feelings of resentment at our darling Ham Spray being thus taken over, but when he came back R. restored me to reason by saying mildly, "After all, they are human beings, you know. And I always feel terribly sorry for the Army."

*March 6th*

The soldiers have taken possession so tactfully and quietly that we begin to feel quite fond of them. An officer or two have gone into

Alice's old bedroom; the batman dosses down in the nursery sitting-room, and goodness knows how many others in the nursery itself. In the music-room typewriters tap, and a stream of despatch-riders appear at the door. Burgo is mad with military fervour, and was out early thinking up things to say to the sentries, with his hands in his pockets. If we went anywhere near he would say, "Don't bother me. I'm having a glorious time with Jack" (or Ted). The guardsmen evidently are "human beings" and neat and tidy as well as friendly ones, but their activities seem as mad and meaningless as those of ants in an anthill.

*March 8th*

Sounds of evacuation began early this morning. Feet running, a harsh voice saying, "Get a jerk on". When I went in to the kitchen to cook breakfast it was full of soldiers making themselves cups of tea.

They are gone. We went into the music-room; nothing remained — nothing except that peculiar soldierly smell and a few cigarette ends. No, not *quite* nothing. Behind the shutter I found some papers marked SECRET, which R. said gave the exact composition of one of our divisions, and was information of great value to the enemy. Just as we were studying it a motor-cyclist dashed up.

"May I look round, just to make sure they haven't left any documents?"

"Well, yes, they have as a matter of fact," said R. "Here it is."

"GOSH! This is *important*!" and the cyclist, a rosy round-faced boy, shot off. It was strange to find military activity so very like a school game.

Over today hangs a cloud of anticipation of R.'s appeal tribunal tomorrow. He is going through a severe attack of stage fright. Lawrence visited us again, to run over some arguments, and papers with snatches of reasoning on them lie all over the room.[1] At the same time R. breaks off his imaginary dialogues and picks up a book and reads it with a concentration I envy and admire.

*March 9th*

The dreaded day is over and with complete success. Craig and Raymond met us at the Ivy. R. said he would rather I didn't attend, so I listened passively while the others rehearsed the proceedings over lunch. Craig jotted down the details of R''s military career and memorised them so quickly and accurately that he reeled them off later without a hitch. Raymond looked huddled and rather unhappy, as I feel sure he was.

[1] For the final statement see Preface.

It showed true friendship to stand up for a pal you entirely disagree with; but he couldn't resist one little dig; "As a matter of fact, I'm sure if Ralph had a gun in his hand and saw a German aeroplane coming over, he would certainly take a pot shot at it." Which is the nearest to a silly remark I ever heard him make.

I visited Janetta during the proceedings, and found her finishing a picture propped on a chair, and eating a lettuce. When an air-raid alarm went I was looking out of the window at Regent's Park, and I saw the Nannies and children hurry off in various directions, while the soaring wail of the siren shot up again and again over the peaceful scene of green lawns and water, children and swans, reminding me of firework rockets – seeming as they do to leave a tall question mark in the air – or the cries of outlandish birds.

Then R. arrived, having cleared his obstacle with a wide margin. He described the proceedings; Craig's excellent manner, Raymond's nervousness, and his own which at once disappeared when he saw the perfect dignity and politeness the judges applied to everyone. He began, "I don't know if I made my position clear in my statement . . . " "Yes, I think it was perfectly clear." They asked a few questions about the date when he became a pacifist, his market gardening activities, and an Oxford don asked. "I think you take up the Absolutist position?" He even cracked a couple of jokes, which made them all laugh, and then thanked them for their consideration. It was over.

*March 10th*

The Padels rang up for news and Lawrence came over to hear every detail. It was as if we had had a baby and our friends were kindly sharing in our pleasure. But if one starts to analyze this baby, I wonder what will be found? Relief from anxieties such as being threatened with prison, or unpleasant scenes with the local Home Guard? Or success in this, as in any other endeavour, especially because it was an intellectual one? I put top the satisfaction of R.'s having acted in accordance with his beliefs, but of course there are a host of minor ones – like wondering what will be the effect on Gerald!

Lawrence has been getting distracted letters from Julia, who said how frightful it was looking after Oliver, and that she was worn to a frazzle by his relentless egotism and hostility, and that she intended returning for a breather at least.

*March 16th*

Ever since my visit to Judy Hubback I have grown increasingly aware of local disapproval for our pacifism, wondering for instance how I would pass off an unexpected meeting with Mrs. Hill. Today, walking to the village, I saw the fluffy white head of Mrs. Thunder approaching me. I fancied she looked startled.

We paid our first visit to Olive[1] since our "trouble". Of course it wasn't mentioned, but she contrived to show her complete loyalty to us whatever mad or incomprehensible thing we should do.

There's a suggestion of audible stillness before the storm conveyed by the news just now. The patient has been wheeled into the operating theatre, nurses stand round in their white overalls and masks, waiting for the surgeon to appear. The suspense is hardly bearable, and one perversely longs for him to stride in, be handed his instruments, blood to gush and the operation begin. R. keeps wisely repeating, "Something will start this weekend." But it's revolting to the reason to be actually longing for hell to break loose.

The Padels have been deluging me with Communist literature, and this evening (after much putting it off) I sat down to read some Lenin. For the theories of Marx and Engels criticising Capitalism I have always had some respect, but Lenin seems almost empty of thought, and I feel he "argues" from his stomach instead of his brain, mentioning "violent revolution" as if speaking of a pot of caviare. What I find quite intolerable in Communism is the assumption that it's *better* to achieve a result by violence than by persuasion; and why turning the State upside down and putting the proletariat on top should solve all problems they hardly bother to suggest. I rehearse arguments by which I can convince these kind innocent people that I am not, never have been and to the best of my belief never will be a Communist.

*March 21st*

An evening speech by Winston was announced. Would it herald some new developments, a Second Front even? After a lengthy and much qualified statement of war aims, the old conjurer suddenly declared that he had received a telegram from Montgomery and the *8th Army is on the move.* So R. was right, and there's an extraordinary feeling of suspense lifting.

*April 21st*

We tore up our roots from Ham Spray and travelled to East Anglia, to stay with Helen Anrep. How lovely to be in someone else's house; and walking into Helen's sitting-room I was overwhelmed by the beauty of

---

[1] The first maid to come to Ham Spray, now married.

163

it, lovely china everywhere, chosen with exquisite taste, as are the stuffs draped over worn furniture and the subtle delicate colours of the room itself. All sorts of things from rare Oriental objects to Spanish or Italian peasant pots are combined and unified by Helen's (and I suppose Roger [Fry] )'s individual powers of selection. The room was a perfect background for Helen's smiling rosy face and untidy white hair, as her slight body moved silently and rather elegantly about, unexpectedly clad in a very dusty tweed suit, with fresh feminine white frills at neck and cuffs.

Upstairs were more beautiful things, vases of beautifully-arranged flowers everywhere, and *incredible dirt.* Only the floors of the rooms seem to have been touched for years. Black cobwebs festooned the windows and walls, and dust lay thick on the piles of books piled on every available surface.

Walked with Helen beside the river. When we commented on its being a remarkable indigo colour, she said, "Oh yes, it's the outflow from some sort of factory — a dye works perhaps", but with no sign of minding this strange aberration. The Suffolk landscape was both intensely English and somewhat decayed: enormous fallen elms lay in the grass, and we passed fine old mills that had become dilapidated and deserted, and overgrown gardens with waves of lilac overflowing their walls. Talk, as usual, about the Euston Road Group, the wickedness of the Royal Academy and the eccentricity of country neighbours. Helen told some very amusing, if scandalous stories about members of the Group. Why they and some of the Bloomsbury painters *worry* so about the Royal Academy beats me.

*May 10th*

Home again. Janetta has been here for a week, and now she has gone off (one now, and soon to be two) I regret the things I didn't say. Kenneth came one night, walking unexpectedly into the sitting-room. After a while he handed her a letter in rather an offhand way, saying, "Oh, here's your father's letter about Rollo." She read it and was obviously shaken. When she handed it to me I saw that it seemed to give absolute proof that Rollo was dead. His papers had turned up on the dead body of a soldier. Of course while the official verdict is "Missing", it is impossible to crush hope altogether.

Burgo has been ill and the weather has been appalling; today it pours and blows, drips, patters and oozes. There is no possibility of going out and I have done badly as sick nurse. I came down to supper almost in tears after a prolonged tussle of wills, and found R. supporting and reasonable. I couldn't get on for a week without him.

Meanwhile Judy Hubback *has* to get on without her David, and said (turning a little pink) that it had become an obsession with her to imagine him coming round the corner of the house. The North African campaign, I should say, goes "wonderfully well", and it looks as though it couldn't last much longer. Yet I don't detect much cheerfulness around. War weariness is naturally on the increase as time drags on, and a general sense of apathy.

*May 19th*

Well – Victory is ours. The Axis is out of Africa. The church bells are to ring.

The blackout comes very late now, so that we don't have to draw the blinds in the passages. I love stumbling and feeling my way along them at night by the mystical light of the full moon which has streamed brilliantly in at the windows lately, and looking out to see the sky full of stars. By day it has been drowsy and still, very quiet except for a chorus of singing birds and the frou-frou of little ducklings running through the grass. The lawn is a hayfield and the garden a wilderness.

We have bought a lovely picture of green apples by Lawrence, and this afternoon Burgo and I bicycled to see it. Burgo amused Julia very much by the way he bent over it like a very old connoisseur with his hands on his knees, saying: "I must say Lawrence, I think it's *marvellous* the way you've done that bit shading away into darkness. And that sherry glass is very lifelike."

*May 25th*

Waking early, I began half-dreaming, half-thinking about conversation, partly as a result of a visit to the Wests and their babies yesterday. It isn't only babies who have to learn to talk – we are all, all our lives trying to learn to string words together better. What are we doing in the world, what do we eat and keep ourselves alive for? Conversation, communication, is the chief purpose of life, I thought, lying with my eyes closed. We think so highly of "good talkers" like Desmond and Virginia because they are the ace performers of the chief function of life. Such sleepy thoughts are always top-heavy though they may have a seed of truth in them.

*June 3rd*

To Well Farm, Welcombe, Devon, where we have taken rooms for a fortnight. The white-washed farmhouse is tucked very snugly into the top of a narrow valley leading down to the sea. It has a tall fuchsia hedge and a little plot of shorn grass bordered by pebble paths. The farmer and his wife, Mr. and Mrs. Cornish, are very friendly, with rosy

165

happy Devonshire faces, but there are some strange figures in the kitchen. When I was in it today two tall pale youths, apparently twins, came up to me with Alice-in-Wonderland gestures and making unintelligible remarks. Mrs. Cornish flapped her apron at them as if they had been intrusive hens, and cried, "Shoo! Shoo! Out you go!" Afterwards she told me they were "M.D. really", and their mother, the "great lady" of the village, had sent them to her to look after.

I wrote to Leo [Myers] asking him what his current beliefs were. Today he writes that he is still a highly emotional Communist who longs to shoot almost everyone — "all Liberals, Cecils, Bloomsbury and City men", and hinted, fairly mildly, that R. and I ought to be shot too.

Walked to the next Mouth, as they call the bays here, to visit the "Indians" — poet Ronald Duncan and his family. What is it that makes a sight of them so pleasant? The beauty of their lonely valley for one thing. It's impossible not to respect people who insist on living in such a place, in spite of its grave inconveniences. They told us that the Mad Boys at our farm are thought quite alarming, and even dangerous to their mother. The sinister air of the kitchen is completed by a whiteheaded crone who works there, and who walks about bent double, weighed down by a vast goitre hanging almost to her waist, which makes her look like a stout white turkey. I stood waiting for Mrs. Cornish; the two idiot boys were sitting in the passage out of sight, but I could see from the shadows on the floor and the reflection of their tilted white faces in a glass door, that they were silently mopping and mowing, and was glad when Mrs. Cornish returned, bringing health and sanity.

*June 10th*

An afternoon excursion to Gull Rock, which has been to us much what the Lighthouse was to Virginia. We made our way painfully over a chaotic wilderness of huge blocks of stone, and at last reached the vast amphitheatre dominated by a copper-green ledge on which the gulls live, and from which they were hurling themselves with hoarse shrieks of mocking laughter. The stratification was so extraordinary that I felt I was actually in the presence of some violent natural upheaval crystallized into a moment of time. Gull Rock itself was separated from us by a narrow channel through which the grey-green water squelched like tooth-water through teeth. We climbed the cliff nearest to it and saw that behind the gulls' kingdom white with their droppings there was a sheer rock, flat as a plate, descending to the sea.

Called on the "Indians" on the way home. They were friendly but not quite at their ease. Then the talk turned to Gerald and conscientious objection and everything livened up. Ronnie said he was a pacifist, and he has let a number of others, as well as a few communists, refugees, poets and I dare say German spies, take over a deserted house on his land, perhaps suitably named Gooseham.

*June 17th*

Back to Ham Spray. No "help" at all, and Raymond comes tomorrow. Much too busy to write.

Nothing could have looked more beautiful than our view this evening, when the light began to fade after a glorious day. The hay in the Park has been cut and lies in long feathery lines, from which wood pigeons rise up flapping their wings and seeming as large as cranes. R. and I sat reading until dark with the sitting-room windows down as far as they would go. We were much aware, therefore, of the outside noises, bird rustlings, advance of a cat on our poultry, settling down of ducks in their coop, weird shriek of owls. A huge moth, whirring like a helicopter, made a sudden entrance into the room and then removed itself with dignified disgust, whirring still.

A letter from Clive with a story that pleased me: Desmond has bought some R.A.F. badges and removed the letters, and he gives his lady friends their "wings" if they have read *The Wings of a Dove* all through. When he was ill Molly was reading aloud to him, got bored and suddenly began reading in a thick American accent to distract herself. Desmond: "Molly, no! Molly, stop it! Or I'll take away your wings."

Our invasion of Sicily has been the new development in the war, moving at first with great speed, then in what seems agonising slow motion. David Hubback is involved. Judy is restless with anxiety, which makes her drop in a good deal on us and on Julia and Lawrence. She told us she was "living on sal volatile" and her knees were physically weak with terror. Poor Mrs. Chandler of the Ham pub has heard that her only son is missing from a bombing raid on Hamburg; the town has been almost blotted out but our losses in bombers are horrifying. All is working up to a frenzy as we gradually move into the offensive.

Burgo's wise thoughts on human character: "If a person can never be kind and doesn't know how to be, then I think he isn't really a person at all. He might just as well be an animal. I hate selfish people worse than anything, and I like them to be generous and loving, even if they're boys. I hate the way people think boys ought not to be kind and loving, only girls — just like they think girls ought to sew and cook and boys only dig. I think boys ought to sew and cook as well, and girls sometimes dig."

167

R. and I to the Bothy for the weekend, cool and refreshing as a plunge into water. Raymond was industrious at his typewriter; Eardley, stripped to the waist, digging in the vegetable garden. Raymond gave us a garbled account of Julia's efforts to get exemption from call-up, writing to various friends to ask them to vouch for her work being "of value to civilization". He assumed that no-one could so perjure themselves. I know for a fact that this was not what she asked them to say, but merely that "she was a serious writer". But in any case, even if one doesn't believe this — and I for one do — is it so dreadful to stretch a point to get an old friend out of trouble? It's Morgan [Forster]'s famous issue between country and friend. I went so far as to say I set enormous value on friendship and very little on patriotism, but I saw this horrified them both, and Eardley in particular looked very shocked.

The weekend passed very happily in talking, reading and gliding off in the punt. One evening when we were walking to the pub to telephone, we stood for a moment to watch an endless stream of bombers going over. As men reeled out of the pub on their way to the men's lavatory most of them looked up and laughed or said, "Somebody's got something coming to them tonight." Raymond murmured: "Verona, Florence, Pisa." Eardley said to R: "Wouldn't it be wonderful to be in one of those bombers going over to bomb Germany?" Why isn't he, then? I couldn't help silently wondering. Raymond and I talked about the curious lack of emotion with which we were watching this gladiatorial spectacle. For this is in effect what it was, and goodness knows how many of those bombers will "fail to return". The light had almost gone, and a pale yellow-white searchlight shot its beam upwards against the Thames landscape of rounded trees and luscious meadows, still faintly coloured blue-green and grey.

*August 16th*

We have had a visit from the Garnetts — Bunny, Angelica and William. Angelica intrigued us by saying that a few days ago Bunny came home from his office swinging his umbrella and carrying a bottle of champagne. "There's good news," he said, "that must be celebrated; but of course I can't tell you what it is. You'll know in course of time, and when it *does* break," he said, chuckling to himself, "it'll be pretty striking."

*August 24th*

We heard from Catharine that poor Gamel had been operated on for
168

hernia and was now in Swindon Hospital. Contrived to find a bus to take us there and visited her. She looked thin, and a bunch of flowers lying on her chest trembled violently with the beating of her heart. It seems her doctor thought she had cancer and she and Gerald spent a week facing the idea of her death, before she could go to a specialist in London. As soon as he heard her American voice, instead of examining her he burst out into a furious attack on our Yankee Allies. She felt so angry she nearly offered to pay his bill and go at once. However the conclusion was that she has not got cancer.

Leaving her, we joined a swelling stream of the citizens of Swindon, all following a series of notices marked "British Restaurant", to a huge elephant-house, where thousands and thousands of human beings were eating as we did an enormous all-beige meal, starting with beige soup thickened to the consistency of paste, followed by beige mince full of lumps and garnished with beige beans and a few beige potatoes, thin beige apple stew and a sort of skilly. Very satisfying and crushing, and calling up a vision of our future Planned World — all beige also.

*September 2nd to 9th*

A week's visit from Alix and James — and a very eventful one so far as the war was concerned. I have passed over in silence the fall of Mussolini, a huge *bonne bouche* that we digested surprisingly quickly. A few days later James, rather pink in the face, announced that the 8th Army had landed on the Italian mainland, and later still, "The Italians have surrendered unconditionally!"

It was the nicest visit the Stracheys have ever paid us. We regaled them on home-grown ducklings, plums, figs and melons, and they have never been more benign and friendly.

James on the psycho-analytical front: "Things have been very bad lately, with so few neurotics, and those there are snapped up by the refugees. However I hope with the approach of peace the situation may brighten up a bit and gradually return to normal." Alix was very amusing about her endless tussle with her mother, to introduce more heat and sanitation into their house. Mrs. Sargant Florence is a remarkable old lady, as handsome in her way as Alix and with the same fine Red Indian features and level blue-grey gaze. She had a considerable reputation as a painter at one time, and has covered the walls of hall and passages with truly appalling frescoes representing a concourse of blind men in a waste place. "We call them the Willies," said James with a wild laugh, "because Alix's Uncle Willy sat as model for them all." Then she discovered some mysterious equation between music and colour, and published a book about it. She has other strange cranky beliefs, such as that water-closets are "wicked" and earth-closets "good". After end-

169

less pleading from Alix, who has delicate health and dreads the cold, her mother agreed to a W.C. being put in, if Alix would foot the bill and promise to remove it the moment the war was over, and if it was promised that the plug should never be pulled "except in cases of extreme emergency". She then must have forgotten all about it. Alix told us: "Then one day I heard a *fearful* caterwauling in the back yard and saw a stately, gleaming white object standing there, with the plumber and his boy in attendance both looking rather taken aback, while my mother waved her arms and shouted, with her white hair flying like King Lear's: 'My whole life's work is destroyed!'" Another story of Alix's: "I've been having tooth trouble and didn't want to go to London, but I found a sort of defrocked dentist in Marlow, who visited people in their houses with a plug-in drill. It made a horrible noise and worked anything but smoothly, and the tooth he mended soon fell to bits. It must come out, he said, and I had to drive and bring him back to Lord's Wood where he gave me an injection and then found he'd left his forceps behind, so I had to drive him to Marlow again with a frozen gum to get them. When he got to work the gum was rapidly unfreezing, and James and my mother, eating their dinner in the room below were electrified to hear wild yells and the sound of me being dragged round the room in a basket chair." It turned out he was a drunkard who had lost his practice thereby.

*September 14th*

To London for the day, and lunch with Bunny and Angelica at Gordon Square. London no longer looks like a centre of life, much less civilization. Everyone struck me as tired, flat and lustreless, though healthy and sane, and I've never seen so many soldiers, sailors and airmen in the streets. Coming home in the train, an airman sitting opposite began quietly unbuttoning his thoughts to us. They were all of the most innocent and dull description — about shooting rabbits with one of his officers, picking blackberries, his wife's cooking, and how he used once to be a delivery man for Harrods. He was as nice and harmless as anyone could be, and quite incurious about us, just full of a desire to communicate — which I found in itself touching. "I lost a wounded partridge the other day when I was out shooting. I hate that. As a matter of fact I don't like killing anything, and I don't like the idea of bombing, whether it's us or the Germans who do it." I note this as an example of something I've often observed in this beastly war: that those personally involved in it are much less bloodthirsty than those who aren't.

There is great local excitement because last week one of the black soldiers from Savernake Forest murdered one girl and raped another, just off the high road to Marlborough. The girls were said to be virtuous wardmaids from Savernake Hospital. Various ladies now come forward to say that black men had "spoken to them" as they bicycled through the forest, and – getting no reply – fired off their revolvers, in what direction isn't clear.

Alix writes, "I don't know whether our stay with you has utterly eaten you out of house and home in the way of Ducks, Honey and Wine. Certainly they – and the pleasant rational society (how heavenly to be able to argue hotly yet with absolute friendliness!) which I liked so much with you, will see us out, like the fat in the camel's hump and the water in his stomach, for many a week to come."

Saxon is spending his fortnight's holiday here. I get more and more devoted to him. His teasing perversity is evaporating with age, and his sweetness of character seems to grow. In the evening R. reads aloud, while I darn and mend, Saxon knits white woollen leggings for Barbara Bagenal's grandchild, and Burgo fetches his knitting too – a dish-cloth.

News from the outside world: Bunny and Angelica have a daughter.

Nicko Henderson, back from Cairo came to see us, bringing messages from old friends – Bryan Guinness and Michael MacCarthy are both miserable and longing to be home. Eddie Gathorne-Hardy says Ham Spray "is the only civilized house in England". Nicko is attached to Lord Moyne in some capacity which involves entertaining visitors from England. He gave an amusing account of Noël Coward, wanting to swim but having no bathing trunks, so he had to accept a long, unbecoming pair of underpants belonging to Lord Moyne. Then he asked Nicko, "Is there such a thing as a lav about?" Nicko pointed vaguely to some large trees. N.C.: "No, no, old chap; big stuff, very much so." So Nicko took him indoors and found a lavatory for him. Soon afterwards Coward came out clutching Lord Moyne's pants, half on and half off, and ran into Nicko with a lady visitor. Nicko rather maliciously introduced them, and N.C. said "Simply *amazing* meeting you like this. Definitely no sign whatever of toilet paper."

A letter from Julia, which I opened rather anxiously. There has been a renewal of air-raids on London this week, one at least every night, and

I wondered how she had been standing them. She writes: "It is some-what like having a nightly purge; one is uncomfortable until one's had it — the raid I mean — one grits one's teeth and endeavours to bear up and numb oneself for the short period it's functioning, and then heaves a sigh of relief and happiness when the all clear goes. The noise is comparatively mild. All the same, Germans circling overhead and trying to kill one are Germans circling overhead trying to kill one." I should think so indeed. "Very much so."

I have been a good deal preoccupied by the thought of London raids, and even dream of them by night. The intense quiet here, emphasized by the peaceful autumn stillness, puts them in strong contrast. Julia's letter is full of references to "little dinner parties", Molyneux coming to buy Lawrence's pictures, visits to his flat at Claridge's, unconsciously I think wanting to make us feel we are missing much of the point of life. I'm not sure whether I do feel it or not. One is alive in one way in the country, in quite another in the jostle of London life. Probably the best thing is to take alternate doses of each.

Yesterday, after a morning's quartet playing, the two old Padels spent the day here, bringing with them a circular chess board, copied (they *say*) from one invented by Tamerlane! Mrs. P. and R. had a game on it. Took Saxon to the station and stamped about trying to keep warm in the piercingly cold morning mist. We were sad to see him go. "The loneliest man in the world," said R.

*November 1st*

I opened a letter from Bunny at breakfast and out fell a bombshell. "I am extremely anxious," he wrote, "that Angelica and the baby should be out of London during the next few weeks. I am writing to ask if it would be possible for them to come to Ham Spray for the latter part of November. It is almost the only place to which I could persuade her to go without me. I would not write this letter, which I do without her knowledge, if I had not a reason (call it a hunch) which I am not able to tell her or discuss at present. All I can say is that I should be much happier if they were outside London during a few weeks: it may be absolutely unnecessary, but the sight of these soft little creatures makes one timorous."

This piece of news, and its implications, exploded very slowly into a soft but ever-widening circle of detonations in my brain. A moment's thought made it clear that Bunny was acting on secret information and it might get him into serious trouble if his indiscretion became known. Then came the thought: had he the right to hand on this piece of explosive to me, to load me up with gun-powder and then say: Don't go off. Or not even to say it, but leave me to guess it. For, of course, if he

172

has some inside information that London is destined to suffer some appalling fate during certain fast-approaching weeks, I should *like* to pass it on to everyone living there whom I love and who could possibly get away. Janetta first and foremost. Damn it all, we aren't playing this beastly war game of Bunny's. Why should we be forced to obey its rules, and not put danger and unhappiness to friends first? Yet Bunny is also a friend, and his danger and unhappiness also has to be considered.

Julia and Lawrence were staying the weekend, and I had read Bunny's letter aloud at the breakfast table before I realised its full significance. They reacted violently. Julia at once began to plan to leave London during the danger period, very naturally. Lawrence said that she must certainly go if she wanted, but he wouldn't dream of it. If his friends were in for an unpleasant experience he wanted io share it. All day long the arguments went on, the ripples from Bunny's letter spreading wider and wider. In the afternoon I wrote to him saying we should be delighted to have Angelica and the baby for as long as they liked.

As we sat over our various activities this evening all the lights went out all over the house. Lawrence had been listening to Beethoven's C sharp minor quartet on the gramophone, and the sudden extinction of the music was more startling than the stoppage of light. I fetched candles and put them in pots round the room, and the rest of us went on with our activities in little pools of light — Julia reading a book, R. and Burgo playing draughts.

*November 2nd*

After leaving Lawrence and Julia at the station, I bought a paper, and the first thing I saw was that a German plane had crashed into Inkpen beacon last night. So that was what fused the lights! It seems odd that just when we had been considering London's peril enemy bombers had been hovering near. Audrey Bonham-Carter saw the crash as she was walking home. There was a huge blaze, and a lot of people from Inkpen hurried to the spot. One of them said he "found himself falling over a bomb". The bomb-load was scattered over the Downs, unexploded; the crew were all dead, two — including the pilot — having been shot through the head.

*November 3rd*

London for the day. I went straight to 41 Gordon Square, where I found Angelica lying in bed cutting up oranges for marmalade. She seemed very pleased at the idea of coming to Ham Spray, but also to realise the awkwardness to us in being let in to the secret of Bunny's

173

"hunch". I didn't tell Bunny, who arrived later, that Julia and Lawrence were in on it. He took that risk in writing as he did, and I can do no more except beg them to be discreet. He said that subsequent events had made him think the danger more remote: "Other people didn't take it so seriously and it was that that alarmed me. Now I think they do, and measures are being taken which may stop it altogether." What IT can be is never hinted at. When Angelica and I were alone together she said she couldn't guess either, but from Bunny's expression when he talked about it she thought it must be something absolutely horrible. The gutter press has been raising a scare about German plans to shell London with huge guns embedded in the cliffs of France.

Lunched at the Ivy with Clive and Raymond, who had a lot to say about these rumours. R. suggested that at that distance the shell could only be very small and the life of the guns very short. "Oh no," said Raymond, "these are to be rocket shells, and they will be much bigger than anything London has yet been subjected to; each one can do enormous damage." It all sounds too Wellsian and fantastic to believe.

*November 19th*

Judy Hubback brought her husband David to dinner; he's back on leave from Sicily. I noticed a reluctance in both of them to plunge below superficialities, or discuss how the war affected those taking part in it. R. says that is the species of coma war produces, and reminded him of his own experiences — the dazed state of trance, and the *modus vivendi* reached only by keeping to a neutral unserious level.

The Garnetts are not coming after all, but going to Charleston, why I don't know. We got an amusing letter from Lawrence on the subject of Bunny's hunch (which has become "the rabbit hutch"): "Perhaps tonight it will come clattering or gliding, rocketting, dripping or whatever it is going to do, out of the sky. Meanwhile I am beginning to suspect that the Hutch is everyone's Hutch. The paper has a column about it every day, and today admitted that it was causing widespread comment, which I translate as 'universal alarm'. I am not at all sure that there isn't a panic on. John Davenport, that well-oiled weathercock, suddenly announced he was going away for three weeks' holiday, and was gone within the hour."

The whole subject has assumed a grotesque appearance which makes it hard to believe anything will come of it all. If it does, our jokes will look pretty silly.

Clive writes, "I sympathise with Fredegond Shove,[1] who hasn't

[1] Poetess; published by the Hogarth Press.

spoken to Maynard for years, but — finding herself sitting behind him at the Cambridge Theatre — leant forward and said, 'You're the only person who has any power; can't you do something to stop this terrible war?' "

*November 25th*

Two days running there has been news of huge raids (the "biggest yet") on Berlin, five times as heavy as the heaviest on London. It's a suffocating thought. We shall go on and on, R. thinks, till nothing is left. Bunny probably knew of these ahead and thought the Germans would retaliate with their famous "rocket-gun". I rang up Janetta, who is due on Friday with Kenneth and the baby, suggesting she comes at once in case of possible reprisals for our raids. Thus I have now in effect passed on Bunny's warning without giving him away. Reports continue to come in of the ghastly destruction our two monster raids have caused. The fires are still burning and the cloud of smoke "has reached the shores of Sweden. The raids won't stop until the heart of Nazi Germany has ceased to beat".

Frenzy rages in some quarters because the Mosleys have been let out of prison. As neither R. nor I accept the principle that people should ever be shut up for their principles or without trial, the question doesn't arise for us.

*November 27th*

Janetta and family are here. A good deal of rocket-bomb talk last night. Kenneth, who is an A.R.P. doctor, was told that none of them was to leave London for the present, cancelling a job in Yorkshire he had been promised, in view of a "possible secret weapon attack on London".

How interminable the war seems! Sometimes I feel I'm hardly more tired of the war itself than I am of my own abhorrence of it, ever with me like a bad taste or hole in a tooth.

I am reading Trevelyan's *Garibaldi*, always cracked up as a moving and exciting book, yet I find it chiefly inspires me with amazement at the frivolity of this horrible game of war, with its barbarous rules and disregard for human life, the unmerited respect and blaze of glory accompanying any mention of it. Nor can I feel admiration for Garibaldi himself — a simple-minded, rather stupid, overgrown boy-scout. The ideal of manliness needs refurbishing and bringing up to date. At present it belongs to the caveman era, and in spite of all progress in science and education young men can only show they *are* men by hurtling through the air or under the sea to hunt down and kill their fellows. Perhaps

175

that's why there are so many homosexuals nowadays. Sensitive and intelligent males, to whom this idea is secretly repugnant, feel they cannot measure up to it, and decide to be females instead.

R. and I walked down to Inkpen in the dark to fetch Burgo from a tea-party. The stars came out one by one and a Christmas-card moon sailed over the Downs. Then a forest of searchlights sprang up and fingered the sky.

1944

*January 20th*

This diary has very little chance of existence these days. I thought I was hard-working before, but ever since Boxing Day I've done the entire work of the house, Mrs. M. having been ill and run down, and most unlikely to return. Also we all spent the last fortnight having 'flu, one after another. Are we to continue life as it is — possible only so long as we have hardly any visitors — or what? The problem is in the offing, but we don't talk about it much. Barring, in my case, one or two moments when I felt I couldn't bear my days being entirely filled with thoughtless chores any longer, I know perfectly well that I can, and I even manage better than I used; but sometimes I think of our existence in terms of struggling across the Atlantic in an open boat, or lost in the desert in a small car with hardly any food. Don't be ridiculous, I hear a voice say, you have a comfortable house, a productive kitchen garden, and your husband and child with you. Look at what most people have to put up with!

Music is my great solace: quartets every week, and the other day our company was swollen to an octet — an occasion I looked forward to and thought about afterwards much as I used in my youth to think of a ball or party. I found it very exciting to be in a small room with so many instruments at once, and in danger of stumbling over 'cellos and violas if one moved.

*February 2nd*

We go on as before, but at breakfast the other day there was a near row between R. and me because I read the *New Statesman* at breakfast out of sheer mental weariness. He exploded, and said that I was always doing this sort of thing nowadays, and not paying any attention to him. I felt a good deal of sympathy with him, but could only say, "Well, if you want me to remain a human being you must find me a 'help'." He went off at once on his bicycle to look for one, unsuccessfully I fear.[1]

*February 10th*

Slowly sinking into the bog, down and down. Dog-tired every evening, I doze on the sofa. Up to bed and sleep lightly, toss and turn, and have visions of dirty plates and vegetables waiting to be peeled. Down in the morning bung-eyed, to see the ancient red bricks of the kitchen floor getting blacker and blacker.

[1] In extenuation of this collapse, I must note that we had at this time no washing-up machine, clothes-washing machine or vacuum cleaner.

However, yesterday, a miracle, a new figure turned up. Honest brown eyes behind specs, strangely fitting false teeth. What joy, what comfort!

As the pressure eases off, the outer world gradually penetrates my consciousness, as it does when coming round after an anaesthetic. At first I feel greedy for it, drink in the sights and sounds so long crowded out, welcome the few puny thoughts that steal into my mind, and eagerly snatch up books and papers, or listen to the wireless to catch the ideas of others. Then I bang my head on the stone wall of reality — the WAR. All England is on tenterhooks waiting for the Second Front; Japanese atrocities are retailed with relish; the miners are in a perpetual state of strike, colonels are still thundering in *The Times* about "The cowardly, dastardly and brutal entry of Italy into the War", assuming of course that the entry of all the Allies into the war was courageous, altruistic and noble. There is great agitation about the possible danger to Rome, which is getting ever nearer the battle zone. Are its ancient monuments worth the life of a single soldier? "Not if it's *my* son," cries one. "My son shan't die for any old building." (Very natural, but you seem to be prepared for him to die in the useless effort to capture a small hill and kill a few Germans.) If only people would realise that their son's dying and killing other people's sons wasn't going to benefit humanity in any way, but almost certainly the reverse. What good did the First World War do?

*February 22nd*

We have had Angelica for a week, with her baby, Amaryllis. She is a delightful companion and has restored our morale, making life in some magical way more exciting. The cold was appalling throughout her visit, and we went about rubbing blue hands together, and with chattering teeth. Cold and music were the chief features of her stay. She played the violin to my piano and vice versa; we played the Bach Double Concerto, and she sang to my accompaniment. We even had a session at the Padels, Angelica playing the piano in the Schumann quintet. Mr. Padel was instantly bowled over by Angelica, and although it was snowing and Mrs. Padel ill in bed, he insisted on bicycling over next day in his tweed deer-stalker to hear her sing. Next evening the telephone rang: "*Could* I have a word with Mrs. Garnett?" She came back giggling, for he had nothing to say except that he hoped to see her again and "What did she think of Epstein?" I've never seen such a case of love at first sight.

This last week scattered raids on London have suddenly intensified into something approaching the old Blitz. The other night I was woken by deep subterranean rumblings which shook the house. "An earthquake," I thought, for it seemed outside all previous experience, but realised it was big guns. It was followed by other "old-fashioned noises" and then the All Clear. For several days after this the children have been picking up strips of shiny black paper in the fields. It seems they are dropped by German planes to confuse our radio location.

### February 23rd

Rose at dawn and travelled to London with Angelica and the baby. Lunch with Clive, Raymond, Angelica and Bunny at the Ivy – oysters, chicken (old hen rather) and Algerian wine. Bunny and Raymond said last night had been even noisier than the ones before, and the bombs more widely scattered. Their faces bore visible signs of their having been through some shattering experience, and we felt as though we were visiting the front line. We were to meet Boris and Maroussa at the Great Western Hotel, Paddington, but on arriving there we found the door boarded up and two eager-looking page-boys who told us no-one could go in: "Blitzed Sunday night", so we went to a teashop nearby. Maroussa was very cantankerous with Boris, obviously in a state of nerves, and said the raids had been horrible, and that she could do nothing but sit with her head in her hands while they were going on. Yet she is loth to leave London, even for a day, fearing invasion or thefts from their flat.

### February 26th to 28th

Julia and Lawrence's long-postponed visit. The fiendish cold unluckily continued and put Julia to a severe test. She wore her false leopard-skin jacket and two pairs of woollen gloves even at meal times. When we apologised for Ham Spray being such a difficult house to heat, she replied, "Well, if it was mine I should have to sell it," thus offending R. greatly. They were both heroic in the help they gave with bed-making and washing-up, and in Julia's case she hates it so much that it *is* heroism. When I said I didn't want any help with the cooking, indeed would rather do it alone, she said, "Ah yes, I understand and respect that," in a voice of great relief. This week of bad air-raids has been a horrible strain on her in ways I recognize: a rather glazed expression, lack of interest in other people, letting her appearance get quite extraordinary, while criticizing others for not being "elegant" enough. Of all the numerous facets of Julia's complex character, her unselfconscious and eccentric side is the one I'm personally fondest of.

Boris and Maroussa. Maroussa thawed, and shook off her irrational fears. She slept well and relaxed, and talked to me with horror of the state she found herself in. She feels mentally tensed up the whole time to ward off the shock of the next raid. Most of their studio has been made unusable by bombing, and she and Boris crouch miserably in one room, listening all day to broadcasts from Moscow. Boris has no job now, and is disgruntled by being treated as an alien who has to get a police permit to come down here for a few days.

From the moment of their arrival on Hungerford Station, when Boris enfolded R. in a bear's hug and kissed him on both cheeks, astonishing the other travellers, their visit was a delight. They are both so appreciative and responsive that one wants to do everything possible for their happiness and comfort. Maroussa had breakfast in bed every day and they went away laden with fruit and vegetables. Leaving them at the station, we drove on to visit the Bomfords, where we found Gamel. "Gerald sends you his love," she said; and I felt a dart of anger at this *geste arbitraire*, which I suppose in his own eyes transforms his unconquerable hostility to R. into something more compatible with his own view of himself.

*March 16th to April 3rd*

Janetta and Nicolette with us for nearly three weeks. Apart from the hovering shadow of the Second Front, this was a lively and stimulating time. The weather was lovely; Nicolette slept in the garden, crawled all over the lawn and grew fatter, browner and more energetic before our eyes. Kenneth came down for a day or two, and told us he had it on the word of a General on the Staff that the Second Front would be launched that night. I foolishly believed it, and lay awake for hours listening to every aeroplane, expecting I know not what. Nothing. This is not the only night I have done this, only to wake to a perfect rustic stillness which makes the very existence of the wretched "Front" seem an impossibility.

Janetta described her horror of the raids all too vividly. She is oppressed all day by the expectation of the siren going, and when it does it is like a stretcher arriving for someone waiting for an operation.

*April 5th*

Burgo and I to lunch with some Inkpen ladies. Mrs. C. was a brassy conventional snob, boastful of the number of V.C.s she knew, of servants her mother kept, and of near relations she had in the thickest danger. None the less I was appalled when she said, "How are we to prepare our children to enjoy the next war?" F. (scarlet in the face with indignation): "Well, I must say I hope they *won't*. I can't think of anything less desirable." Mrs. C.: "Oh, but many of them do enjoy it." Our hostess: "But, Mrs. Partridge, what are we to do? It's better than that they shouldn't be able to stand it, like Philip." (Her son, who has had a nervous breakdown and left the Navy.) F.: "Able to *stand* it perhaps, but not enjoy it." Mrs. C.: "It's such a pity my brothers are out of it all in Ireland all this time." Our hostess: "I think you ought to be very glad. They are your brothers you know." Mrs. C.: "Yes, but then they're tough — it's such a *waste*."

I came away boiling and fuming and boiled and fumed all the afternoon.


*April 15th*


To lunch with Alec and Frances Penrose. There we met a very tall, dark American officer with enormously long black eyelashes, a Professor of Philosophy at Harvard in private life. We talked about the future of Europe after the war. No-one made any attempt to sustain a belief in the "war to end war", but the question was how the next alignment would take place. How would sides be picked when the next match began? Russia and Germany? Germany and the Anglo-Saxons? The American declared he had no hopes for the future peace of the world and I was amazed that he could bring himself to take part in the present horror, if he assumed it was paving the way for the next.

From time to time R. and I express to one another the constant feeling we have (which like permanent toothache hardly seems worth mentioning) of *isolation* in a mad world. Isolation of the sane, we feel — yet it's daunting to accept that nearly everyone else is mad.

In Hungerford the Tutti men were going their annual rounds, but far more attention was being given to the Second Front. Mr. Pike the shoemaker said: "Any day now." Mr. Barnard the grocer thought it might have started already and waved aside my enquiry whether my sausages had come. "Not come through," he said with glee. "Things won't, ye know. Not now. People don't understand that though; all they think about is getting oranges and silk stockings." Even when I found the sausages and prepared to carry them away, he preferred to ignore the fact. "No. Things won't get through now. Not *now* they won't."

Bunny and Angelica have taken a furnished villa at Oxted, next to old Mrs. Garnett, and they invited us all three for the weekend. It was a very ugly yellow brick castellated box, built by two suffragette lady doctors, and gazing out onto what at first sight seems an extremely secluded rustic English scene. A closer look, and one observes other dwellings similarly peering out, discreetly enough, as if anxious not to spoil each other's view. The side of the wooded hill is in fact thickly populated, for in a number of little houses – some homely, some arty-crafty, some mere shacks roofed with black tar – there lives a colony of intensely lively old ladies: widows of Persian professors, Russian revolutionaries, and Constance Garnett herself. They spend their time gardening away besottedly, tottering round to see each other, peering out of beady inquisitive eyes at any stranger, keeping a lot of cats. Bunny's mother is not a very sociable person though full of charm. She lives in a world of her own thoughts, and the pumpkins she grows in her garden are probably as important to her as human beings. but she looks out at stray visitors like ourselves with mild blue eyes, in which intelligence and humour are combined, through the thickest spectacles I ever saw. I suppose she has almost blinded herself with years and years of translating Russian masterpieces for a mere pittance.

The weekend passed drowsily. The weather was hot, and Bunny's voice was muted as he talked away softly about bees and pruning fruit trees, while Angelica presided somewhat silently. General subjects never arose; the war might not have existed and there were no newspapers in evidence. Yet they often get air-raids, and they took us to see where a stick of incendiary bombs had fallen not long ago, unopened and all in one place in their woods. We brushed our way through blue-bells and saplings, and then – what a strange sight! – there were two or three great yawning chasms lined with raw, yellow earth. Nature, in the form of moschatels, anemones and primroses, came right to the edge of the ugly gashes man's ingenuity had made and filled with tortured masses of twisted metal, crumpled like balls of paper in a giant's hand, and tubular pieces of aluminium. Great clods of clay had been hurled far and wide among the spring flowers and trees.

One evening Bunny read us a delightful paper on Dorothy Edwards written for the Memoir Club. But I felt lost and at sea, as if my identity would only return when I was back at dear Ham Spray. Perhaps I'm not fit to leave home any more. Ham Spray, resounding with shouted arguments and laughter, and rushings up and down stairs and general hullabaloo, seems a centre of life compared to this murmurous bumble bees' nest.

These few days back at Ham Spray have confirmed my feeling that whatever else it is – ramshackle, not very warm, untidy – it is, at times at least, a centre of life.

Allen Lane has for some unexplained reason asked me to write a book on wild flowers, to be illustrated by an artist called Richard Chopping. He came to do a few days' preparatory work on it, and in an instant a thousand practical questions were buzzing round our heads like a cloud of mosquitoes. We sat up till the small hours going over our plans, and then my head was too full of plant-names to sleep. Richard endeared himself greatly to both R. and me. He is, I think, a very sweet character – affectionate, gentle, kind and inquisitive. Tall and good-looking with rather slavonic features, he is quite remarkably *clean*. We were much impressed by the way he went off and washed his socks every day and hung them on the line. Meanwhile I managed to dash off for an afternoon of quartets, Eardley came for a night, and the Tidcombe boys came over with a pasque-flower to show us for our book.

All last night we were kept awake by extraordinary noises – of low-flying aeroplanes followed by loud explosions which shook the house. I suppose they were of enemy origin as the siren had gone. Before going to bed we saw a red flush waxing and waning over the Downs, and a flight of aeroplanes flying north. Other green and red lights were moving everywhere. But by day, too, a new phenomenon has begun – bangs of a shattering loudness burst from time to time on our ears without any warning, making one give a huge jump like a baby when a door is slammed and spill anything one happens to be holding. Audrey Bonham-Carter says that they are so loud at Inkpen that their teeth rattle in their heads, but the local Colonel tells her this will all stop when the Second Front begins. It is degrading to be waiting day in and day out for something so horrific.

Hester has been here for two nights. The days passed in ceaseless talk, and though much of it was very amusing I sometimes longed to switch it off like the wireless. She is a very good mimic and had lots of stories about the negroes she serves at her canteen. One said to her sadly, "De Red Cross dun do *nothing* for de soldiers. Dey dun give us *no* nice ladies. De ladies dey gives us is *bad*."

Since then our hearts have been warmed to the cockles by a visit from Raymond. How we both enjoy having him here – and in spite of our standard of comfort not measuring up to his I really believe he enjoys being here too. He had just come back from five weeks lecturing in North Africa, travelling out in a military aeroplane, unable to see out or sleep, on a seat made of aluminium scoops. He described enthusiasm for England and cries of *"Vive l'Angleterre"*, principally based − he thought − on a reverse feeling towards the Americans: *"Ils sont des barbares."*

### June 2nd to 6th

We have all three been for these last days at dear old Well Farm, the Cornishes in Devon. When I came down to breakfast this morning R. was smiling strangely. "Mrs. Cornish says it's on the wireless that the Invasion has started." How to describe the effect of this announcement, coming after so long a wait, and so differently from the myriad ways I had imagined it? Something seemed to turn over inside me and then re-balance. There I was, just as before and yet not the same. Something from outside had entered in and become part of me.

We asked if we might listen to the nine o'clock news in the kitchen and found three chairs drawn up in front of the wireless and an atmosphere of church reigning. One half-witted twin was shooed away. Mrs. Cornish knitted peacefully. An elderly woman with bright eyes under a flat hat sat on the sofa. Then in a solemn hush the King stammered forth his banal generalities in which God as usual figured largely. The long-planned invasion had begun early this morning, with gliders, parachutists, "ducks" and troops streaming across the Channel and landing on the Normandy coast between Cherbourg and Le Havre. Difficulty and losses were far less than expected. So far so good. I could hardly draw a deep breath throughout the broadcast, and looked at the tossing trees outside the window with a sudden stab of realization that our fate now hangs in the balance, as individuals and as a nation. And this, here and now, is what we have expected and waited for with such a horrible mixture of dread and longing, for months.

### July 3rd

Of course, as soon as the war came alive again it became impossible to write, and write I have not for three dramatic weeks. While at Well Farm we listened each day to the progress of our armies in France. It was extraordinary how soon the whole position was assimilated into one's being, and ceased producing those "dentist's pains" and pangs of anxiety and hope of the first day. Now, three weeks later, it is clear that the Invasion has been a success and less costly than expected. Meanwhile the Russians have started a fresh onslaught on the Eastern front, and are hurling the Germans back fast. They are in retreat in Italy. We bomb them incessantly. What prevents them from collapsing utterly? The fact is that I quite soberly feel they may do so at any moment. But there is one thing I haven't mentioned, and that a most unpleasant one — the doodle-bug.

The day after we reached Ham Spray we were rung up by friends to say that they had heard from London that they were being attacked all day by wireless-controlled pilotless aircraft! Could anything be more Wellsian? Since then these pilotless planes, facetiously christened doodle-bugs, have been the chief topic of conversation. Horror falls on some. Others are exempt, for the range of these monsters seems to be strictly limited, and we — thank heavens — are just outside it. But "evacuees" begin again, and Ham has many new faces in it. The worst of this death-watch beetle is that it goes on day and night; there is no respite from it.

I rang up Janetta, to ask if she would like to bring Nicolette down. "As a matter of fact I've hardly noticed it; I slept all last night."

"What's it like?" I asked. "Very noisy?"

"Well, there certainly are some rather odd noises. But so far I don't mind it much. There was one half an hour ago."

Soon after this came Julia, our first doodle-bug refugee; also Saxon on ten days' sick leave, arriving covered in dust from a doodle-bug which had landed between Percy Street and Tottenham Court Road just as he was leaving for the station. It blew in some of his windows and filled his rooms with black oily smoke.

"Did it make a tremendous explosion?" we asked.

"No. I didn't hear anything. But then I didn't hear *much* when that land-mine fell in Great James Street."

People vary greatly in their reactions. Some dislike it more than ordinary bombing "because it's uncanny", or for such curious reasons as "because you can't do anything to it" or "because it's hardly human." Others less, "because it isn't looking for me", is "random and aimless", and even "helpless to defend itself". Everyone jokes about it unceasingly, but in a somewhat horrified way. Saxon suddenly burst out, "I can't think why everyone wants to talk so much about this doodle-bug." (I can think of several reasons.) An article in the *New Statesman* described English villagers typically referring to it as a "chap" — "and then I looked up and there was another chap coming along".

The object now emerges as a robot plane about twenty-five feet long, projected from a concrete base in France; it flies low and with considerable noise and has a light in its tail. When the light goes out and the noise stops the doodle-bug is about to descend and everyone is advised

187

to take cover instantly. Other doodle-buggiana: a letter from Dorking: "Have you seen these damn things? I couldn't sleep for curiosity about them, but now I'm satisfied, and have seen several at night and one very close here by day. It flew just over us and crashed into Leith Hill. It was slim and elegant and going with tremendous purpose, like those games where you make a dash for 'home' when the 'he' is turned the other way. There seem the hell of a lot of them, and they've certainly got a fascination that raiders never had." Julia on arrival from London: "I've not heard any good of them so far." Saxon, in a letter: "The All Clear went as I was in the taxi from Paddington, an alert as I walked to Dr. Gould's, and others most of the day. Barbara [Bagenal] was with me in my flat, marking some clothes, when a 'chap' whistled overhead and came down by the Whitfield Memorial Chapel. Some few minutes later we heard another arrive and saw the smoke — apparently it hit the Regent Palace Hotel. Barbara and I went to the National Gallery; the picture 'on view' for the time is Goya's portrait of Dr. Peral. Against the wall opposite him sits an attendant. When three bells go he takes the Goya downstairs and when one goes he brings it back again. He must have walked quite a long way today." R. is much struck by this last fact and thinks it ought to be put on record. For more than a week it has rained steadily from heavy grey clouds. If it hadn't been for this there would have been fewer doodle-bugs. As it is our fighters have shot down seventy-five per cent of them.

Old Mrs. Garnett's little house at Oxted appears to be on the doodle-bug path to London, and they were so frequent that Bunny has sent Angelica and the baby to Charleston. As for Constance herself, he has bought her a helmet which she keeps beside her while weeding her flower-beds.

There's something obsessional about this new development, which I'm well aware of myself. Anything may happen in this war now, is the feeling, and meanwhile we prepare for the return of refugees. Janetta and Nicolette are expected any day, for six months, while Kenneth is in Cairo.

Last weeks we took Burgo to do his entrance exam. to Newbury Grammar School. We all felt anxious, and Burgo broke into last-minute wails and said he could not, would not go. Then he went to the lavatory and came out having pulled himself together: "I'm not going to be silly any more. But just tell me this, when you put up your hand do you do it sitting or standing?" When we called for him afterwards he was bouncing and radiant, and had thoroughly enjoyed himself.

We have had nearly six-weeks of refugee-life and I cannot say we have stood it well. Old scars are reopened and old irritations begin to grumble. We are most fortunate in our refugees but I find I long for that delicious flump of relaxation between spells of working "all out". At breakfast today Julia declared, with the obvious intention of making me feel I had nothing to complain about: "At Swallowcliffe I did all the cooking and housework for three years." (She had forgotten she had a full-time resident maid, and only Tommy[1] and herself in a small cottage. Thus petty have I become.) Our idea of pleasure is now to flop somewhere, away from our refugees. Why is this? For I'm very fond of all three and so is R.

The doodble-bug situation is no better than before. There has been an official evacuation of children from London, and an unofficial one of everyone else who can get away. Country rooms and pubs are crammed.

Richard Chopping and I were summoned to meet our publisher, Allen Lane, at the Carringtons for tea. Delicious cakes on a table on the lawn, bees buzzing and flowers blooming in a summery peaceful hum. Then the telephone rang and it was Lane, saying that the doodle-bugs had kept them up all night and were falling round them still and he couldn't leave his wife, who is pregnant.

Clive writes, "The 'chaps' are brought down round Charleston in great profusion; they set up the most fiendish din imaginable when they come at all near, and combined with the guns and screaming planes scare the natives considerably."

The other morning at breakfast Julia described a loud noise she had heard in the night. "It shook the house till I thought it would fall down," she said. "I'm sure it was a doodle-bug." No-one else has heard it.

"Pooh!" said R. "Probably a door banging or a carthorse stamping."

But it actually *was* a doodle-bug, which had fallen on Inkpen Beacon, just a mile from this house. Coombe Manor, the same distance in another direction, had its windows broken. The Penroses, six miles off, were startled out of their beds. The Tidcombe Boys, eight miles off, got up and made tea.

A few days later we went to look at the crater; a deep but unimpressive cavity in the clayey earth of the field. People were streaming up to look at it, grinning vaguely and saying, "There isn't much to see, is there?" Sheepishness is one of the odd by-products of the war, I've noticed.

[1] Stephen Tomlin, Julia's first husband.

The last entry seems to have been written in a phase of temporary insanity and I re-read it with amazement. The exacerbation produced by refugees is like an inflammatory disease, growing out of all proportion to its original cause and then continuing to exist on its own. It disappears as suddenly as the measles, and one wakes one day cool and without spots. And why can't one just think of them as *visitors* for heaven's sake?

Two days ago our neighbour, Colonel Boord, arrived at the door, very affable. We share the water tank over our garage with the dairy. "Would we be so kind as to go easy on the water, as two thousand gallons had mysteriously disappeared in the night."

"Good gracious!" we said, and added with perfect truth that we hadn't taken a drop.

R. asked: "Do you mean you don't want us to take any?"

"Oh no, of course not, but just go easy."

Yesterday there was a violent explosion – no doodle-bug this time. Nearly all of us happened to be in the drive, except Julia who was leaning out of her bedroom window, when Boord arrived from the farm purple and screaming, and quite beside himself. "Look here, Partridge, I've cut your water-pipe for you! You really are a *bloody* man." He and R. then disappeared into the back regions, while Julia remarked distinctly from above: "The man's barmy." I followed, thinking they might come to blows, and saw Boord shake his fist in R.'s face and say, "I'd like to bash your face in, and if I did the whole county would be pleased. I know all about your history. I know you wouldn't join the Home Guard." R.'s face had become as pale as Boord's was purple; he merely said, eyeing another figure skulking in the background, "Major Huth[1], I give you six months' notice to remove your tank from my garage." Legally speaking, the tank was R.'s but Major Huth paid £5 for it, on condition that he allowed R. to draw what water he wanted for the garden. It was for watering our tomatoes, which need it just as much as Huth's cows, that the pipe was now being used. Should the water not be available Huth has to move the tank and pipes. All this left us in a fine stew and R. wrote off to Craig [Macfarlane] at once.

This morning, Sunday, no milk was delivered. So this is Huth's reply. He knows no-one can get milk without registering in Marlborough, so he cuts it off without notice. We have fixed up with an Inkpen farmer, but we must register first and then we will only get half as much as before. At first I felt in despair; milk has been our life-line. It means

---

[1] The owner of the farm, and Boord's father-in-law.

butter (as we have a hand churn), milk puddings and plenty for Burgo to drink, not to mention our refugee baby (Nicolette). But on the whole I'm relieved at not being dependent on odious Huth.

*August 14th*

Milk-water crisis continues. It seems that two thousand gallons has gone again. Evidently he has a leak somewhere in his bloody system. All the cottages who draw their water from his supply (not our tank which only serves the dairy) are bone-dry and fetching water in buckets, poor things. Of course we no longer take a drop; our own well is deep enough for most of our needs. Meanwhile Vic the cowman reports that Huth is swearing every sort of vengeance. Craig telephoned to say that our position is better than we thought; Huth having broken the contract the tank at once becomes our property. And Boord had legally committed an assault. R. is all for peace, however, and has written a temperate but firm letter to Huth.

This private war has not blotted out the public one, which is suddenly going incredibly well. This evening terrific news: "The Battle of Normandy is won," shouts the wireless. "The Germans can put up no effective resistance." It really looks as if it might be over in months if not *weeks.*

*August 23rd*

Burgo has been accepted by the Newbury Grammar School, and today we took him to see his future headmaster, packing into the car with a lot of baskets of fruit and vegetables. We liked Mr. Starr and were cheered up by the interview; for one thing it was clear Burgo had passed easily, and on his merits. Lunched at the Chequers Inn, and were aware that the news was just starting in the Lounge. Then we heard the Marseillaise. "Paris must have been retaken!" I said. And so it had. Here is a piece of news that brings nothing but pleasure. An old dog of a Lesbian, dressed as a man, with a stock and cropped grey hair, sat down beside us: "Glorious news, isn't it," she said, "and especially that the Free French did it themselves."

*August 24th*

R. and I lay in bed last night thinking and talking of nothing but the fall of Paris and the probability of peace soon. I woke feeling "I must get up — things are happening." Janetta said she had been far to excited to sleep, and when I took some eggs to Mrs. Mills, the baker's wife, she said, "I couldn't sleep for thinking peace might come soon." So we all sit, like people in the waiting-room of a hospital while a life or death operation goes on . . .

In the evening James and Alix arrived, bringing with them as they always do a sense of immutability. Even their eccentricities are continuous. James had been talking to some Russian who said he knew all about the various German secret weapons — V.2, 3 and 4. Also we hear, as we often have before, that the War Office is taking V.2, the famous Rocket gun, extremely seriously, and is prepared to evacuate London on a much larger scale should it come into operation as they think it well may. According to James its range is so long that it can be fired from Cologne and still hit London, so that our capturing the north coast of France will make us no safer. In fact nothing will put us out of range except peace. It is a horrible thought, and I can't help feeling that Hitler might well let it off in one last mad Guy Fawkes explosion, even though he saw he was beaten. Miles, the aircraft designer, told Anthony West that there were some technical problems connected with the Rocket that the Germans had apparently not solved yet. He described our reconnaissance aircraft flying over the place where the doodle-bug was tried out, and observing the craters it made. Then one day a crater *eighty yards wide* was seen, and this was made by the rocket. Another rocket story is that the first one was sent off three weeks ago and has not come down yet, which is not quite as mad as it sounds — the theory is that if it goes too high it disintegrates. So — we are a mass of rumour and speculation.

Alix wanted to start an argument this evening about population, and how important it was to reduce it instead of increasing it. This is my favourite theory and I heartily agreed, which didn't prevent her going on with her attempts to convince me.

A good Alixism: "Really the things people say about Dried Household Milk are *quite* untrue. It's perfectly all right. The only thing it does taste slightly of is *plaster*."

A letter from Heywood asking if we have any of Lytton's books in Swedish for a new customer, a Swede, who is badly in need of something to read. He went to "Boompos" and was given a translation of *The Well of Loneliness*. "It is Tomboys", was his comment.

*August 25th*

Faith and Nicko Henderson bicycled over to tea, eaten on the lawn in deck-chairs. A rather gloomy conversation about education. James said all boarding-schools were awful, and he was dead against them. Alix and I discussed the eternal question: what is to be done with the Germans

192

after the war. Alix: "I think it will be a good thing if quite a lot are executed, and all the Gestapo, SS etc. are deported to a sort of Devil's Island and not allowed to reproduce themselves. After that, treat everyone else well, take no territory from them and give them the Sudetenland. I also think it might be a good plan to *force* them to make a lot of obsolete armaments, hopelessly old-fashioned dreadnoughts and so on, on the principle that if we thwart their desire to make weapons it will only make them crave all the more to do so."

From there we went on to the well-worn question whether the instincts of cruelty and aggression are increased or decreased by gratification. The desire for destruction is, I think, commoner in young males than females — one of the few advantages possessed by the latter. Could it possibly be converted into construction or other forms of activity, just as a child will stop idly cutting up paper or stuff if given something it likes doing? Or could the especially aggressive be employed in abattoirs or clearing building sites? I see I'm getting like Alix!

I've just been reading my diary during the Fall of France and comparing our feelings with those of today. I felt quite tremulous as I read of those awful days, more awful because we didn't fully realise the appalling danger we were in. And how irritated we were by poor M.A.M.'s optimism, which is shown to be more wildly unjustifiable than it even appeared at the time. Now only the Rocket gun looms over our heads.

*August 26th*

The lost summer came back today; the Downs emerged from pearly mists. Burgo and I weeded the front flower-beds, and then, beaten by the heat, I pulled a rug into the shade. But whatever one does just now, whatever one's eyes rest on, more than half one's mind is like a sponge soaked in thoughts of the approaching end of the war. What will peace be like? Alix confessed at lunch that she viewed the letting-up of restrictions with dread: "Just think of the appalling responsibility of having to *choose* how one's life is to be led!"

Still feeling hopelessly restless I got Burgo to walk up the Downs. He persisted in talking about death, burial and suicide, asking a lot of questions about all these subjects. How much had R. minded the deaths of Lytton and Carrington? In a trembling voice he said how much *he* had minded the death of M.A.M. and Rollo. He said, "It's particularly sad when young people die — as if a hammer got lost before it could hammer in any nails." As for suicide, he asked about the ways of doing it and I told him, but gave what I hoped were good reasons for *not* killing oneself. He replied: "Oh, I feel sure I shall commit suicide some-

193

how."[1] Then he talked about Alix and James: "I can't imagine them as parents. It's like Protestants and Catholics – some people are one and some the other." We were talking so hard that we saw little of our surroundings as we descended the Downs, pale with drought. As we approached Ham Spray garden there were two dark-clad figures drooping across the lawn, like suits of clothes on hangers – the Stracheys themselves.

Julia returned from telephoning Lawrence to say, "The *on dit* in London is that the rockets will begin on September 1st. I just tell you for your information."

*August 31st*

The spectre of GAS has again reared its ugly head. The wireless announced that Hitler was evidently determined to use it on England before he explodes, and that trains full of gas were arriving in Holland and Belgium. One was bombed and gas escaped, causing a panic. R. says he will certainly do it by means of doodle-bugs, which will be very disagreeable and frightening but bound to be a failure. However that may be, the thought of gas always takes the wind out of my sails and the breath from my lungs, though why it should be worse to be suffocated than burst into fragments it's hard to say. This hateful war has gone on five years today.

Dr. Boulton came today to give Nicky her diphtheria injection. He stood in the hall gloomily holding his little bag. "Are you very busy?" I asked, trying to make conversation. "Oh, *awful*! Never known a summer like it. There's a lot of this dysentery – and then people's hearts are giving out. They've had about all they can stand of the war. Most of them better out of it in my opinion. And the peace is going to be just as bad. Nothing but muddles." He jabbed poor Nicky's arm rather viciously and cleared off.

However, there's no break in the goods news – Dieppe, Verdun, Sedan. I catch myself thinking what sort of covers to put on the chairs. (As they have needed the sacrifice of clothes coupons they are pretty shabby.) The poor old house has weathered the storm somehow, but she badly needs a coat of paint.

We bicycled to the Downs beyond Oxenwood to meet Craig and Elspeth [Macfarlane]. While R. and Craig discussed the Boord situation Burgo and Mungo dug for buried treasure in a barrow, the breeze ruffling their hair and blowing a pinky brown flush into their cheeks; and Elspeth and I lay on the short turf spotted with eyebright and purple gentian, with the smooth seal-backs of grey stones rising out of it.

[1] He didn't, but died of a heart attack at 28.

Elspeth is living near the Guinnesses at Biddesden. The Victor Pasmores have been staying in the big house, and the servants nearly gave notice because they brought no pyjamas.

Tonight came the news that the English have entered Brussels, followed inevitably by the Brabançonne.

*September 5th*

At breakfast, while reading her post, Janetta's face became grey and set. Afterwards she showed me a bleak letter from her father saying that Rollo's body had been found in Tunisia, buried beside his aeroplane, and reburied in the military cemetery, with only a plain wooden cross, but "later it would be possible", etc., etc. I found it very difficult to know what to say to her or gauge the exact contents of her mind, and was ashamed, for there are few things more important than being able to interpret other people's thoughts.

Bicycled up Ham Hill to look for mushrooms. As always I enjoyed being on what seems like the domed roof of the world. A great wind was blowing but the sky was very blue, and everything looked its loveliest, with the stooked fields in the distance and long ribbons of grass bent by the wind and turquoise blue from the reflection of the sky. Mushrooms were few, and the field was full of swarthy black heifers with coarse faces and stocky bodies; compared to our lovely Guernseys they looked like Australian aborigines.

Julia was back, after a short visit to London for a spell of what she calls "things *mondaine*". We do not know for how long, nor does she seem to. She appears rather stupefied, and I think surprised to find fellow-pacifists following the progress of the war so closely. We greeted her with a certain stupefaction also, although there was friendliness on both sides.

During lunch a conversation arose about the menace of Religion in general — Julia seemed to feel especially strongly about Catholicism, though I can't say I make much distinction. Thence to what is called the "mystical experience" and what it consists in. We decided it was a flash of conviction that the Universe is One and Undivided, and that every part of it has significance when considered as part of the whole. R. described having something like it during the last war when he lay on a wire mattress in a French wood and watched the dawn. I don't think I have ever experienced it, nor do I understand how things like torture and atrocities fit into such a vision of the cosmos. From there we went on, inevitably, to the results of the war. As I talked and thought, the terrible conviction came over me that the *only* lesson that will be learned from it is that England should be armed and strong. The

195

armament race will, so I believe, begin at once. R. thinks there will be a reaction from this insular jingoism towards internationalism and individualism. I wish I could agree.

Returning from a bicycle ride I found Julia stretched on a rug on the lawn, odalisque style. I joined her, and we both soon became aware of a deep and distant reverberation, like the beating of a giant's pulse, which continued for about an hour and obviously came from a long way off. A *very* long way as it turned out, for this evening the wireless tells us that "today London and the South of England heard the guns in France".

In the evening Julia, Janetta and I sat round our wood fire, and a lively conversation sprang up and lasted until bed-time about love and the changing attitudes towards it. We questioned Janetta about the contemporary picture. She answered readily enough, calling up a (to me) dreary vision − of hopping into bed at the smallest provocation, no courtship, no gradual approach or Stendhalian crystallization, much unkindness, that utterly useless emotion jealousy, of course, and desperate attempts to preserve a cynical outlook. Perhaps no generation can find the attitude of another to this important subject entirely sympathetic. I wonder why such analytical discussions crop up so rarely these days. Is it just war-preoccupation, or can it be that as one grows older subjects of talk get worn out and threadbare with use? I don't believe that. The inveterate talker will descend into the grave still talking.

*September 16th*

There have been vague rumours of explosions in London. We could get nothing lucid out of Saxon on the telephone. "Oh yes, we get plenty of noises, you know." But a letter from Julia who rejoined Lawrence there five days ago says: "We are being shelled, believe it or not, by some sort of V.2 or other, but as we only receive one every two days it hardly seems to count. Neither the newspapers nor the wireless say anything about it, as you know, but as you can imagine London is buzzing with rumours. Altogether, since last Friday I gather there have been six of these mysterious explosions."

*September 21st*

Our private D-day was three days ago when Burgo, excited but fairly on the spot, dressed himself in full school kit, tie and cap and was whirled off to a new life at Newbury Grammar School, and returned *all right*, as far as we could see, and full of comments. However, it's now clear he is going through a considerable strain and needs a lot of support. It's not the other boys, but the rules and regulations, the terror of doing something wrong that obsesses him. "My essay was the worst in the whole school," he almost screamed at me today. I saw his book later and it was marked "17 out of 20. *Good*." R. is much better with him than I am. Every sight of me prompts a collapse, and "Please, *please* don't send me to this awful school." When he left him there this morning R. luckily ran into the headmaster and had a word with him. "I'm very glad you told me," said Mr. Starr. "I've been cracking down on him rather – I thought he was being rather superior and needed taking down a peg." I think he greatly erred in not spotting B.'s intense anxiety and lack of confidence.

He has a delightful distraction at weekends in his new friends, four Italian prisoners working on the farm; he takes them apples and figs, and talks to them in slow pidgin English accompanied by stiff courtly gestures.

*September 27th*

We have made a dramatic airborne landing at Arnhem in Holland, and for all the talk of "a heroic episode" and "it will live in History", we somehow sense that it hasn't gone as planned. One section has obviously been cut off and forced to withdraw. It is as if, playing a game with dice, we had reached a square saying "Go back to square 43". I'm quite surprised with what ease, as well of course as discouragement, I have given up the belief that the war is about to end, and accepted the fact that it may well last till Spring or later. In a sense I feel that this war or something indistinguishable from it will *always* be with us. I said so to R. in the bathroom this morning and at breakfast the theme continued. I had cooked it largely out of dried egg powder and dried milk powder. "So you've sunk to my level," said Janetta, who has, I'm afraid, been terribly depressed lately. And yet, though hopeless in the sense of being without much hope, I don't feel altogether sunk – I accept the future, come what may, but from a lower rung on the ladder.

*October 2nd*

A telephone call from David [Cecil] saying that he and Rachel could not come and stay today as Lord Salisbury is ill. I felt childishly disappointed at being deprived of the pleasure and stimulation I know their visit would have brought. We don't see very many intelligent, quick-minded people these days, and they both have a remarkable gift for immediately understanding one's lightest remark, and a responsiveness which I got a tantalising taste of even in my telephone conversa-

197

tion with David. Autumn has suddenly enveloped us, and instead of withdrawing life back into its roots, seems to induce a desire to expand and exchange warmth with other human beings — a feeling more appropriate to Spring.

Burgo, at home with a cold, is very happy making presents for his beloved Italian prisoners. He came running in wearing on each little finger a ring made out of a threepenny bit and set with tiny pieces of coloured glass. They were so tight we had to soap his hands to get them off.

Unexpectedly summoned to the Padels, who had a clarinettist staying with them. We played both the Brahms and the Mozart quintets. I have seldom got such pleasure from a sound I was helping to make. What exhilaration!

*October 25th*

Going in to the dining-room to lay the table just as it was growing dark, I looked out at our view — which I would exchange for no other in the world, which is always changing and never ceases delighting me. The sky had cleared and was a very pale blue, with half a silver moon hanging over the Downs. A white mist had magically materialised out of the ground, swathing the fields and in it the cows were ambling gently to and fro.

Listened tonight to a programme of music by the sons of Bach — all of it pretty. To end up with they played something by their father and the effect was devastating. R. said, "My God, what an awful father to have!"

*November 8th*

As it grows colder and colder, the war gets slower and slower. In fact it seems to have *stuck* — and we must face the fact that it will probably remain so until the spring. Yesterday a few large flakes of snow drifted out of the sky, and in the night a great gale got up and belaboured the house with rain which oozed in at all the tightly-shut windows. Indoors all the mirrors fog up and the walls drip and perspire — liquefaction outside and in, a dreary spectacle.

I'm reading two books at once, one about Milton, one about Beethoven. I went to bed feeling crushed and towered over in the darkness by these two massive figures, the thought of whose thwarted genius (one blind and the other deaf) I somehow found indigestible, like our present daily help's "turbulent" pastry, as R. calls it.

Or perhaps I was suffering from the knowledge that our pig is to be killed tomorrow.

An uneventful day in London – no alerts, no explosions, no V.2. Check up with my doctor, who looked surprised and detached when I spoke of my gloom about the state of the world. He could only see the universe in biological terms, he said, whereby our civilization could be interpreted as a small and trivial phase. Possibly human beings would stop playing their all-important part, and some other form of life – the white ants, for instance – would shortly come to the fore. I was quite fascinated by this unemotional, remote stream of words issuing from the lips of a small, oldish man, with a face like a distinguished French clown.

A plentiful dose of humanity at the Ivy, lunching with Clive, and drinking a lot.

A beautiful autumn day. I sat out on the verandah, where there was everything to please the senses and soothe the eternal inner sense of tragedy and decay. We had told ourselves so eagerly that we shouldn't have to go through another winter of war and now it is evident that we must. Though all arms seem to be raised to strike Germany her death-blow, that blow doesn't fall. In the park in front of me, the light shone white on the backs of wheeling rooks, locked in combat as they clattered out of the ilex with the noise of the opening of a wet umbrella.

Thought a good deal about the passing of youth. Here is Janetta in the full bloom of youth and beauty, able to make anyone's heart beat faster, yet does she seem to realize the advantages of her lot? Or its impermanence? Not a bit. But for many women the loss of the power to attract is a deadly tragedy, all the more disquieting because it is gradual and indefinite, even intermittent. It must be appalling not to be able to convert it into the pleasure of being liked, or interest in other people, or enjoyment of the attractiveness of the young. It's as impossible to regret the passing of youth all the time, as it is to grieve all the time for someone dead.

Burgo has been lately in a state of abnormal mental activity – I suppose the result of the stimulation of school. Or perhaps ideas were put into his head by his coming out top of his form in the I.Q. tests, with a mental age three years older than his true age. I have been hard put to it to answer all his questions. During his "rest" he compiled a life of Piers Gaveston from the *D.N.B.* By bedtime he had taken to *The Tempest.* "I'm looking up this 'blasphemious' in the dictionary." Then he had developed a passion for the gramophone and one day played it from two o'clock till bedtime without stopping — everything from Fred Astaire to Benjamin Britten.

*December 10th*

It is the dead season of the year and I have little desire to write in this diary. But we have been through anything but a dead period. In the weeks following our pig-killing numbers of visitors came to help eat it, and this sudden burst of hospitality livened us both up no end. Among others, we have had David and Rachel, Clive, Anthony West, Richard Chopping and Boris and Maroussa.

David and Rachel were charming and animated as ever — David undeterred by suffering from mushroom poisoning, talked entertainingly and without pause between hasty dashes from the room. Boris soused us in his usual richly-spiced soup of Russian flattery. He arrived wearing an elegant suit of lichen-green Irish tweed, the trousers tapered round his massive legs, and black Italian shoes with perfectly square toes, made of the softest leather. Next morning, however, he appeared for breakfast in a cowboy shirt in gorgeous red and green checks, and to remind us of its beauty he several times during the day lifted his pullover from over his stomach to reveal it, while an ineffable smile spread over his broad Slavonic features. He always likes to come into the kitchen and help with whatever is going on, ties an apron round his capaccious waist and sits patiently stirring a mayonnaise, enlivening it with some marvellous addition of his own. He has often directed our wine-bottling. Even cutting up parsley needed respectful attention, and he teases me for my sketchiness. He was in his element, therefore, chopping up head, trotters and entrails of our pig to make brawn, carefully seasoning them and adding herbs, and our brawns have never been so delicious. Then he played chess with Burgo as seriously as if he had been an adult; and though I'm sure he would deny being musical, he appeared to be irresistibly drawn to my piano, and sat for hours overflowing the music-stool, picking out with great delicacy of feeling but infinite slowness whatever music happened to be on the desk. He even insisted on accompanying me and my violin, and we crawled like snails through the slow movements of Handel and Corelli sonatas, Boris occasionally laughing softly to himself and refusing to agree that we shouldn't play because we weren't good enough.

His conversation is always a delight, with a brilliant choice of words, surprisingly modulated in tone. Some Borisisms: "There's no sense in marriage; I prefer *collages* – associations that everyone knows about." Of Picasso: "He is a clever crook, who cashed in by *épatant la bourgeoisie* – a *couturier*, a Dior, always thinking up new models." Asked what a certain lady was like, he thought for a moment and said, "Coarse." I remember once a very stupid woman saying at luncheon that she "simply detested cruelty, especially to animals and children", whereupon Boris smiled up at a corner of the ceiling and said in dulcet tones: "I rather like such cruelties as these." The only reference to the war I can remember him making on this visit was, "So low is our moral disintegration in this sixth year of the war that I hardly can get up from my bed in the morning, and it is only due to Maroussa's cruel determination of not bringing me the breakfast up that I come down moved by pangs of hunger. Somehow I float in idle contemplation of the world, waiting, waiting . . ."

And so do we all.

1945

Ham Spray and its inhabitants forge through this sixth war winter like an ice-breaking ship going through Arctic seas. Partly because we have been subjected to intense cold. First frost and ice, and now light snow, but with it stillness, exquisite pearly skies, and air sharp and intoxicating to the taste as one draws it into unwelcoming lungs. All this sparkle and beauty has helped to keep up our spirits pretty well. This morning we were all out in the snow — Janetta stalking about on Burgo's stilts with her long hair swinging; Nicky trotting purposefully about, a tiny Father Christmas, in her red siren suit frosted with snow; Burgo making snowballs.

A letter from Julia contained the news that a V.2 rocket had fallen horribly close to them, and only a few hundred yards from Alys Russell's house which is wrecked and has all the doors blown out. She writes: "We were woken by an *almighty* earthquake and thunderclap of thunderclaps, heaving at us out of nowhere; the sky blazed, the house was shaken like a medicine bottle, and splintering glass from windows all round the square (our own included) filled the air. When silence fell one just lay and waited for the walls to crumble and topple slowly over onto one, because it seemed they could not possibly have survived it."

*January 12th*

A lot of conversation all day. At lunch about whether the end ever justifies the means. R. believes emphatically that it does not, and this belief is woven into the very roots of his pacifism. "There are some actions," he said, "that one couldn't possibly perform for any end whatsoever — torture for instance." And it did indeed seem self-evident.[1] As for me, though I think generalizations are the breath of mental life, I'm inclined to mistrust moral ones unless they are treated as averages, like household accounts; the more particular a moral statement is, the more accurate, and the more general, the less so. And I can't subscribe to a summing-up like "Deliberately killing another human being is always wrong", because I believe in euthanasia for one thing.

*January 16th*

School begins again today. Not a trace of anxiety or resistance on B.'s part, how wonderful! And he returned in the evening all sweetness and

---

[1] I wonder what would have been his feelings had he been alive now, to see it (torture) an element in the training of almost every policeforce and army in the world.

desire to please. The other thing which has sent our morale soaring is that the Russians — whom we had been inclined to forget about — have suddenly launched an offensive on a massive scale, and it seems to be going better than our wildest dreams. Warsaw has fallen, and they are less than two hundred miles from Berlin.

This ice-cold life we lead in the middle of a white, snow-covered landscape, causes what I can only describe as a sort of boisterousness, and there is a feeling of adventure about these arctic conditions. Every morning we get up in pitch darkness, tearing ourselves from our warm bed and rushing along the bathroom passage. Getting up, dressing and bathing, has always been the time of our liveliest conversations.

By the time B. has been despatched to school the sun has come over the Downs, illuminating every twig and leaf, still carrying its white unruffled dressing, but with a crisp outline of frost. Perfect stillness. We live in a huge ice-box. The evening is the only time we are really warm, with a heaped fire of roaring logs.

*January 26th*

Colder still, no doubt about it. Hardly a trickle came from the taps this morning, but luckily there *was* just that, and it thawed them out at last. The milk in the larder was a solid chunk. Winter has declared war on us delicate pink human beings and we feel its claws. Even the cats look scared. The snow on the road is flattened to creaking white linoleum.

*January 30th*

Last night a gale got up, blowing the front door open and filling the hall with snow from end to end. R. and Janetta went to Ham and reported drifts six feet deep. Janetta's eyes were sparkling and her cheeks pink. "It was wonderful!" she said. The Russians are wonderful too, advancing with such speed that BERLIN is suddenly in the picture.

B. in bed with earache, I was reading him *A Flat Iron for a Farthing*, but today it couldn't be found. With muffled grunts he admitted he had hidden it in a drawer under his shirts "because it's so sad when the mother dies and I didn't want to have bad dreams".

The excitement of hearing about the advance into Germany puts us into a frenzy of impatience, and I am well aware of wanting to forge along through time as quickly as possible, looking forward each day to evening, and then to the start of a new day, and so on. I said to R. how much I deplored this scrabbling through our lives.

"Yes, I want to get on to the end of the story," he said. F.: "What? To old age, decrepitude — the tomb?" R.: "Yes" (in a serio-comic voice), "the tomb — that's where I want to get." "And separation from me!" I cried. "Don't you realise that's what it'll be, even if we are lucky enough to die at the same moment — the end of all our happiness together!" "*Don't*," said R., "that's something I keep trying to shove out of sight, like Burgo and the *Flat Iron for a Farthing*." And he rushed from the room, leaving me in tears.

*February 14th*

St. Valentine's day. Nicky has received a valentine from Saxon.

The snow has all gone and been succeeded by rain and deliciously soft springlike air. Janetta and I pushed Nicky in her pram to the snow-drop wood, and picked a large bunch of them to send to her friend Diana Cooke, who has just had a baby. We took them home and packed them in a big cardboard box with aconites, violets and ivy leaves.

This afternoon to play quartets. I asked Mr. Padel if he thought the war would soon be over. "Oh yes, and then the *real* war will begin." (He is a dedicated Communist.) I dared say no more, but good God, if this war isn't real I should like to know what is.

While we were playing I thought how chamber music could be a model for the conduct of personal relations — which, as is easy to forget — need constant attention of each part to all the others.

*March 13th*

There's an incredible sense of spring at the moment. The birds sing; old Tiger capers round the lawn like a kitten; the warm sun comes through the glass roof of the verandah and bathes us gently. Janetta sits out reading; I grub in the rockery to tidy it for the bulbs already bursting out of the earth. It's the beginning of that vegetable *rush* which will carry us breathlessly through spring and summer and dump us, exhausted, in the brown gloom of November. Another month has slipped by and everyone is saying "It can't be long now." On the Western front we have advanced to the Rhine and crossed it in one place. I was talking to Mrs. M. in the kitchen; her two sons are in this campaign and she has been terribly anxious. I said how good it was that we were across the Rhine. "Oh, is the Rhine a river?" she asked. "Yes, a very broad one," and then curiosity made me go on, "What did you think it was?" "Oh, *fancy*! I thought it was some kind of a moor."

Our daily diet now consists in descriptions of our conquering armies in Germany, and reports about the German reaction to defeat. An ambivalent note is very clear here: on one side "they are crushed, and do what we tell them, and pretty harmless on the whole", and on the other, "we mustn't for a moment forget, just because they look like ordinary old people, girls and children, that they are fiends – no less." Every hour of the day injunctions are broadcast to the American troops not to fraternize – which I take as pretty good proof that they are doing so. Descriptions of the efficient underground life the Germans had organized in these much-bombed Rhineland towns, with thousands of people living together in huge shelters, makes a cold hand grip one's heart. If two such horrible things can co-exist – the bombing and the underground life – why shouldn't they go on for ever?

*March 16th*

A flying visit from Phil [Nichols], who is due to leave in a week's time for Czecho-Slovakia. His ambassadorial life has hardened him into a conventional mould, beneath which he is deeply emotional. He spoke of his brother Robert's[1] death with unconcealed agitation, and I couldn't help remembering how cynically he used to talk about his love affairs, and all the brilliant suggestions for winning the war he used to keep posting off to the War Office. Now it was "Since Robert died I don't feel I mind about the war or anything."

We talked about the appalling revelations of German atrocities now coming to light: mass executions of Jews in gas-chambers. "Why doesn't the man in the street mind them more?" he asked. "Probably because the world has for several years been one huge atrocity," I said. It seems to me frightful but true that if people are fed on stories of the mass blowing to pieces of civilians and burning them alive in their houses by bombing, they lose some of their sensitivity to further horrors, however ghastly. R. mentioned the gloating way we now talk of burning the Japs in their wooden houses, and are building up a view that the Japs are subhuman, just as the Germans believe the Jews to be. The soldier who controls the gas-chamber, like the bomber pilot, may well be just carrying out orders because he dare not do otherwise. But how can either activity fail to have a bad effect on those who perform them?

On to education. R. said that boarding-school violated a child's desire for privacy and hampered its struggle to remain an individual by forcing it to lead a gang-life by day and night. Phil: "But adult life is a gang-life and children must be prepared and trained for it. How should I have got through the gang-life of the last war if I hadn't been prepared for it by boarding-school?" He was disregarding the vast majority of soldiers in the non-commissioned ranks, who did get through it, perhaps less scarred than he was, though they never went to boarding-school. And any way,

[1] The poet.

even were his premiss true, what an appalling idea that a boy's youth must be devoted to preparing him for the gang horrors of the next war!

Our next subject was promiscuity — in my opinion a natural state of youth, exciting and stimulating without being a great source of happiness. To prolong it often comes from timidity, the fear of risking too much in a more solid relationship. People are laughed at when they have too many shots at marriage, failing and trying again. But they shouldn't be, for they are after the best thing.

*March 28th*

The speed of our progress towards victory has been headlong this week. Someone suggested the Germans might still have something up their sleeves, and they have certainly been sending over more rockets lately. The other night Nicko Henderson described one falling beside Goodge Street Station when he was just getting off a bus. "It was only twenty yards off. There was no sound of the impact, just a terrific *roar* that seemed to go on and on and on for hours. All the women in the bus screamed and the men caught hold of them and shouted, "It's all *right!*" We all put our heads down, not knowing what was coming down from above. I asked where it was, and there it was just beside me — not a crater, but a huge pyramid of bricks and rubble. I was the first person on the spot, in evening clothes, and without the faintest idea how to attack this mound of horror. I saw a woman stripped naked by the explosion and with her foot apparently blown off. Ambulances arrived in a very few moments and by the time I had got back again, after going to my rooms and changing, a huge crowd had collected and it was all cordoned off."

Julia and Lawrence have been anxious to get out of London, and asked me to look for rooms in this neighbourhood. I have taken a good deal of trouble, been to dozens of rooms and rung Julia up every night to talk about the length of the arms of armchairs and suchlike details. R. has been highly sceptical about it all. We asked them for the weekend to look at various possibilities, and Lawrence seemed very keen on several of the rooms. "I'm sure the Swan will do. We'll stay there two months; it'll be wonderful." Julia had a cold, far-away look in her eye. "I dare say it'll be *bearable* for a month," was all she would commit herself to. After tea they went to see two other sets of rooms, that had seemed to me more possible. When they returned, "Well?" I asked. "Both absolutely *appalling*," Julia said shortly. "It's no good, I should be too bad-tempered. One really can't be happy in the surroundings those cottage women think nice. And the fact is I can't bear to stay in any rooms that aren't Georgian." So she prefers to remain in London with the rockets, though she admits they frighten her a great deal, to

209

living in a non-Georgian room. It's heroism of her own peculiar sort. On Sunday evening she asked me how I thought Lawrence was looking, and said she was very worried about his health. "Don't you think perhaps a stay in the country would have done him good?" I asked her maliciously. But I do find it strange that she has to support her happiness on so many material things — fenders and fringes of bobbles — instead of taking it about with her.

*March 29th*

Janetta and Nicolette returned after a visit away, and Nicko turned up to supper. He gave a brilliantly vivid account of the assassination of Lord Moyne, illustrating with a pipe and matchboxes the positions of the characters in the drama. The assassins shot him through the neck and body, and the poor man had no chance from the first, yet they took him to hospital and kept him alive for a bit. "What a nuisance!" were his last audible words.

*April 18th*

Lying on the lawn this afternoon in weather more appropriate to July than April, I could neither read nor think — only wonder. I wonder, for instance, why our present situation seems more like the last years of peace than the earlier part of the war. We haven't had a single rocket or bomb on England for two weeks. The attempts made to encourage bitter hatred are common to this fag-end of the war and the last weeks of peace. Perhaps we should pull ourselves together and shake off this uneasy waiting state and try and accommodate ourselves to the new order of things. R. says we are like returned prisoners-of-war — we need rehabilitation. The pressure has let off, the prison bars are being raised, but we don't know how to get used to freedom. Dick Rendel, who was here a short while ago, was telling us about our prisoners, returning in their thousands from German camps. Their state is really pitiable. They get home and find their wives look older, or have fatter legs or a lover, or they don't care for them as much as they thought they did. Going to bed together isn't a success, and the wife has got so used to running the house and family single-handed that she doesn't want his interference. He feels guilt at ever having been a prisoner (a very "loaded" word after all), resentment against the country and the system that ever let him in for such an experience — and the net result is that he sits silent by the fireside groping for some sort of orientation. His wife tries to drag him out to parties "to cheer him up". He feels miserable, has forgotten how to behave, is even rude. And so on. Dick is now in charge of a rehabilitation centre at Hatfield House. He plans to put on a naked show from the Windmill Theatre there.

*April 19th*

The weather continuing like midsummer, we determined to treat it as such and set off in thin clothes for a picnic by the splashing mill-pool at Hamstead Marshall. I had bought newspapers in Newbury, and turned the pages as we drove. My horrified eyes fell on a page of photographs from one of the German concentration camps opened up recently by the Americans. A lorry stood stacked with naked corpses; others in the last stages of emaciation lay in ghastly rows, waiting to be buried. Gaunt invalids lay in straw; a man in pyjamas was hanging from a gallows. The text was just as appalling. Then there were photos of plump, quiet bourgeois Germans being taken to see the camp and harangued by the Americans. Many fainted, and others burst into tears, but the photo also showed many smug, placid faces, like those of people waiting for a bus.

Well, R. and Burgo got for a moment into the cold waters of the mill-stream and then we sat eating hard-boiled eggs and watercress beside it. The day was unbelievably beautiful, the grass positively sparkled, heat poured from the blue sky – but none of this could dispel the horror and disgust brought by the newspapers. They haunted me all day. I feel as though the world's sanity had received a fatal blow, and I can't stop thinking of it and all it implies. Reaction in the kitchen: "Isn't it terrible? Why don't we do it to *their* men, that's what I want to know!"

*April 28th*

The war is shaping to some vast Wagnerian finale. The Russian army has completely encircled Berlin and is pressing through the suburbs towards the heart of it. Hitler is said to be there, personally directing the battle. Mussolini is a prisoner. And Winston has announced that there are no more blackout restrictions. It's quite difficult to leave windows uncurtained and blazing away into the darkness. We have indeed got used to our imprisoned state.

*April 30th*

A different response from the kitchen this morning: "How terrible it's been! How glad we shall be when it's all over!" Mrs. C.'s feelings had suddenly been touched by a picture of a German mother and the two children she had killed before committing suicide herself. The world

211

tragedy dwindled to a size she could assimilate. Supposing *we* had been invaded. Supposing *she* had been that woman. Mr. Mills, bringing our bread, hoped "it wouldn't be long now. And then I shall be just about glad to get a letter from the boys. The wife's away at Reading for a month; there's more company to take her mind off things, and I reckon I'll be glad if it cracks before she comes back. Mr. T. he made me mad the other day. I said I'd be glad when it's over, and he said, 'It didn't *ought* to be over. We ought to go and kill every blooming German.' I said to him, 'You just take a rifle then, and go out there and do it. You know jolly well you can't or you wouldn't say such things. The boys out there don't feel like that.' "

R. sits by the wireless all day, with an anxious face, tuning in to stations, like a doctor taking the pulse of a dying man. The patient is already speechless, but last night we heard our own broadcaster to Germany saying slowly and weightily: "Es ist das *Ende*." And all today anticipation of that end has been like a great undischarged *gasp* filling one's chest.

*May 1st*

To Hungerford to meet Saxon. The newspapers are again objects of horror to shudder away from, plastered with photos of the heaped corpses of Italian Fascists, or of Mussolini and his mistress strung up like turkeys. It seems incredible to have them handed over the counter by a mild girl in specs, with a front tooth missing.

11 p.m. Have just switched on the late news and heard a portentous voice say: HITLER IS DEAD. I went up to bed before R. and heard his voice and Saxon's from the music-room below. "What were you talking about?" I asked when he appeared. "Horses for the Guineas," he said. "Trust Saxon never to mention anything of such immediate interest as the end of Hitler."

*May 5th*

Waiting, waiting for the end. The last two nights I have started awake after the first dimming of consciousness into sleep, to find myself lying with a wildly pounding heart, as if listening for something. The church bells pealing for victory? Anyway all I heard with unnatural distinctness was the sound of Saxon clearing his throat in his bedroom, forced along the tunnel of the passage.

Before lunchtime we heard that all the German armies in the North had surrendered. Holland and Denmark are free.

Molly arrived to stay. I had forgotten what an effort it is bawling at her, and how stupid one's bawled remarks sound, while hers are all subtlety, wit and imagination. She is as much out of this world of today as anyone could be, her deafness and her originality combine to prevent her modulating herself to the times.

*May 7th*

Molly lies in bed till nearly lunchtime and then comes downstairs waving and blowing kisses, with a bunch of the flowers out of her bedroom vase stuffed rather wildly into her bosom. She had been thinking nostalgically, she told us, about the "gentlefolks" who used to have lots of servants and didn't know how to boil an egg.

All day long we were kept on the hop by the wireless telling us that the Germans had signed unconditional surrender but that the announcement had not yet come through – we could expect it any minute. If the war is over then it is over, and I am bewildered to explain this fever of anticipation. The voices of the B.B.C. announcers betray increasing irritation, and everyone is on tenterhooks waiting for the inevitable.

Then at eight this evening the telephone rang, and it was an Inkpen neighbour asking if Burgo was going to school tomorrow or not. (We have been sharing transport.) "It's just come through – tomorrow will be V-day. Churchill will announce the end of the war in Europe at 3 p.m. It's all very flat," she went on. "We've just been drinking a little weak gin." So here it was at last. Nothing could have been more prosaic than this way of receiving the news, yet on returning to the music-room I found all my restlessness had gone in a moment. Oddly enough, the news of peace actually brought a *sense* of peace, very refreshing like a good drink of water to a thirsty person. R. and I sat through our evening quietly, enjoying the relief from tension. Before we went up to bed we went out onto the verandah and looked up at the sky in which a few stars twinkled mistily, and I thought of the night nearly six years ago when the war began, and how I had done the same, wondering what was in store for us all, and gazed on by those same impersonal eyes.

*May 8th*

At three o'clock Churchill delivered the promised announcement.

Afterwards we drove to Newbury to fetch the other Inkpen children from school. Every cottage had a few flags hung out, and in most of them a dummy-like figure of an old person could be seen at an upper window, hoisted out of bed probably to see what little fun there was to see. Near Newbury we had a narrow escape from a drunken lorry-driver veering from side to side of the road – he made the V-sign as we passed.

213

Bicyclists were hurrying in to Newbury dressed in their best; little girls wore satin blouses and red, white and blue bows in their hair.

*May 10th*

I feel happier and more conscious of peace even than I expected. I am very much aware this morning of something that has just gone: – a background to our daily existence as solid as one of the scenes in Burgo's toy theatre – a background coloured by the obscenity of violence, and my own disgust at it. The fields, Downs and woods *look* peaceful now, seen with eyes that know the murder and destruction have stopped. If my pleasure in our being at peace is a more or less steady quality, R.'s is growing gradually, as though it was something he hardly dared trust to, and it makes me very happy to see signs on his face that the load is lifting. This morning he was radiating good humour, which was no doubt why the girl cashier in the Bank leant over the counter and confided all her marriage plans to him; when he's in a benign mood no-one I've ever known attracts more confidences than he does.

I have been reading Flaubert's *Letters*, and have just reached the Franco-Prussian war. How his reactions remind me of ours! First, horror at the bestiality of human beings. As the Germans invade he develops a more conventional desire to defend his country, followed by the most frightful agitation and despair, such as only a literary man can indulge in. *No-one*, he feels sure, can hate the war so much as he does; he resigns from the Home Guard, returns to his views about the beastliness of human beings, is physically sick every day from sheer disgust, and dislikes his fellow-Frenchmen almost as much as the Prussians. As for "evacuees" they are the worst feature of the whole war.

News of V.E. Day in London: Janetta writes: "I've found the crowds very depressing indeed, and the flags and decorations pathetic although often very pretty. Some bonfires were wonderful, bringing back the old ecstasies of staring into a fire, but also having that appalling smell of burning debris, too terrifyingly nostalgic of blitzes. And I so loathe the look of masses of boiling people with scarlet dripping faces, wearing tiny paper hats with 'Ike's Babe' or 'Victory' written on them."

Julia: "We walked to Buckingham Palace, and there found a spectacular scene – all the fountains, balustrades, not to mention trees, were crowded with these little pink penguins in their droves, all facing the Palace, which was brilliantly illuminated with beautiful golden light, and draped with red velvet over the balcony. It was charmingly pretty. Everyone was fainting by the roadside, or rather sitting down holding their stockinged feet in their hands and groaning. A few faint upper-class cries of 'Taxi – taxi!' came wailing through the air from voices right down on the pavement; whilst cockney tones, slightly more robust, could be heard saying, 'I'm fucking well all in now'." Of her own reaction to peace she goes on: "It's something to do with the war having gone on just *too* long, one was at last crushed, and personally I no longer feel human any more; I mean the dynamic principle has given way and one feels like a sheet of old newspaper or pressed dried grass."

At Hungerford Station we ran into Dora Romilly, who had news of the celebration of peace at Charleston. Quentin made a lifesize image of Hitler to burn on Firle Beacon, Duncan defended Hitler in a comic mock trial, and the "Baroness" (Lydia Keynes) had "thudded away in an abandoned Russian drinking song".

This evening we drove to Shalbourne to give Olive a present of bacon. I remembered how after the First War some pacifists had been turned on by the merry-making crowds, for instance how Cambridge undergraduates had pushed down Harry Norton's garden wall; and wondered if our village neighbours, and "old retainers" like Olive, might say to themselves, "Well, *they* did nothing to help. *They*'ve no cause to rejoice." But the warm way Olive and her family welcomed us and exchanged handshakes and kisses did nothing to confirm my fears.

After all, surely it's only logical that pacifists — of all people — should rejoice in the return to Peace?

# INDEX

Air-raids (*see also* London in the Blitz), 35, 39, 42-4, 46-7, 70, 80-7, 90, 105, 143, 148, 151, 170, 173, 180-1, 184-5, 210; 'Baedeker', 131-2; ours on Germany, 168, 170, 175, 187

Anrep, Boris, 52-3, 81, 97, 131, 181-2, 200-1

Anrep, Helen, 34-5, 48-51, 53, 56, 163-4, 200

*Arandora Star* Torpedoed, 49

Arnhem, landing at, 197

Asquith, Margot (Lady Oxford and Asquith), 52

Bach, 25, 129, 180, 198

Bagenal, Barbara, 99-100, 171, 188

Baker, Mary (the 'Shy Bride'), 97, 108

Beaton, Cecil (Sir), 90

Beethoven, 33, 54, 76, 103, 173, 198

Belgium, German invasion of, 38, 40, 42-3

Bell, Angelica (*see* Garnett)

Bell, Clive, lunching with, in London, 23, 38, 80, 97, 107, 110, 114, 144, 174, 181, 199; at Ham Spray, 29, 45, 89-90, 108, 139-40, 200; his pacifism, 48, 55-6, 67, 75, 103; letters from, 52, 56, 75, 87, 167, 174, 189; helps Gerald Brenan, 63; and Angelica's marriage, 133-4; and Ralph's Tribunal, 156

Bell, Colonel Cory, 63

Bell, Julian, 87, 138

Bell, Quentin, 87, 94-5, 215

Bell, Vanessa, 56, 65, 87, 97, 112, 133, 138-9

Berlin, 60, 81, 175, 206, 211

Bevin, Ernest, 84

Blitz (*see* London in the Blitz)

Bloomsbury, 9, 29, 159, 164, 166

Bomford, James (Jimmy), 44, 47, 182

Bonham-Carter, Audrey, 43, 48, 173, 185

Bonham-Carter, Victor, 43, 48

Boord, Colonel, 190-1, 194

Bowra, Maurice, 142

Brenan, Gamel, 22, 24, 34, 36, 41, 43-6, 48, 51, 54, 63, 66, 76, 123-4, 127-8, 134, 168-9, 182

Brenan, Gerald, 22, 34, 36, 38-9, 41, 43-8, 51, 53-4, 59, 62-4, 66, 76, 166, 169; relations with Ralph, 9, 62-3, 99, 102, 106-8, 115, 123-4, 128, 134, 145, 151, 182; attitude to pacifists, 39, 99, 106-7, 128, 162; in trouble with the police, 49, 53-4, 62

Brenan, Miranda, 123

Brittain, Vera, 26

Britten, Benjamin, 158, 200

Brooke, Rupert, 26

Brüderhof, 39, 80

Bunyan, John, 150

Bury, J.B., 118

Carrington, Catharine, 24, 115, 123, 145, 168

Carrington, Dora, 10, 54, 71, 123, 138, 193

Carrington, Noel, 10, 24, 115

Casals, Pablo, 46

Cecil, Lord David, 21, 31-2 37-8, 66-7, 197-8, 200

Cecil, Rachel (Lady David), 21, 31, 37-8, 67, 197-8, 200

Chamberlain, Neville, 33, 39, 50, 52